IMAGES
of America

UNION COUNTY

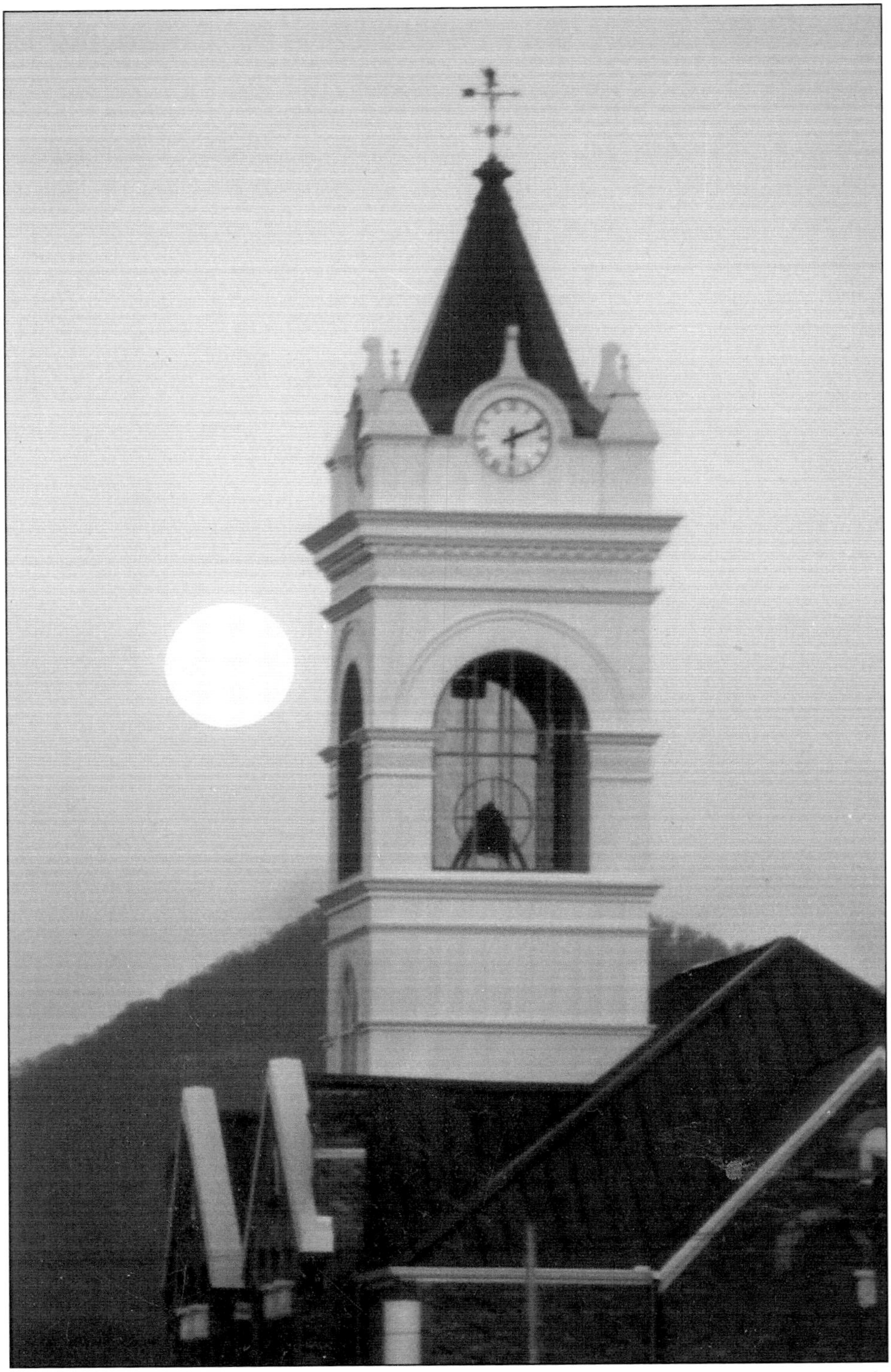

A full moon shines next to the replicated clock and bell tower atop the historic 1899 Union County Courthouse. This tower was placed on the old courthouse in 2001 and it replaced the original tower that was removed in 1960. (Photograph by Norman Cooper.)

IMAGES
of America

UNION COUNTY

Union County Historical Society

ARCADIA
PUBLISHING

ISBN 978-0-7385-1588-5

Published by Arcadia Publishing
Charleston, South Carolina

Printed in the United States of America

Library of Congress Catalog Card Number: 2003111112

For all general information contact Arcadia Publishing at:
Telephone 843-853-2070
Fax 843-853-0044
E-mail sales@arcadiapublishing.com
For customer service and orders:
Toll-Free 1-888-313-2665

Visit us on the Internet at www.arcadiapublishing.com

Contents

ACKNOWLEDGMENTS

The Union County Historical Society wishes to extend its appreciation to
Norman Cooper
for his efforts and contributions in the creation and completion of this publication.

The Union County Historical Society extends its appreciation to the following committee members for their efforts and contributions to this publication:

Dale Elliott	Steve Oakley
David Friedly	Betty Jane Shuler
Martyne Jokela	Jane Thompson

The Union County Historical Society extends thanks and appreciation to the numerous individuals, families, organizations, and others who have contributed to the publication of this book. Many people have contributed photographs and/or information, which have been valuable assets in the book's creation. Individual donors of photographs are acknowledged with the photographs whenever and wherever possible.

Over the years, many individuals, families, groups, and organizations have contributed photographs to the Union County Historical Society Museum and Cultural Center. Many of the photographs in this publication are part of the Union County Historical Society's collection, which includes the Henley Hamby Collection.

The Historical Society extends thanks and appreciation to those who purchase this book. We value your interest in the history of Union County, Georgia.

Introduction

Union County is in the heart of the majestic and beautiful North Georgia mountains. Located in the Southern Appalachian Mountains on the northern boundary of Georgia, Union County has remained relatively unchanged since its beginnings in the 1800s. A combination of longtime residents, retirees, and a younger generation of families have chosen to make this paradise home. These families maintain the characteristics of those who lived here years ago—resourcefulness, independence, and a willingness to work hard. These are persons who have a desire for living in a wholesome community with old fashioned values. Many pioneers helped shape the county.

Businesses of years gone by provided the needs of area residents for decades. Education has played a major role in the development of the county. The county's educational past dates back to a time when small one-room school houses, heated by potbellied stoves, were scattered throughout the county. Today, in the unincorporated town of Suches, the students of Woody Gap School continue to have classes in the historic rock building. In the town of Blairsville, the ever expanding school campus has four schools, including a facility for the high school, similar to a college facility. Throughout the years, the county has been noted for outstanding teachers and administrators. Religion plays a major role in the life of the community, with churches from every prominent denomination present. God is worshipped, morals are taught, hymns are sung, preaching is emphasized, ministers are respected, and members are noted for their faithfulness.

About half of the county is covered by the Chattahoochee National Forest; much of this land has been wilderness for centuries. From the mountain peaks to the lake and along the roadways and wilderness trails, Union County features flowing streams, waterfalls, abundant wildlife, spectacular flora, and magnificent views of abundant forests. The county includes the following: Trackrock Archeological Area with ancient petroglyphs of unknown origin; Vogel State Park, one of the most popular parks in Georgia; Lake Nottely; Lake Winfield Scott; Brasstown Bald, the highest peak in the state; Suches, the highest elevation town and home to the smallest public school in the state; Brasstown-Russell Scenic Byway, the only National Scenic Byway in Georgia; and a section of the Appalachian Trail, which includes the only spot on the entire 2,100-mile route that the trail passes through a building. Much admired for its scenic qualities, environmental resources, and recreational opportunities, the region has never depended upon financial prosperity. The residents of years ago worked hard and managed on very little. The Great Depression actually improved the economic outlook of the region by bringing government assistance programs such as the Civilian Conservation Corps (CCC), Works Progress Administration (WPA), and the Tennessee Valley Authority (TVA) to the area.

Union County has a proud history that includes many noteworthy individuals as well as numerous outstanding accomplishments. Families, education, religion, music, politics, and community life have figured prominently in the history and development of Union County. Focusing mainly on the 20th century, this book provides a pictorial history that memorializes the good people who have worked this hard land and the many characters who have colored it. Notables include the following: Joseph Brown, who served as governor of the state and in the United States Senate; Byron Herbert Reece, a poet laureate of Georgia; "The Barefoot Ranger" Arthur Woody, one of the first forest rangers in the country and a pioneer conservationist who restored wildlife to the depleted forests; Mauney D. Collins, state school superintendent for 25 years; and William Henry Duckworth and Thomas S. Candler, both of whom served as Justices of the Georgia State Supreme Court.

The 1899 courthouse on the town square, built to replace a previous one that had burned, is a focal point for the town and has an interesting history within the community. The taxes to pay for the courthouse were levied in one year, causing many residents to sell their cattle and land to pay the taxes. The Romanesque Revival building had an original clock and bell tower, which weighed two tons. The bricks for the structure were made locally. The old courthouse was threatened with demolition in the 1970s but was saved and restored by the Union County Historical Society.

Formed from the land once inhabited by the Cherokees, Union County came into existence in the early 1800s. Descendants of Scottish, Irish, and English lineage became the predominant settlers in the area. Many generations of mountain people survived with determination, endurance, resourcefulness, and self sufficiency. Union County was created by the Georgia Legislature on December 3, 1832. John Thomas, chosen as a representative for the new county, when asked to suggest a name, is reported to have said, "Name it Union, for none but union like men reside in it." However, naming of the county has often been erroneously connected with the Civil War. The naming of the county took place some 30 years before the advent of the Civil War. Prior to the formation of this county, all of Cherokee had been surveyed and divided into 160 acre lots and 40 acre gold lots and given away by lottery to Georgia citizens by the state of Georgia. The Union County area was remote and enclosed by mountain peaks and ranges making access from the south more difficult than from the north and east. The 1850 federal census shows that a majority of the early settlers came from North Carolina, South Carolina, Tennessee, and Georgia. These early settlers were hardy and self sufficient with the skills of many generations of mountain people. The settlers included craftsmen, blacksmiths, wheelwrights, millwrights, gunsmiths, tanners, and carpenters. Union County was one of the early sites of gold mining in the state, which attracted many to the northeast Georgia mountains. Union County has a rich military history; its citizens have always answered the call to duty. Since the formation of the county, men and women from the county have fought in every war. They are honored, revered, and respected.

This book does not attempt to contain the entire history of the county, but a fascinating pictorial glimpse of yesteryear. The purpose of this volume is to show that Union County is a unique blend of a modern America, which maintains the charm of the legendary Appalachian era, a developing community surrounded by pristine forests, a land of scenic beauty, and friendly people.

Norman Cooper, September 2003

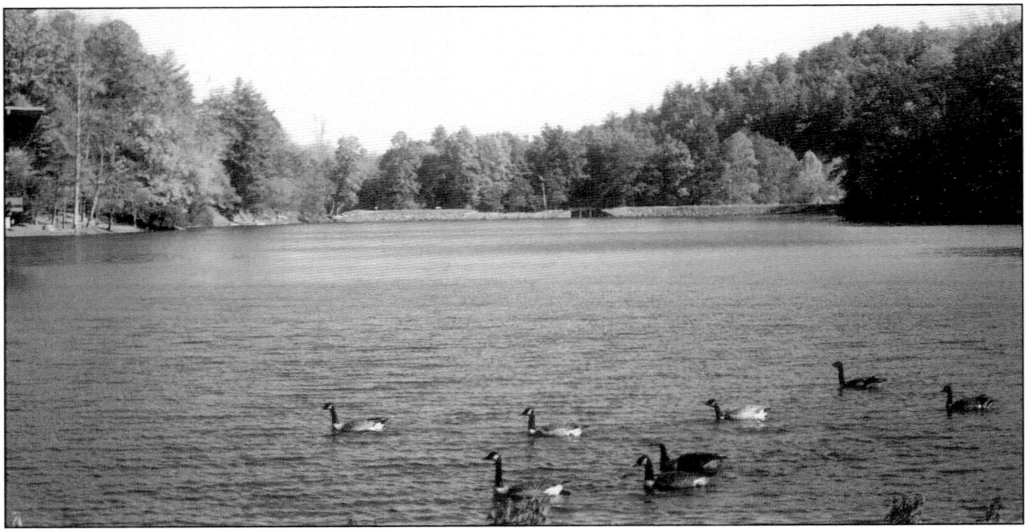

Pictured here is one of the many scenic views in Union County. (Photograph by Norman Cooper.)

One

Historic Courthouse

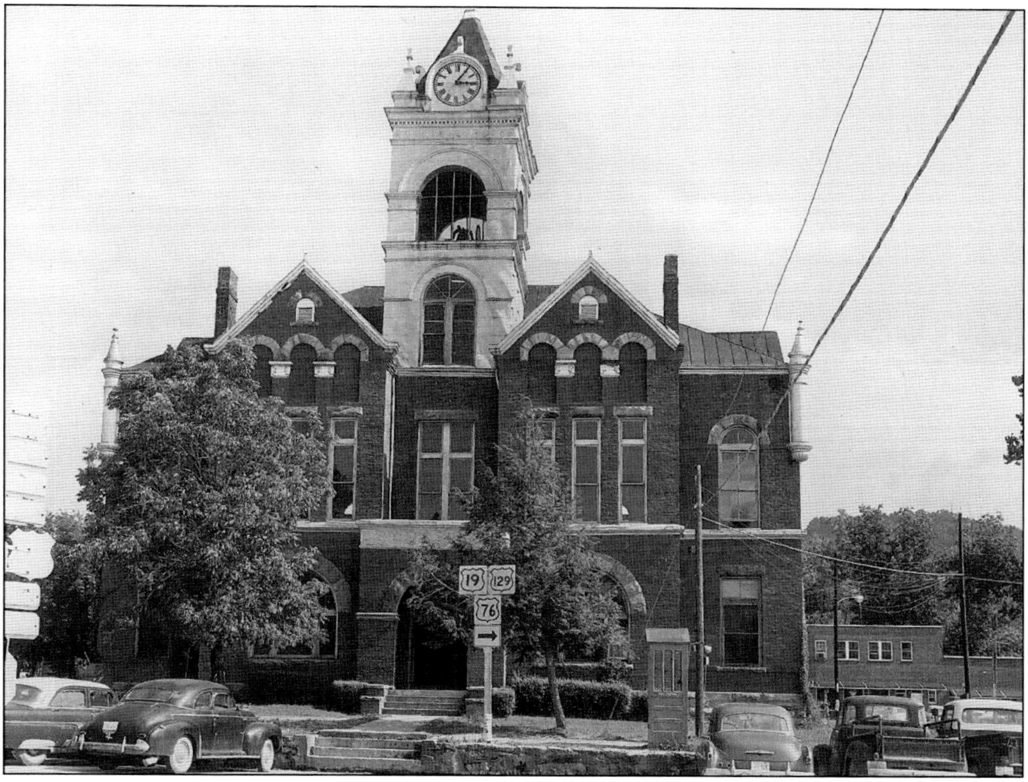

The historic 1899 Union County Courthouse sits at the center of town square. The building is the third of the county's four courthouses. The brick and granite Romanesque Revival style structure serves as the home of the Union County Historical Society as well as a local history museum and cultural center. The exact location of the first courthouse, a log structure, which was destroyed by fire in 1859, is uncertain. The second courthouse was constructed in the middle of the town square, and was ravaged by fire in 1898, along with it most of the county's records. The existing courthouse was born amidst great controversy and debate. A lawsuit was filed to prevent construction and a public referendum was held in an effort to move the county seat westward to an area known as Bunker Hill. The suit was dismissed but efforts to finance a new courthouse through the issuance of revenue bonds also failed. County Ordinary John T. Colwell, along with County Commissioners J.W. Souther, J.A. Butt, and W.W. Erwin settled the matter of the building's location by placing it on the site of the previous courthouse. The above photo was taken in the late 1950s. (Courtesy of Union County Historical Society.)

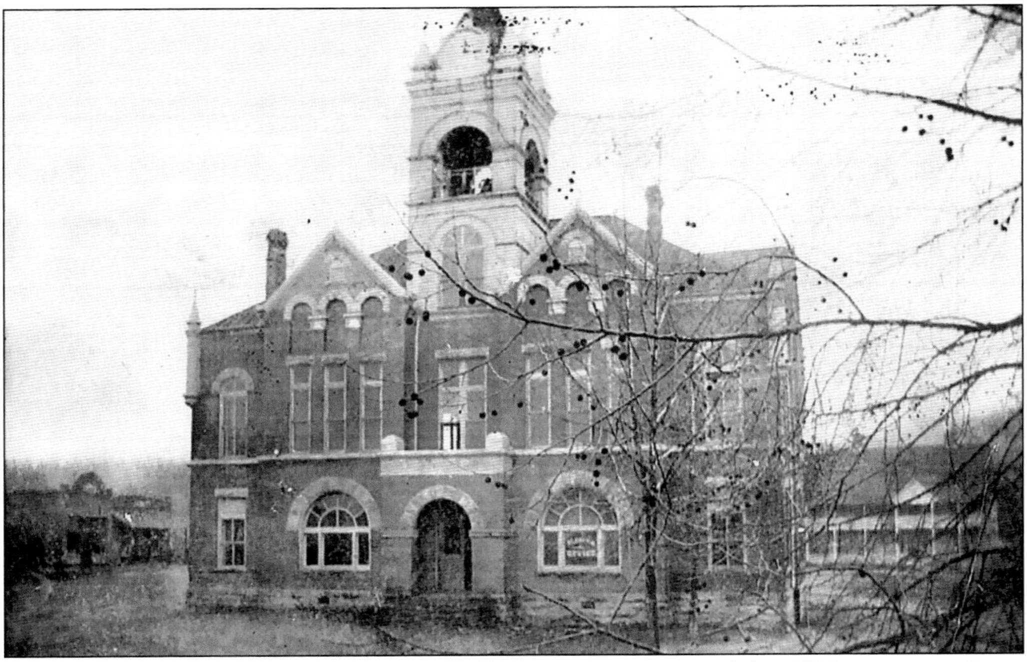

This rare photograph, believed to be the oldest existing picture of the 1899 structure, shows the old courthouse with no sidewalks and no walkways. The red bricks used in the structure were hand-molded in the area. Architects Golucke and Stewart were retained along with contractor M.B. McCinty who bid to construct the building for $12,000. The entire amount was levied against the property taxes of the county in one year, causing an extreme hardship on the citizens, many of whom are said to have been forced to sell their milk cows and other stock to pay their taxes. (Courtesy of Union County Historical Society.)

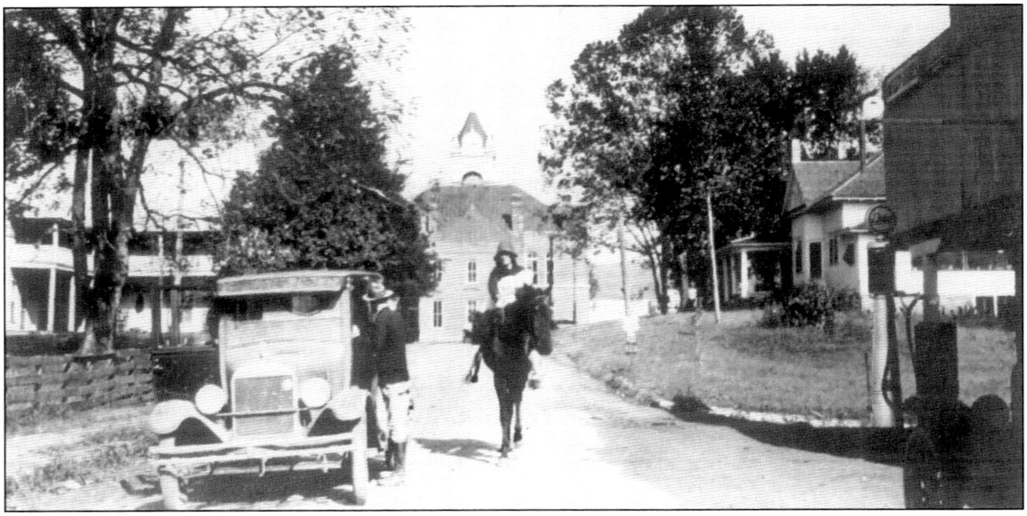

Pictured above is Cleveland Street in the late 1920s, on the south side of the old courthouse. Joe Rich is believed to be standing beside the 1927 Model T. The unidentified rider on the horse holding a child is believed to be a circuit nurse. The gas station on right was a Chevrolet agency started by Sylvan Butt and Rouse Waldroup. The U.S. Post Office was located in offices on the south end of the courthouse building. When the mail was delivered on horseback, the day's delivery was handed out a window to the riders. (Courtesy of Tom Gilliland.)

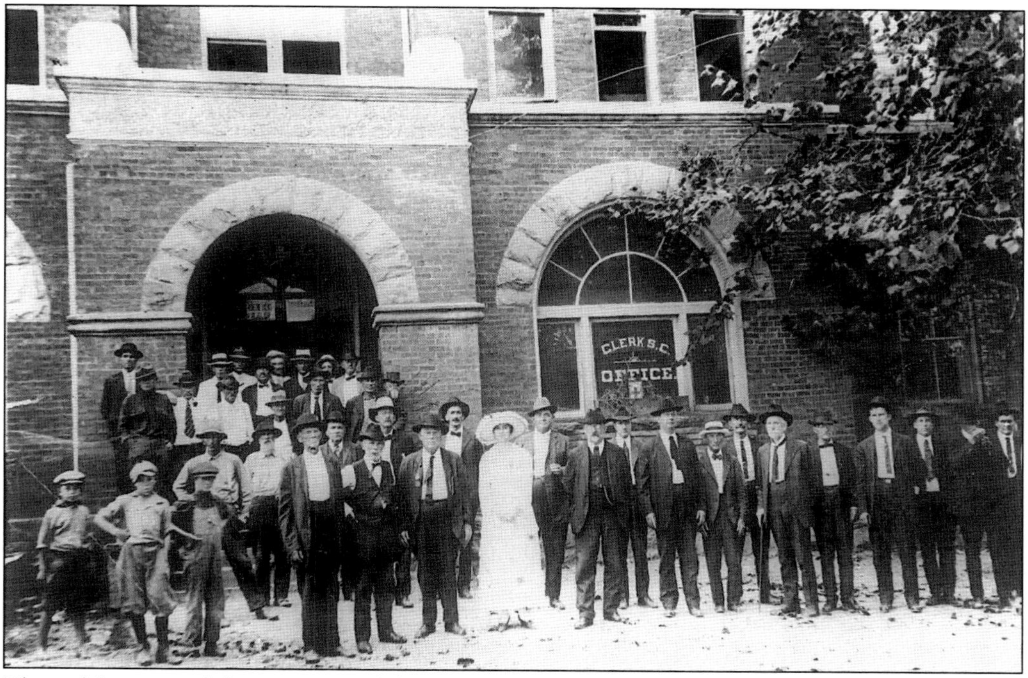

The celebration of the opening of the highway from Blairsville to Murphy in 1926 is shown here in front of the Union County Courthouse. The Union County delegation is on the left and the North Carolina delegation is on the right. Note the window identifying the office of the Clerk of Superior Court. (Courtesy of Union County Historical Society.)

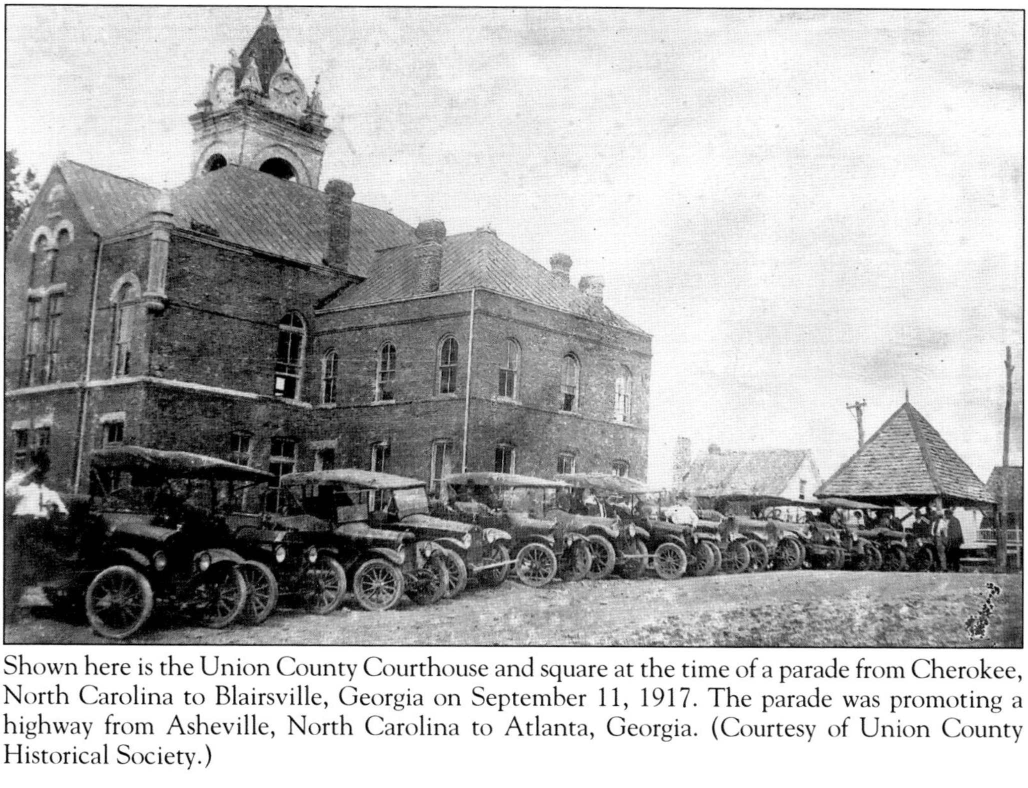

Shown here is the Union County Courthouse and square at the time of a parade from Cherokee, North Carolina to Blairsville, Georgia on September 11, 1917. The parade was promoting a highway from Asheville, North Carolina to Atlanta, Georgia. (Courtesy of Union County Historical Society.)

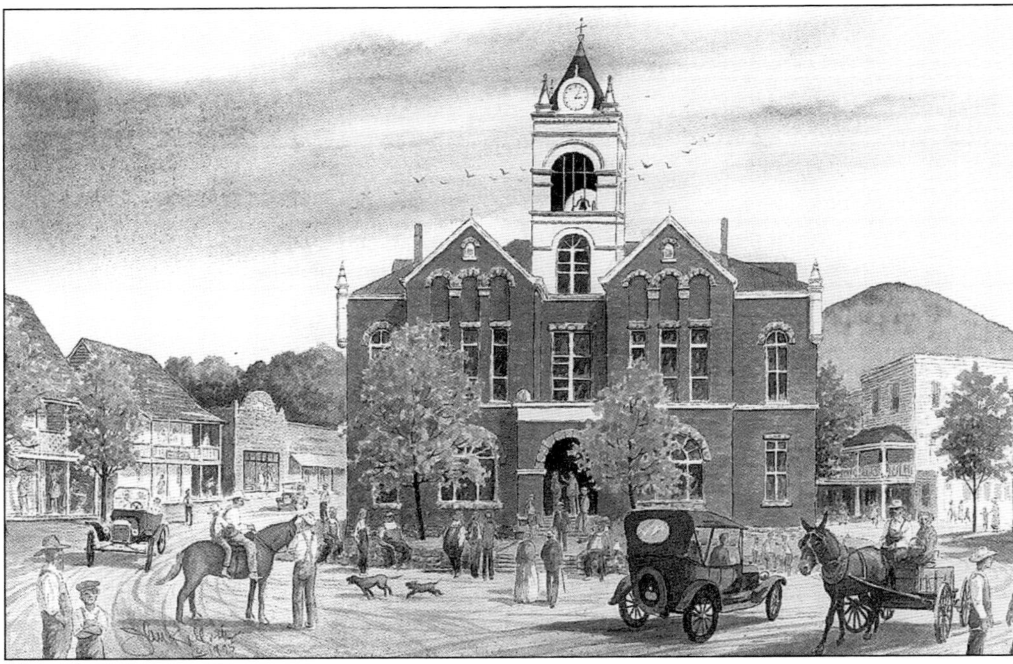

Scores of paintings, sketches, photographs, and drawings have been produced over the years of the courthouse in Union County. In putting together the details of the above watercolor, depicting a scene from 1930, John Kollock used mostly old photographs and personal remembrances since most of the wooden hotels that stood around the square had disappeared. (Courtesy *Watercolor Memories of the Hills*.)

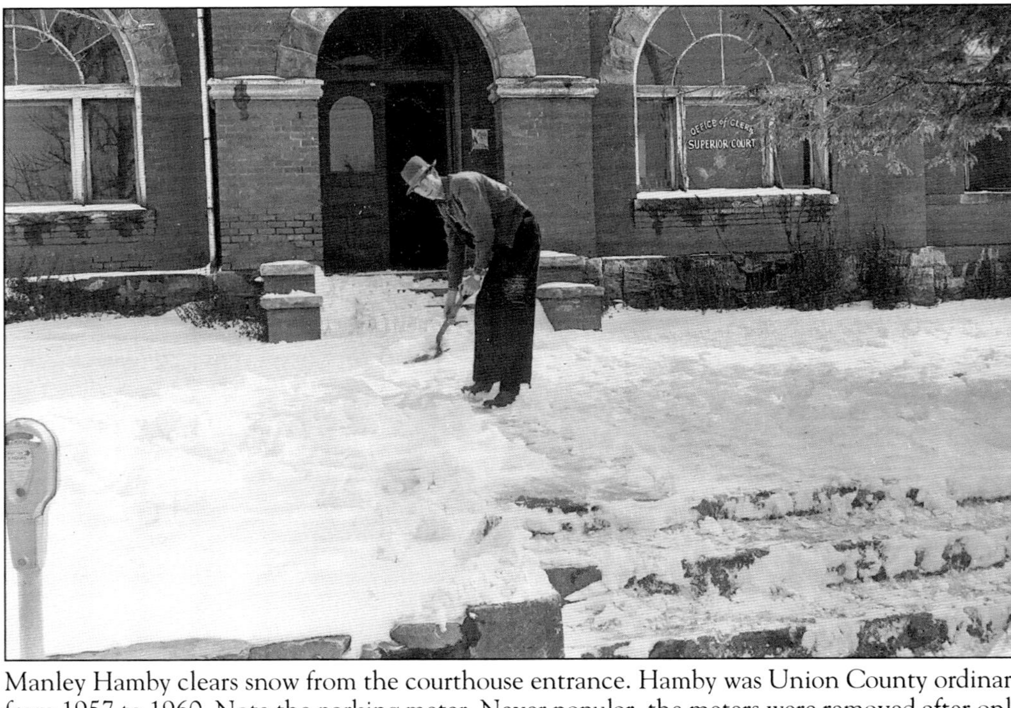

Manley Hamby clears snow from the courthouse entrance. Hamby was Union County ordinary from 1957 to 1960. Note the parking meter. Never popular, the meters were removed after only a couple of years. (Courtesy of Union County Historical Society.)

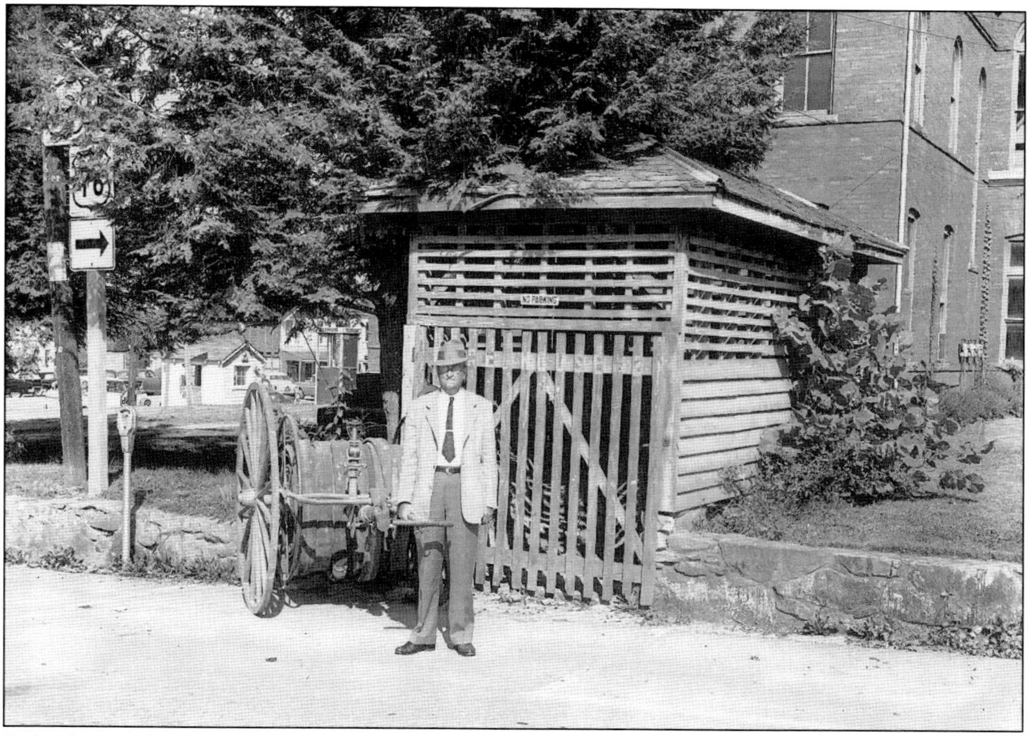

Bob Christopher stands at the firehouse on the square at the old courthouse. (Courtesy of Union County Historical Society.)

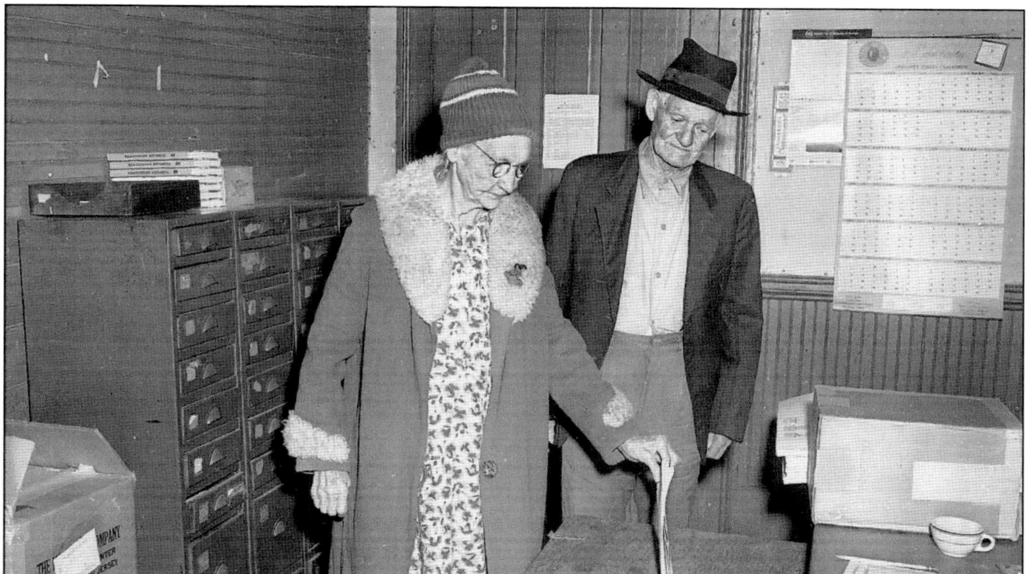

The courthouse was the focal point of community life and activity. It served as the center for school administration, housed barber shops, shoe shops, moving picture shows, trials affecting both life and property, libraries, fiddling contests and singing conventions. It was also a place for voting. Mr. and Mrs. J.M. Wilson cast their ballots. (Courtesy of Union County Historical Society.)

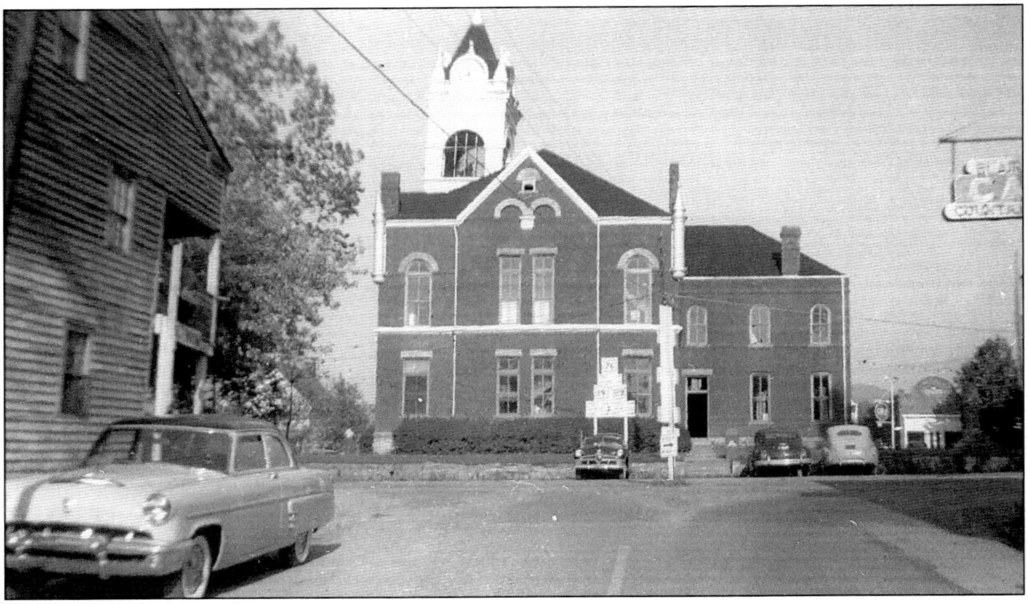

The 1899 courthouse was born in controversy and its life was marked by the neglect of succeeding political generations. Examinations of the grand jury presentments reveal an on-going plea for maintenance and repair. These pleas were usually ignored. In April of 1927, the Union superior court records show that the grand jury recommended "that the roof of the county courthouse and all windows and doors be placed in first class repair immediately; that the plaster be replaced inside the building, all necessary painting that is needed be done, the clock be put in order, and that a public toilet be furnished and made sanitary for the court and public." For decades grand jury presentments continued to reference the declining condition of the courthouse. The declining courthouse is shown here.

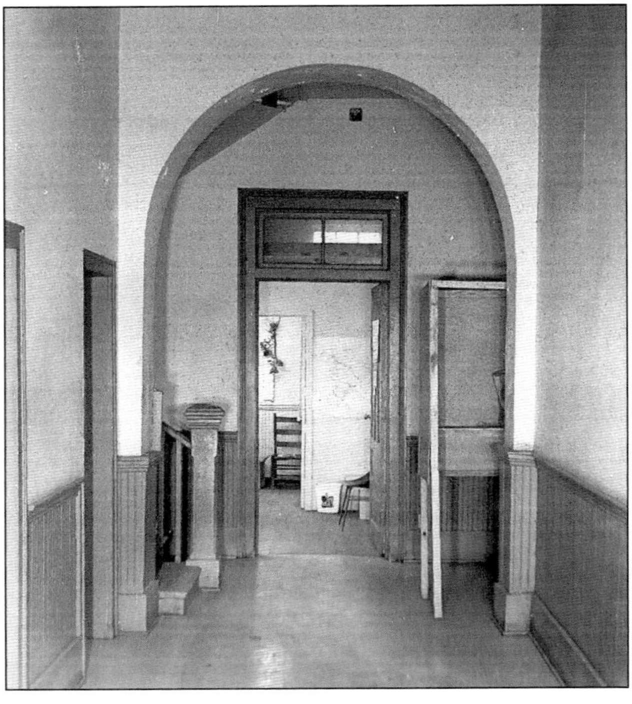

Shown here is a view inside the courthouse prior to renovation. The photograph was taken from the lobby looking south sometime in the late 1970s or early 1980s. In 1976, the county functions were moved to a more modern structure and the old landmark became the home of the Union County Historical Society. (Courtesy of Union County Historical Society.)

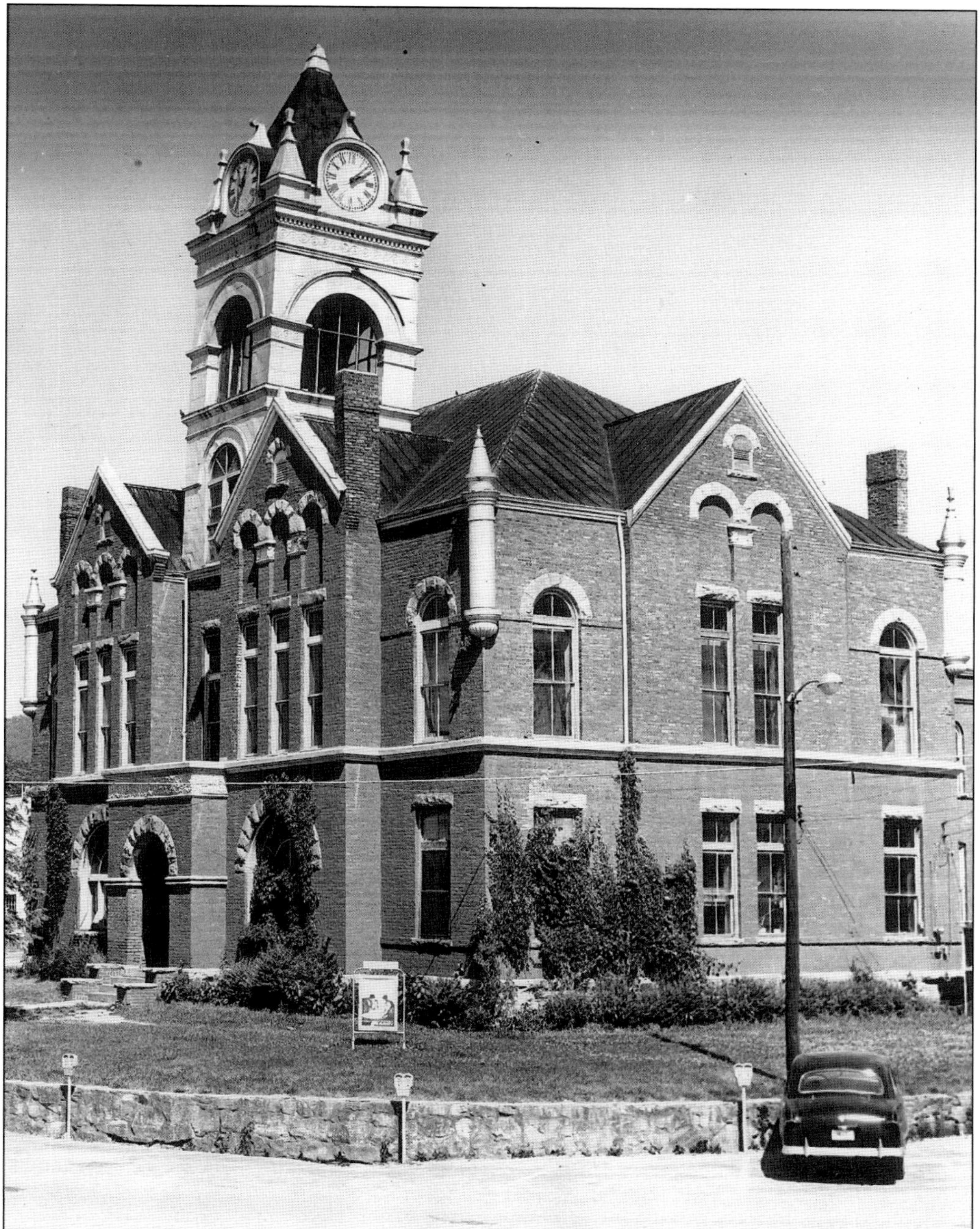

This photo, taken in 1960, was made just prior to the removal of the leaning tower. Judge John Frankum stated that the tower was unsafe. Judge T.S. Candler and a group of citizens met and inspected the tower. In July 1960, Judge Candler and his committee advised that the tower should be removed. The final bill for this work was paid on July 25, 1960 and the work had cost $555.05. All parts of the clock, except the four faces which could not be saved, were stored in the county's warehouse on Haralson Drive. Between 1961 and 1964, the old metal roof was replaced with asphalt material, the wooden window frames were replaced with aluminum framed windows. (Courtesy of Union County Historical Society.)

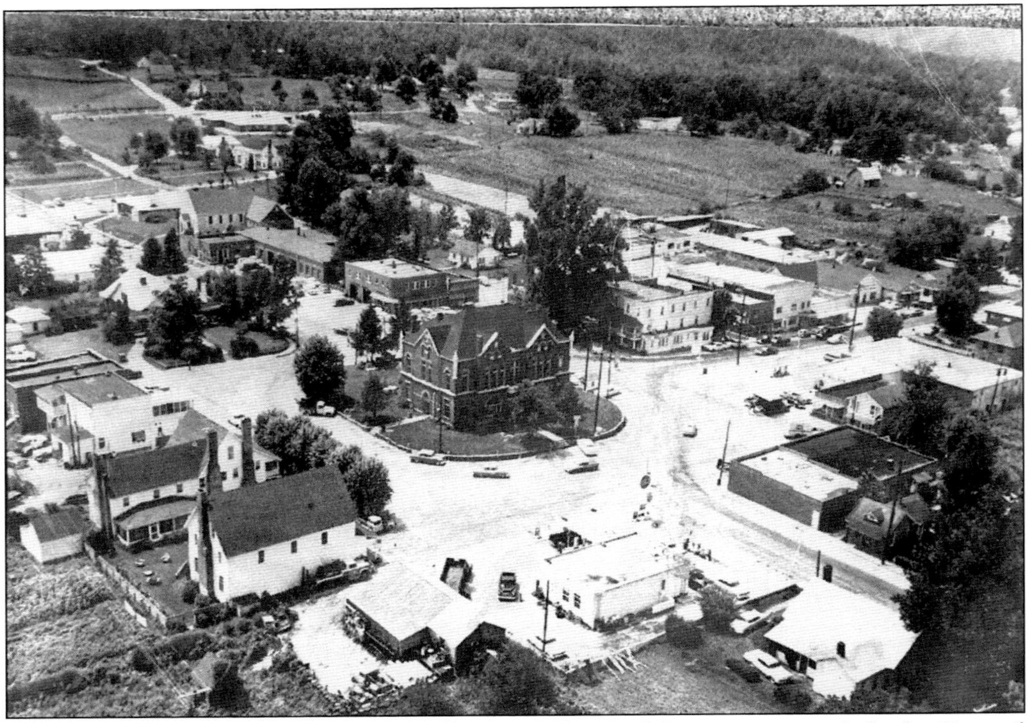

The above photo is believed to be from the 1960s. Some of the structures include the General Store, the Wellborn House, Tom Candler House, Chevron Station, Christopher Hotel, Jones Building, Kings' 5 & 10, and Jesse Colwell Dress Shop. (Courtesy of Union County Historical Society.)

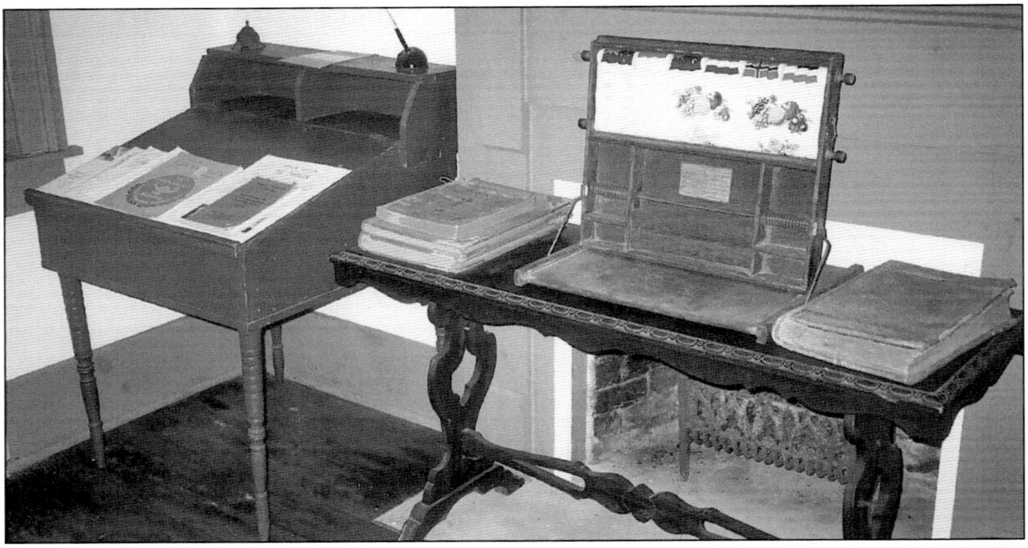

The Union County Historical Society was created in 1976 to preserve and promote the history and culture of Union County. The museum features the original clock and bell mechanism from the courthouse tower, weighing in at two tons. The internationally renowned Margarita Morgan Miniature Collection; *Rapture*, an excellent example of American primitive art; and displays of noted Union County natives are shown in the museum. (Photograph by Norman Cooper.)

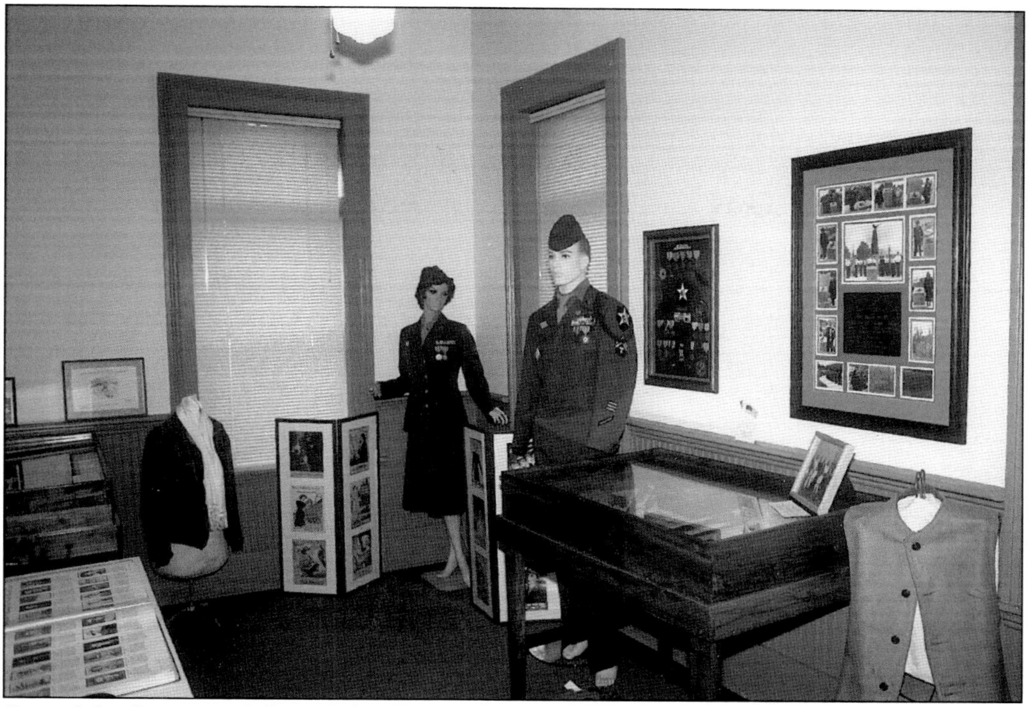

One of the favorite exhibits in the museum in the old courthouse is the military room, which includes artifacts, uniforms, and other items. Many of the items donated to the museum are from the Frank and Florence Ford Collection. (Photograph by Norman Cooper.)

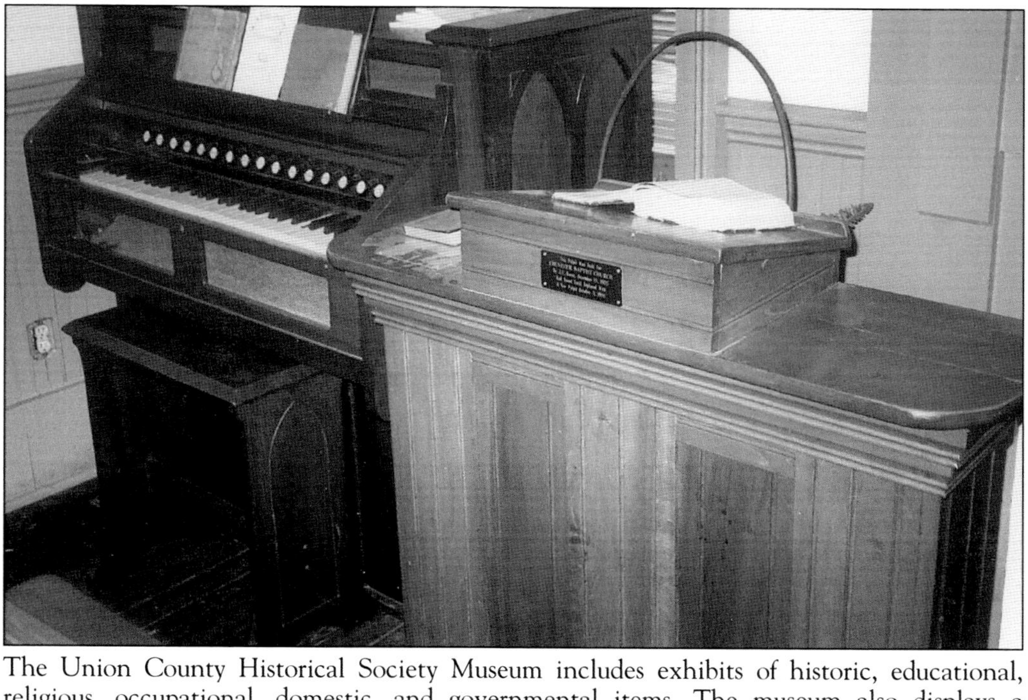

The Union County Historical Society Museum includes exhibits of historic, educational, religious, occupational, domestic, and governmental items. The museum also displays a collection of Native American artifacts, including projectile points, pottery shards, and an intact ceramic vessel. (Photograph by Norman Cooper.)

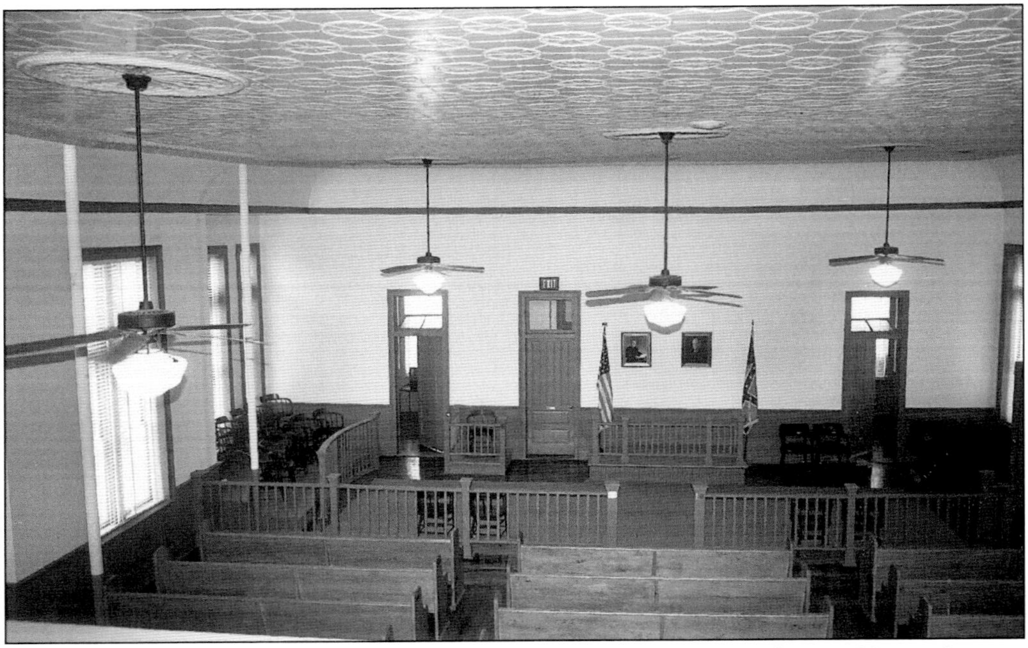

The Candler-Duckworth Courtroom in the old courthouse is a showplace in Union County. The courtroom is used for city court and has been used by the Superior Court of Union County. Cultural events such as concerts, lectures, and plays are held in the facility. The courtroom features an American flag and the Georgia flag in existence at the time of restoration. The two portraits on the wall are of William Henry Duckworth and Thomas S. Candler, both of whom served on the Georgia State Supreme Court. (Photograph by Norman Cooper.)

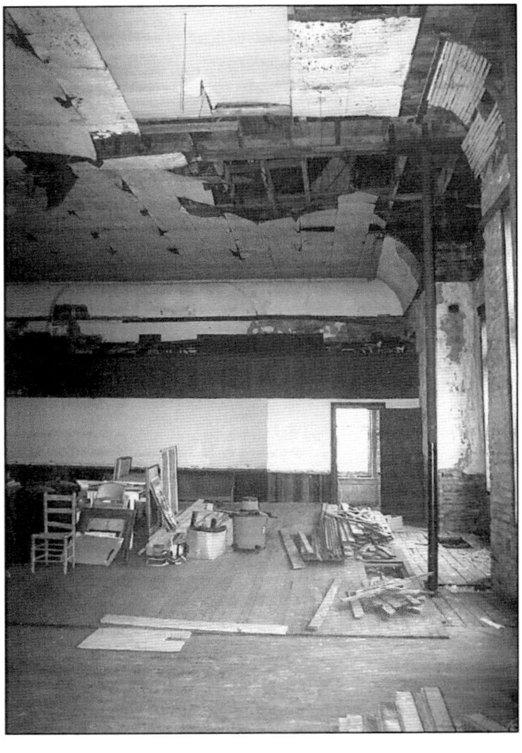

Before the restoration, when the courtroom was still showing the horrible signs from years of neglect, one observer commented that the only restoration the courtroom needed was with a match. The completion of the renovation of the Candler-Duckworth Courtroom proved a valuable kickoff toward the restoration of the clock and bell tower. (Courtesy of Union County Historical Society.)

An exciting day in the history of Union County occurred when the pieces were placed on the old courthouse to form the new clock and bell tower. The new tower is a replica of the previous tower. The Union County Historical Society insisted on a replica of the original tower. The tower was made in several parts in Kentucky. It was then shipped in on flatbed trucks. In this photo, the first part of the tower is being lifted by crane. It took several hours to install. The tower was placed on the front slope of the roof, in the same location where the original tower was located. The roof returned to metal, giving a more authentic appearance of the 1899 courthouse of yesteryear. The roof was reinforced by Head Westgate Corporation and a steel brace was installed. Many generous donors supported the project. (Photograph by Norman Cooper.)

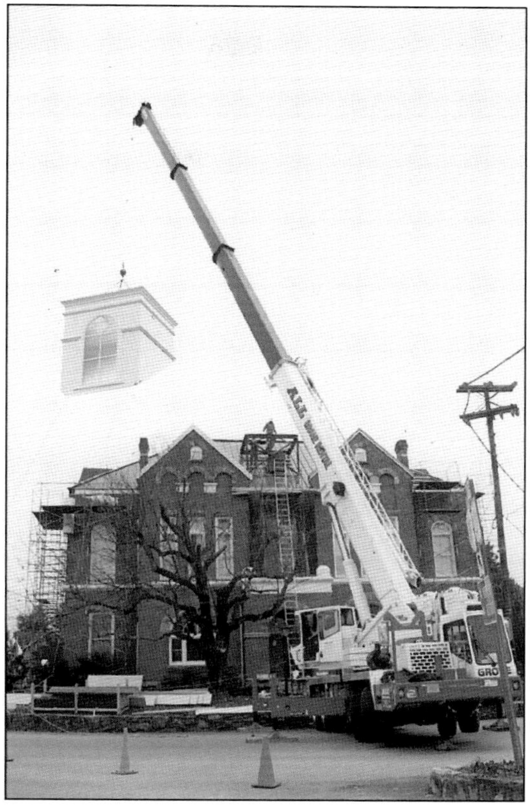

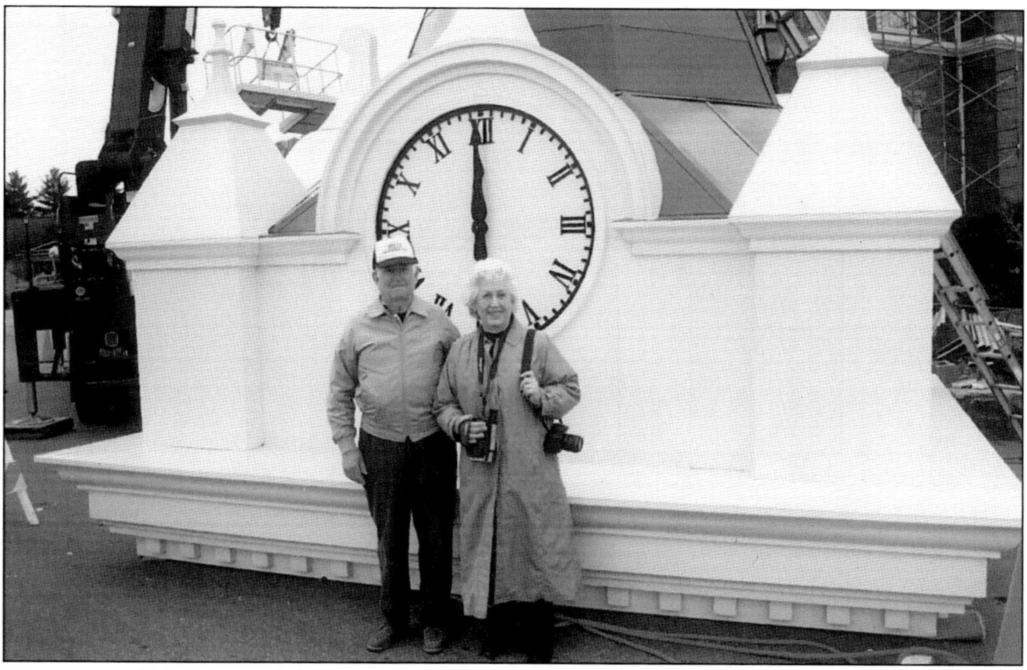

The vision of Maurice and Ann Farabee led to the replacement of the clock and bell tower. They provided tremendous leadership in the Historical Society and were instrumental in obtaining help from the community. (Photograph by Norman Cooper.)

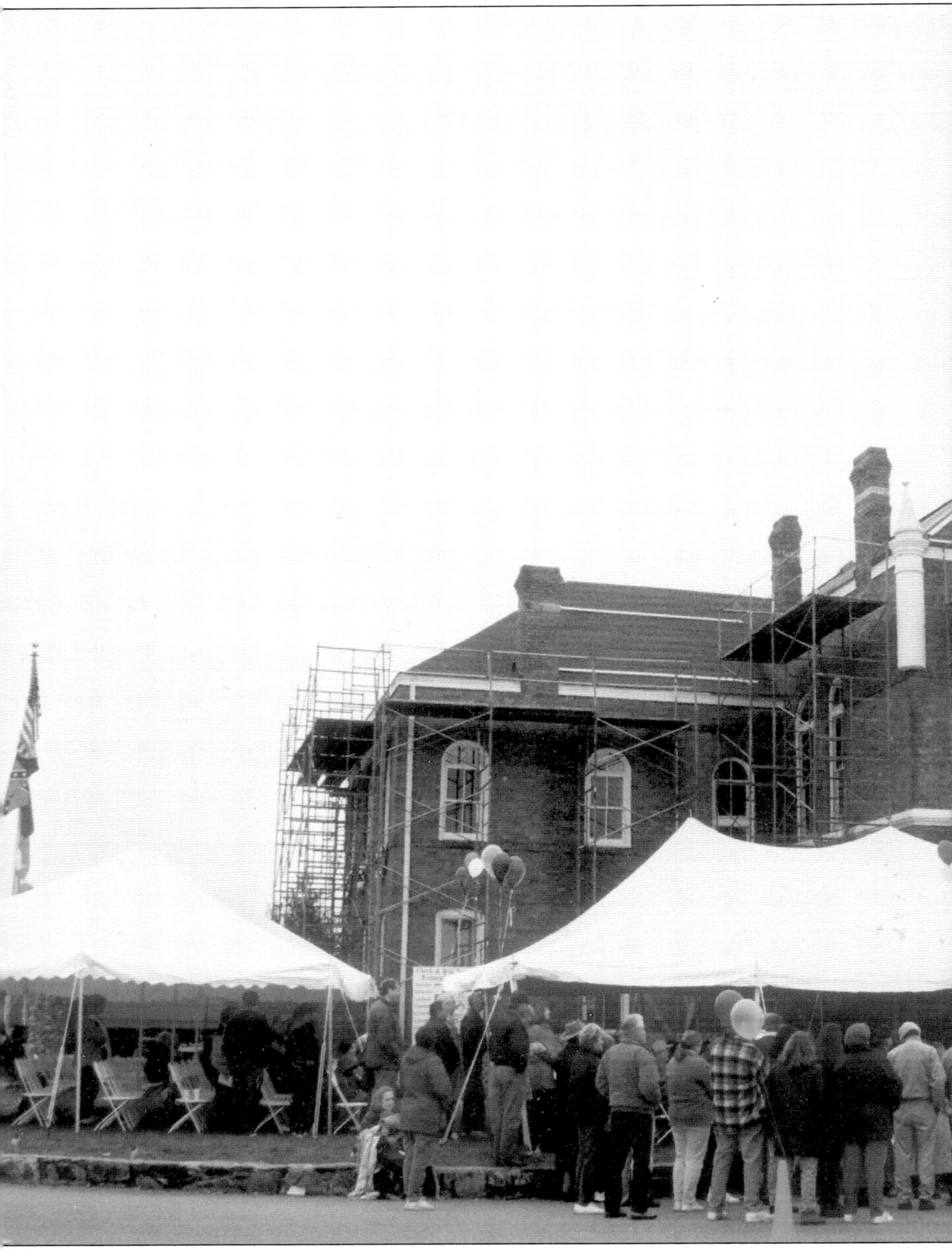

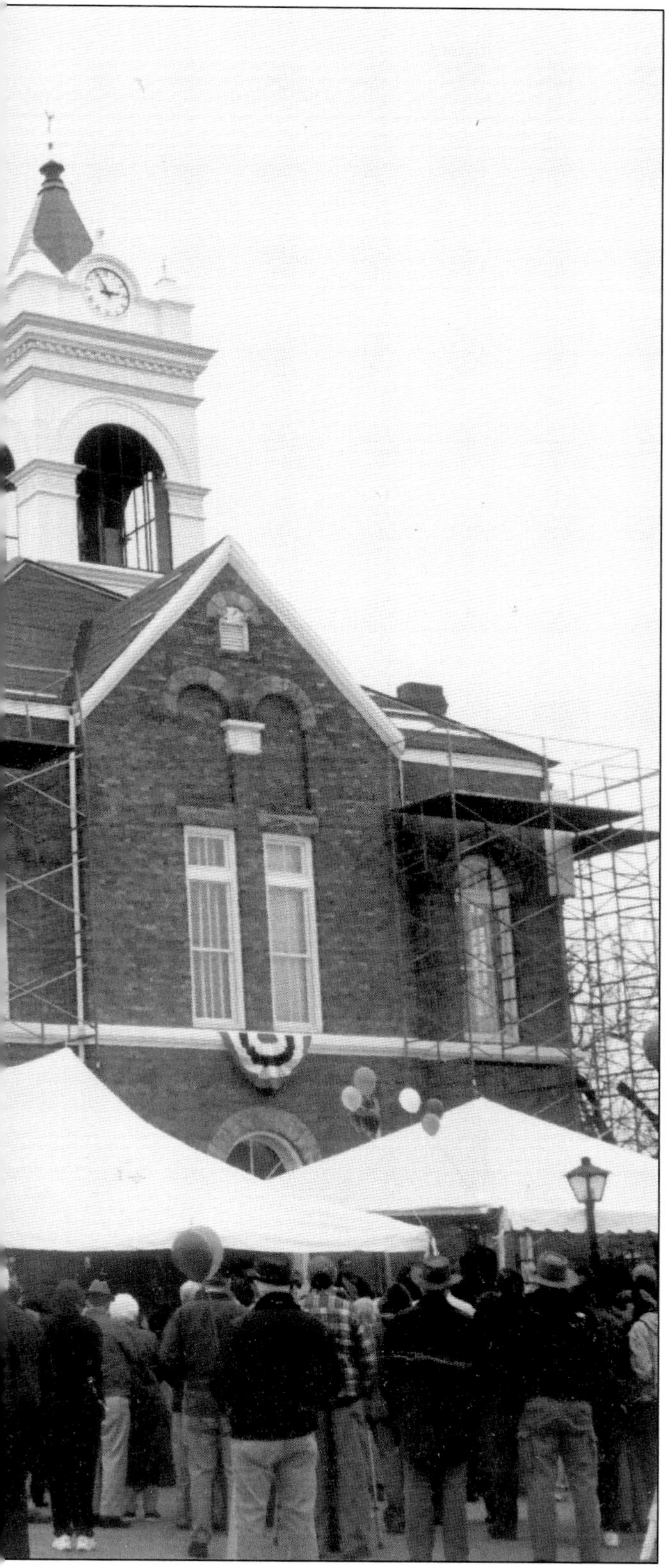

Dedication day for the clock and bell tower was held in November 2000. The day was overcast and very cold but the spirit and enthusiasm of those attending made for a day to be remembered. Keynote speaker for the event was the Honorable Zell Miller, a popular two-term Georgia governor who, at the time of the dedication, was a distinguished United States senator. Senator Miller thrilled the crowd with stories of days gone by and his memories of the old courthouse. Senator Miller talked about the kind of people who originally settled in the area and those who have lived in the area throughout the decades. Senator Miller said "Mountaineers possessed the characteristics of the love of liberty and personal courage. They had the capacity to withstand and overcome hardships. They had hospitality, loyalty, and trust in God and possessed a wonderful sense of humor." One overriding characteristic of mountain people was independence. A musical tribute about the courthouse was written by Sam Ensley and performed at the ceremony. Many notable speakers gave comments and other honored guests attended. Ann and Maurice Farabee were acknowledged. Others who had a part in past years in the preservation of the courthouse were noted, including Edith Paris. Scaffolding seen around the courthouse was used in the installation of a new roof. On the flag pole are three flags, the flag of the United States of America, the 1956 Georgia flag, current at time of the dedication, and the state flag, which flew over Georgia when the courthouse was erected in 1899. This photo was printed in the November 2000 edition of the *North Georgia News*. (Photograph by Norman Cooper.)

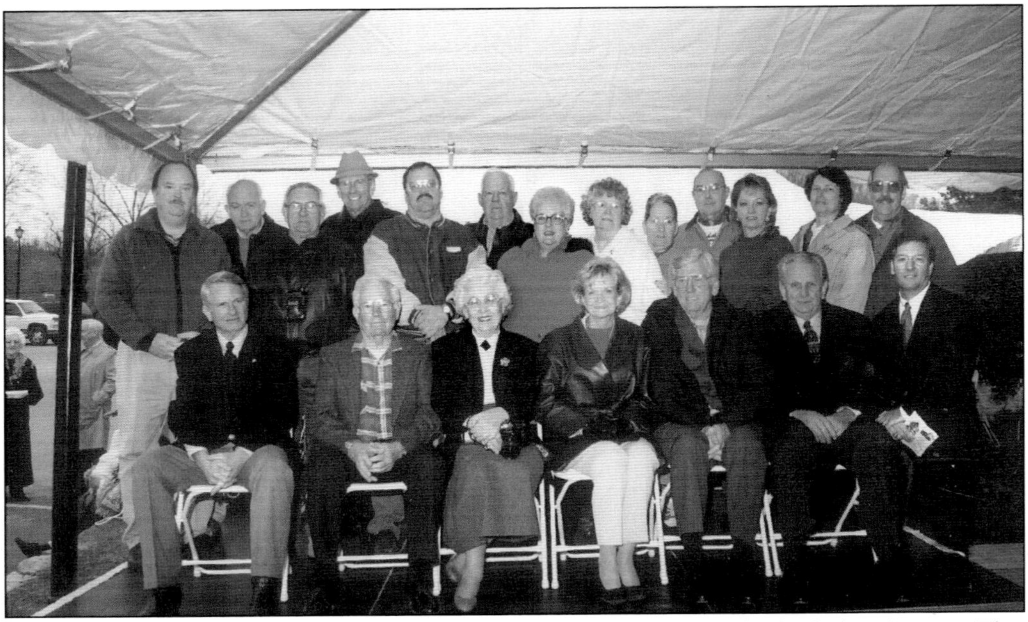

The restoration of the clock and bell tower was made possible with the help of many. This group photo includes many of those who served on the Clock and Bell Tower Restoration Committee, those who participated in the Clock and Bell Tower Restoration Dedication Day Ceremony, and others who had roles in the restoration. Those pictured, left to right, include the following: (front row) United States Senator Zell Miller, Maurice Farabee, Ann Farabee, Georgia State Senator Carol Jackson, Georgia State Representative Ralph Twiggs, former Georgia State Representative Carlton Colwell, and Jim Williams; (back row) Norman Cooper, Robert Head, Bud Akins, Charles Jenkins, Ron Brown, Rodney McCombs, Betty Williams, Martyne Jokela, Paula Johnson, Glenn Fite, Karen Daniels, Barbara Collins, and Lamar Paris. Betty Jane Shuler was assisting guests inside the courthouse when the photo was taken. (Photograph by Norman Cooper.)

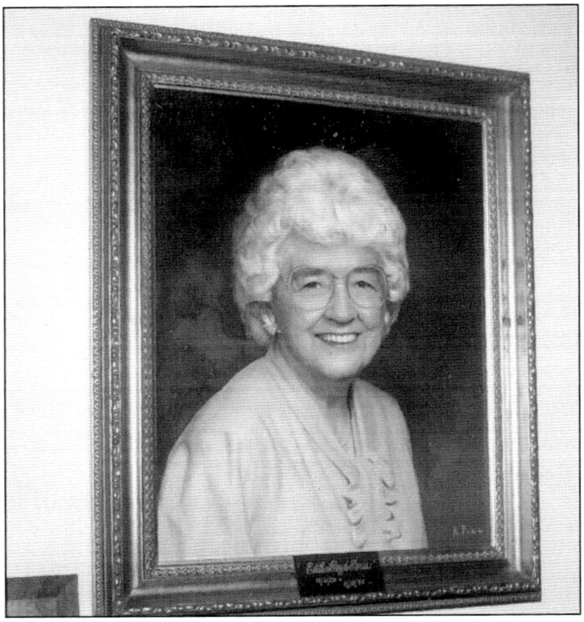

Edith Paris is pictured here. Edith's tireless efforts were instrumental in saving the historic structure. She is remembered as a person who was always soliciting support and donations to keep the old courthouse from being torn down. Without Edith, there would have been no historic courthouse to restore. (Courtesy of Union County Historical Society.)

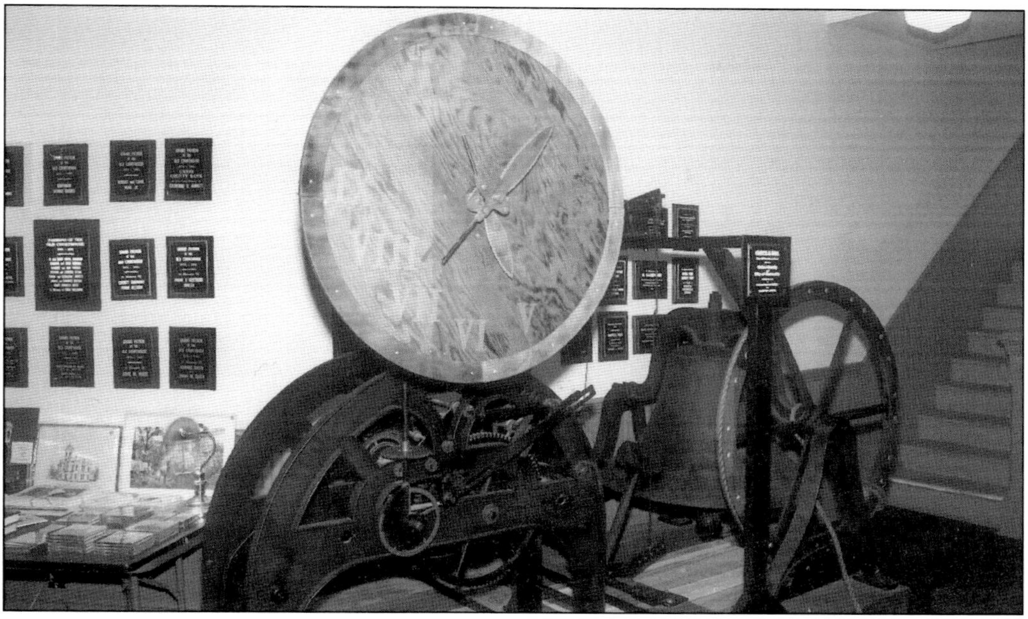

Ordinary Neal Collins had placed a legal ad in the North Georgia News advertising that the clock and bell (salvaged when the original tower was removed) would be sold at a public auction. Gene Sprayberry and Don Wintermute Sr., both with the Jaycees, appealed to fellow members that the bell should be saved. The Jaycees felt that the clock and bell were part of Union County's history and should not be sold. Collins agreed, withdrew the ad, and gave the unit to the Jaycees. Lamar Paris and Mac Orange inspected the clock in Ed Mauney's barn. It was found to be in poor condition. Jaycee Junior Bridges moved the clockworks to the school. Students took the works apart and cleaned the parts by sandblasting. The high school vocational class made the new face for the clock. This project was completed in June 1976 and the clock and bell were featured in the July 4th parade. Note the clock has Roman numerals, with the numbers nine and eleven both appearing as IX. (Photograph by Norman Cooper.)

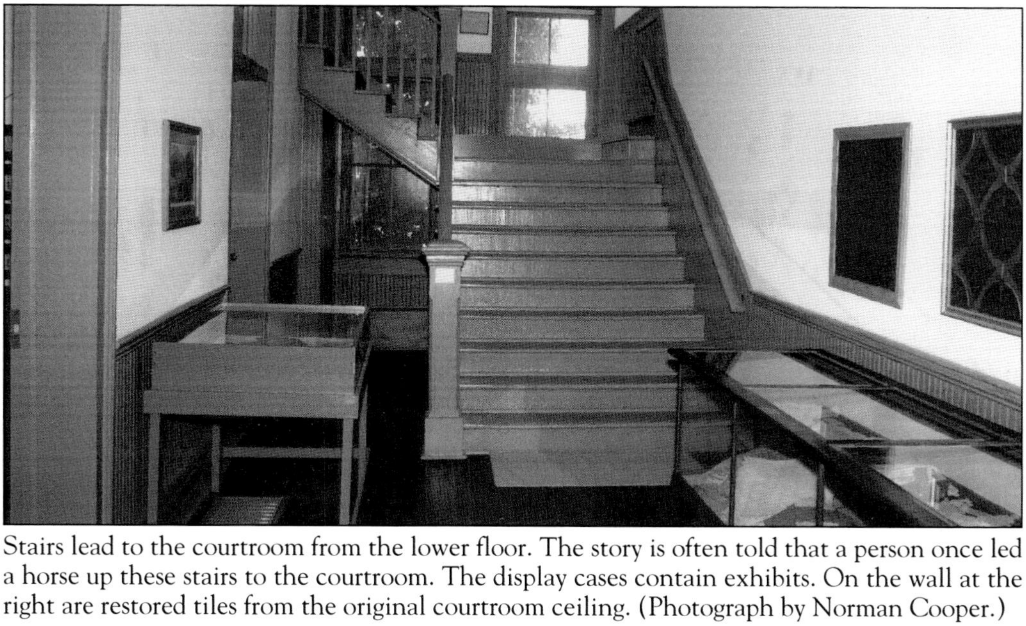

Stairs lead to the courtroom from the lower floor. The story is often told that a person once led a horse up these stairs to the courtroom. The display cases contain exhibits. On the wall at the right are restored tiles from the original courtroom ceiling. (Photograph by Norman Cooper.)

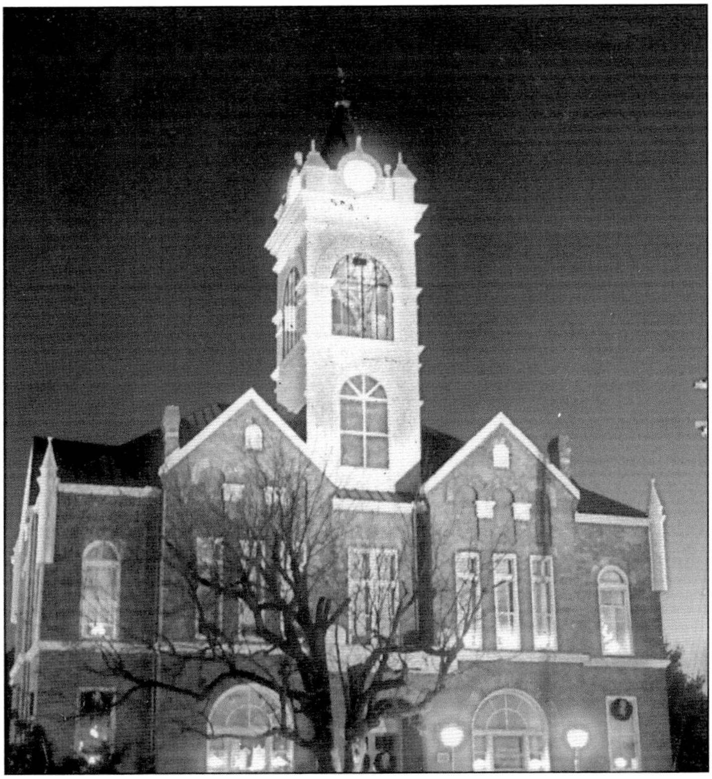

A ceremony was held on the square for the official lighting of the tower in 2002. (Photograph by Norman Cooper.)

The photograph below shows the southeast corner of the old courthouse after the roof was replaced. This is the view of the courthouse seen when approaching the building from the south. (Photograph by Norman Cooper.)

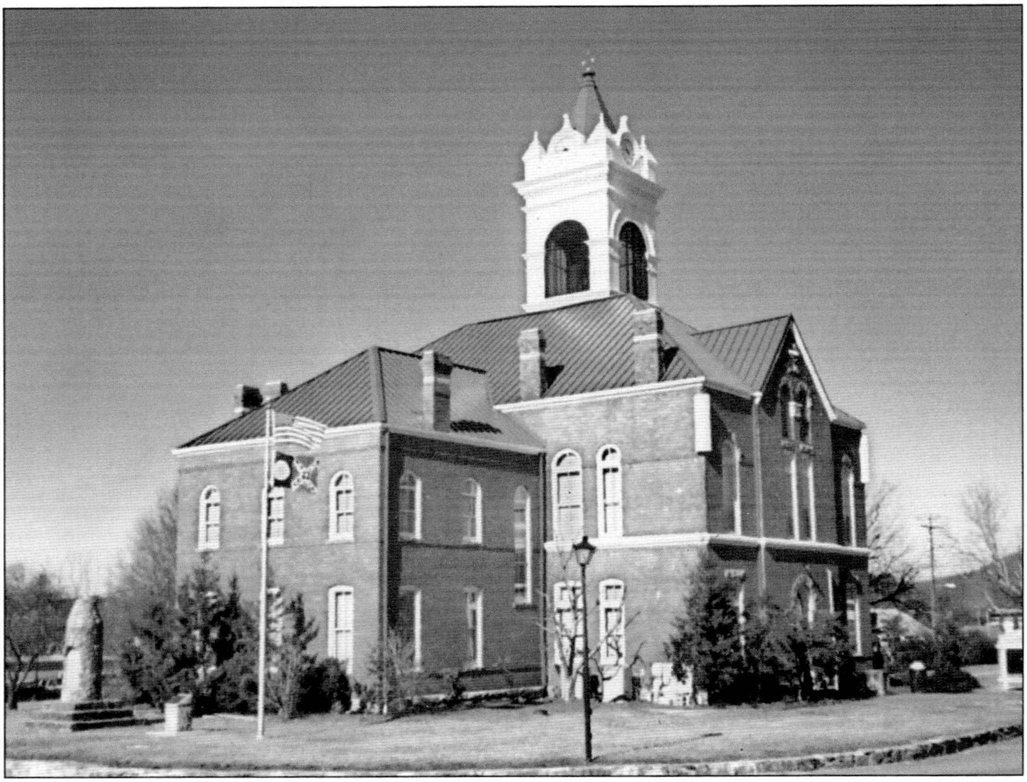

Two

EDUCATION

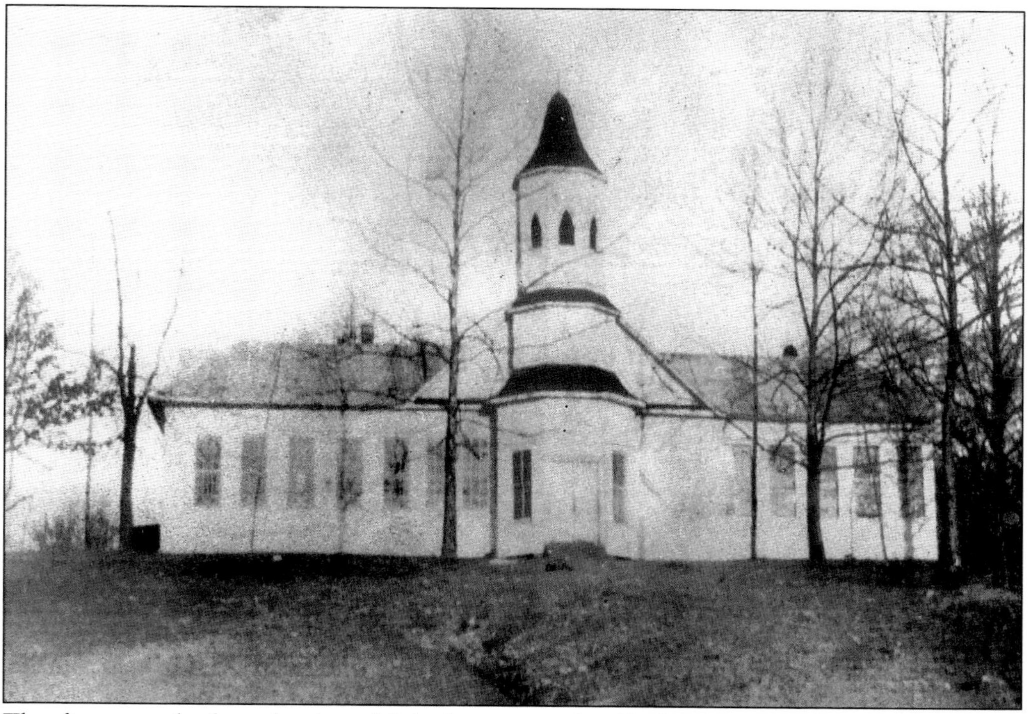

The first record of a school established prior to the Civil War was Blairsville Academy, founded in 1859. In 1904, plans were made by the Notla River Baptist Association to establish the Blairsville Collegiate Institute, pictured above. In 1928, the school was sold to the Union County Board of Education for $1,000 and was renamed Union County High School. This photo is believed to be taken around 1906–1907. (Courtesy of Union County Historical Society.)

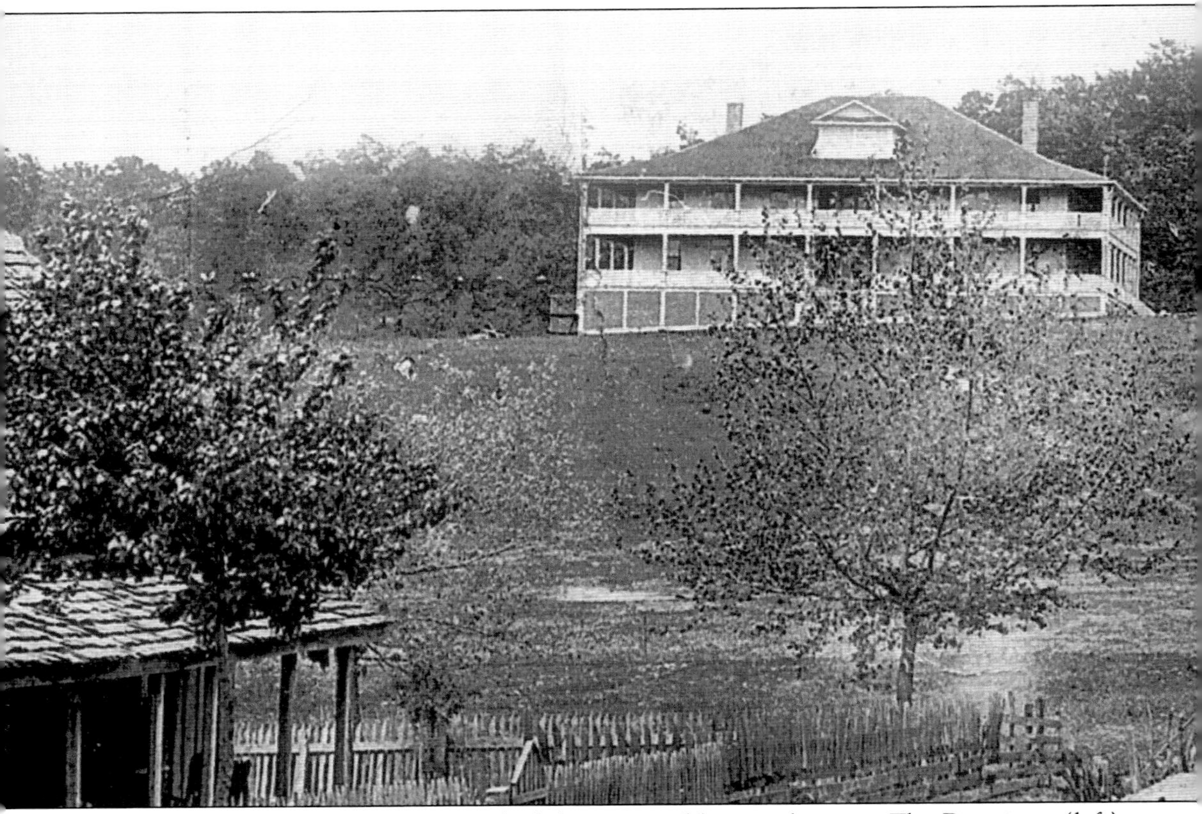

The Blairsville Collegiate Institute (right) is pictured here with tower. The Dormitory (left),

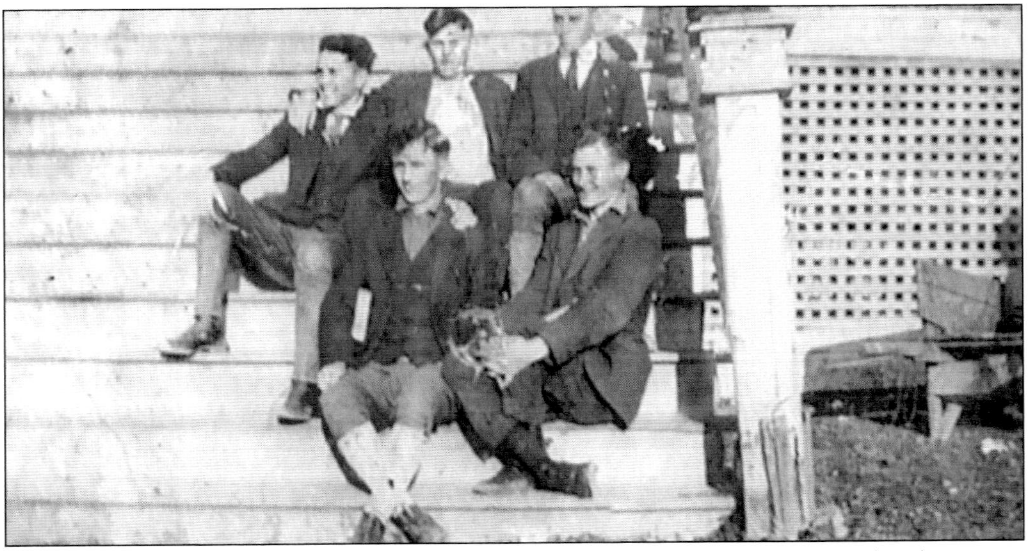

Blairsville Collegiate Institute students and a teacher pose on the steps at the dormitory. Members pictured are as follows: (front row) two unidentified; (back row) J.P. Press Davenport, unidentified, and Vernon Dyer. (Courtesy of David Friedly.)

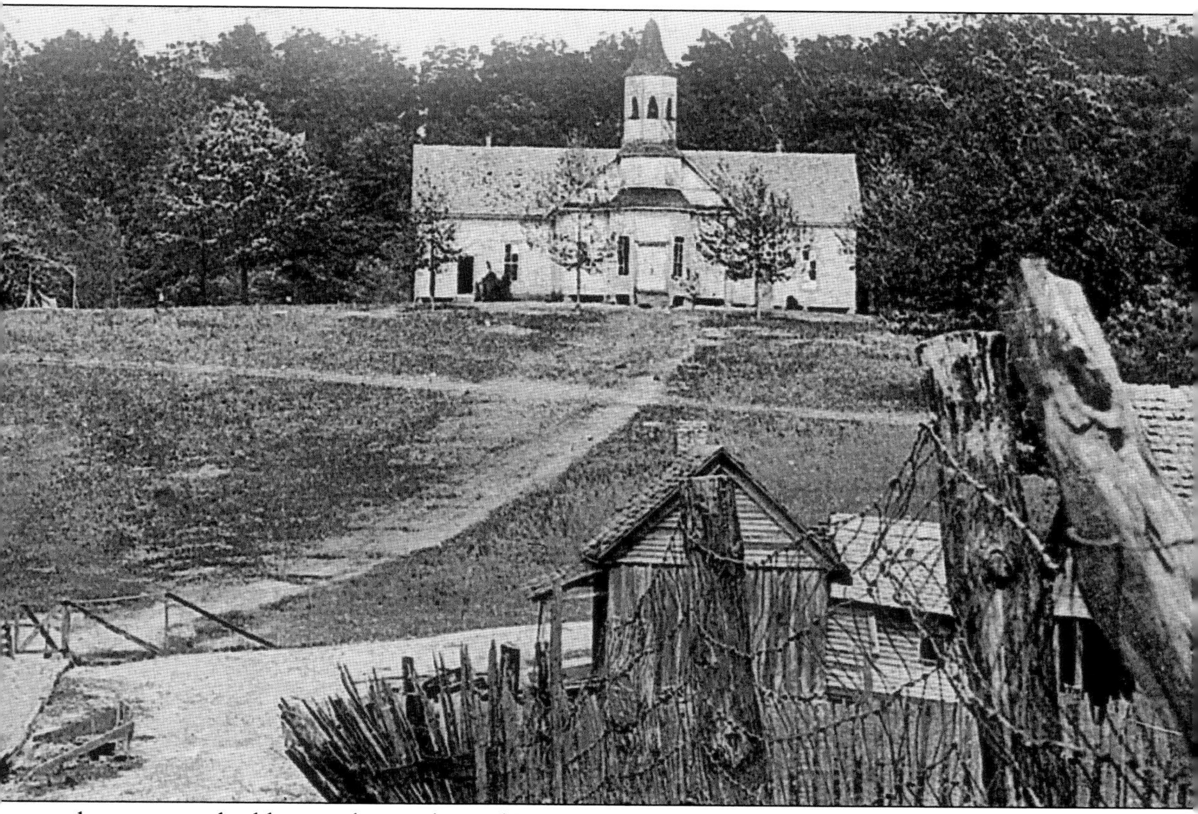

the two-story building, is shown above. (Courtesy of Union County Historical Society.)

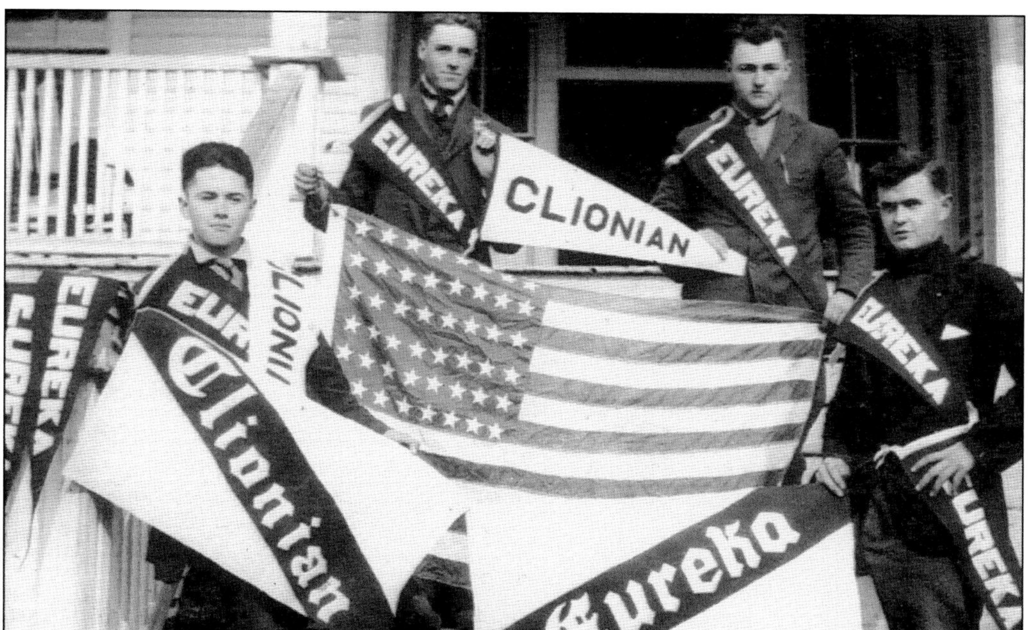

Blairsville Collegiate Institute Debating Society students pose on the steps of the dormitory. (Courtesy of David Friedly.)

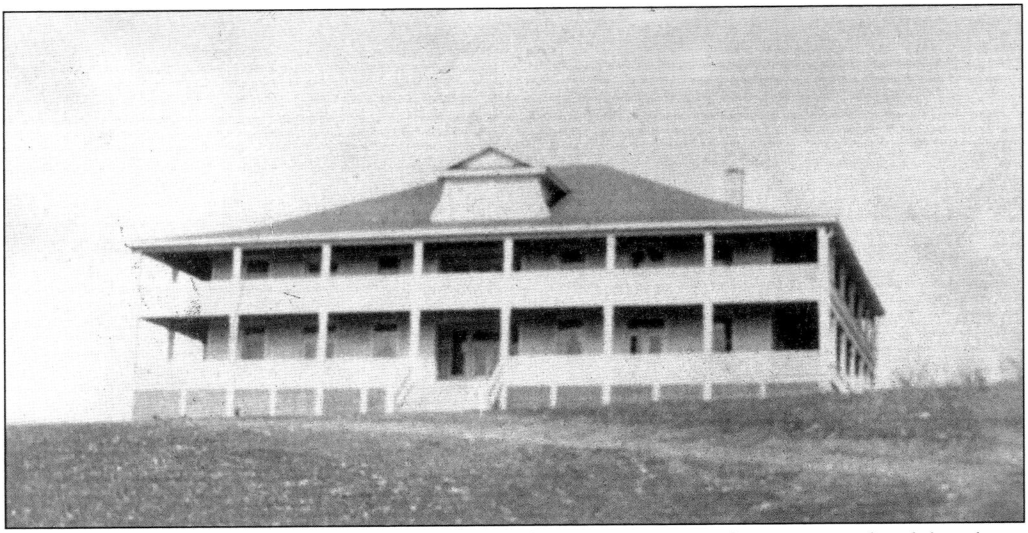

Blairsville Collegiate Institute is pictured here. The inscription on the reverse side of the photo reads, "Old dormitory where I lived when I first came to Blairsville 1929." (Courtesy of Geneva Smelser Hughes.)

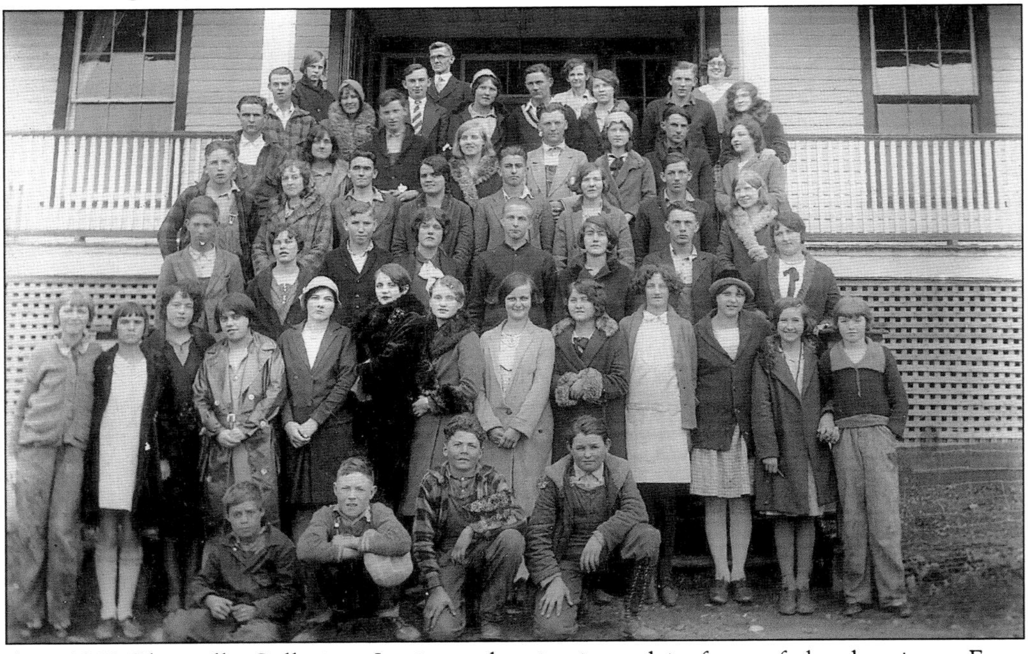

A c. 1928 Blairsville Collegiate Institute class is pictured in front of the dormitory. From left to right are (first row) Gene Foster, Robert Butt, Charlie Wimpey, and Neal Jackson; (second row) two unidentified, Alice Mauney, Mary Lizzie Foster, Ethel Wimpey Rawlins, Mabel Ross, Eva Souther Jenkins, unidentified, Florence Jackson Hunter, Nellie Dyer, three unidentified, and Austelle Colwell; (third row) unidentified, Mary Dyer, Clarence Shuler, three unidentified, Woodrow Dixon, and unidentified; (fourth row) unidentified, Evelyn Cagel Hill, two unidentified, Cecil Everett, and unidentified; (fifth row) all unidentified; (sixth row) unidentified, Lotus Lance Conley, two unidentified, Frank Charters Penland, unidentified, Marion Chambers, and Mozell England; (seventh row) all unidentified. (Courtesy of Jane Thompson.)

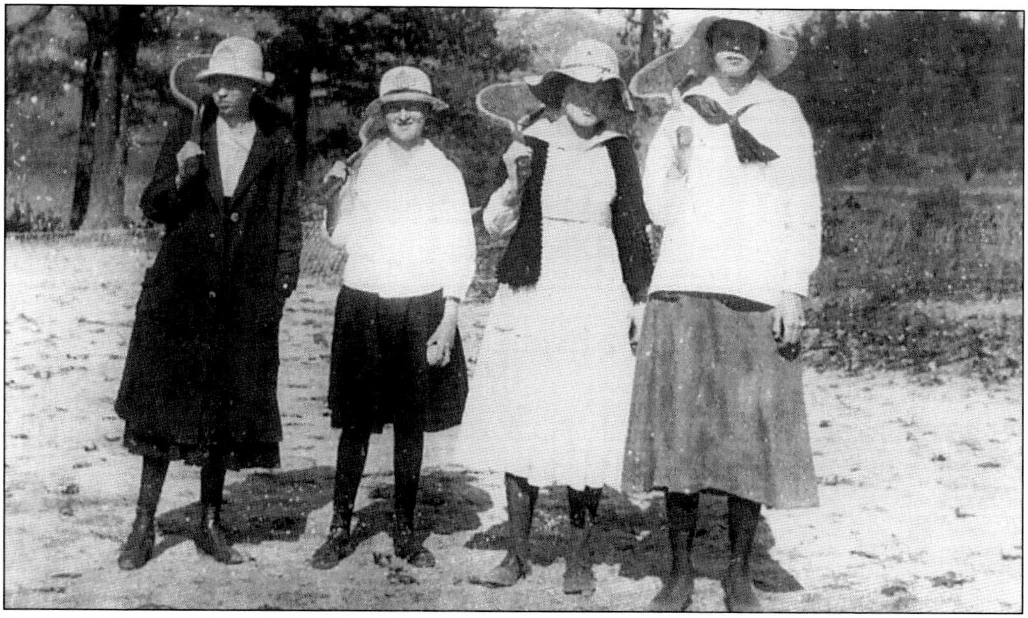

Pictured above at the Blairsville Collegiate Institute in 1917. Seen from left to right are Edna Jarrett, Irene Wellborn, Gertrude Reid, and Bess Cook. (Courtesy of Mrs. Grapelle Colwell.)

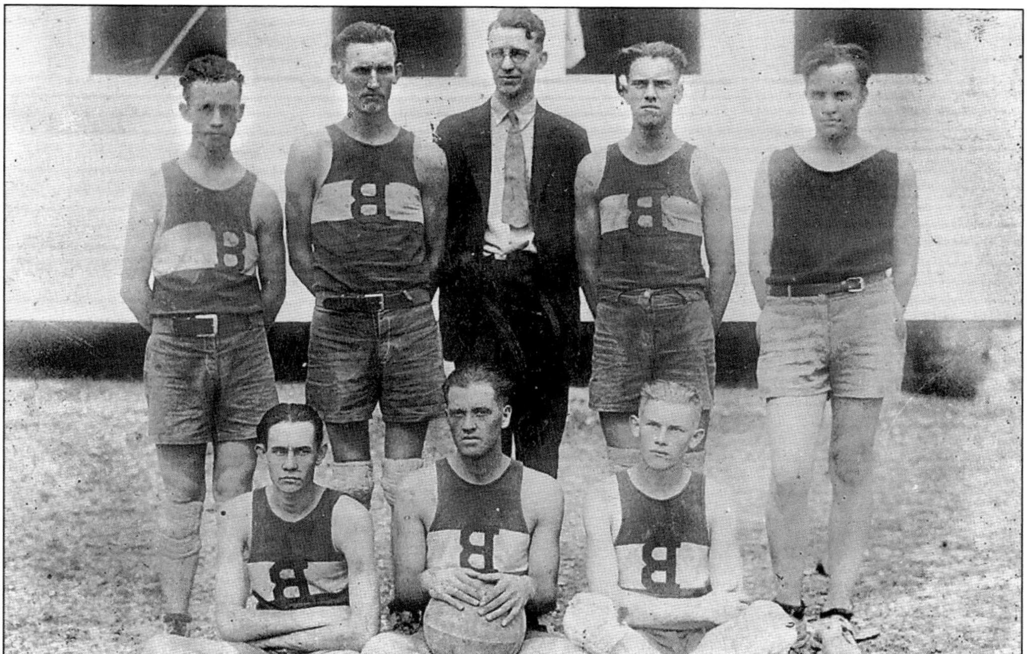

The First Basketball team in Union County at Blairsville Collegiate Institute included, from left to right, (front row) Roger Cobb, Iven Collins, and Oscar Collins; (back row) Hub Collins, William B. Ledford, Harry V. Smith (coach), Roscoe Collins, and Tom Berry Shope. Not pictured are Wayne Stroud and Olvie Collins. The team played in 1925–1927on a dirt and gravel court. They once won three games all in the same day, and they won a game against Epworth by a score of four to two. This photo appears to be printed in reverse—note the backwards "B" on all but one jersey. (Courtesy of Union County Historical Society.)

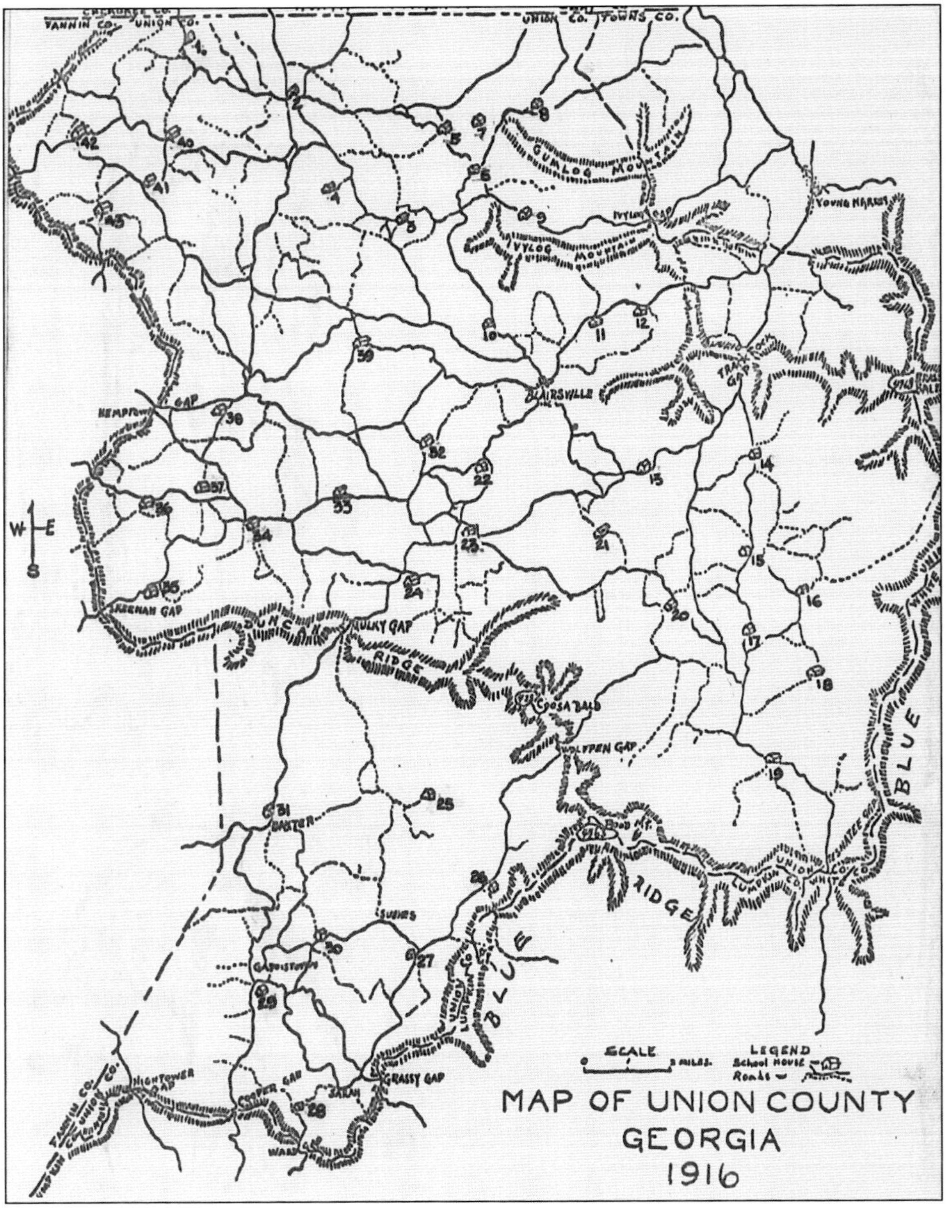

Around 1915, there were 43 separate elementary schools, grades first through seventh, and one high school in the county. Those small elementary schools had enrollment ranging from 25 to 55. There was no electricity or running water. Textbooks were in short supply and the *Blue Back Speller* was frequently the only text available. The schools were Bethany (1), Ivy Log (2), Antioch (3), New Hope (4), Russell (5), Ebenezer (6), Smyrna (7), Bell (8), Pleasant View (9), Pleasant Hill (10), Windy Hill (11), Brasstown Zion (12), Harmony Grove (13), Track Rock (14), Old Liberty (15), New Liberty (16), Choestoe (17), Pine Top (18), Hood (19), Berry (20), Shady Dale (21), Coosa (22), Mt. Pleasant (23), Spriggs' Chapel (24), Zion (25), Mt. Lebanon (26), Mt. Airy (27), Pleasant Valley (28), Mt. Pleasant (29), Corinth (30), Center Hill (31), Bunker Hill (32), Young Cane (33), Timber Ridge (34), Camp Ground (35), Confidence (36), Bethlehem (37), Providence (38), Mt. Zion (39), Union (40), Bruce (41), Mt. Olivet (42), and Blairsville (43). (Courtesy of Union County Board of Education.)

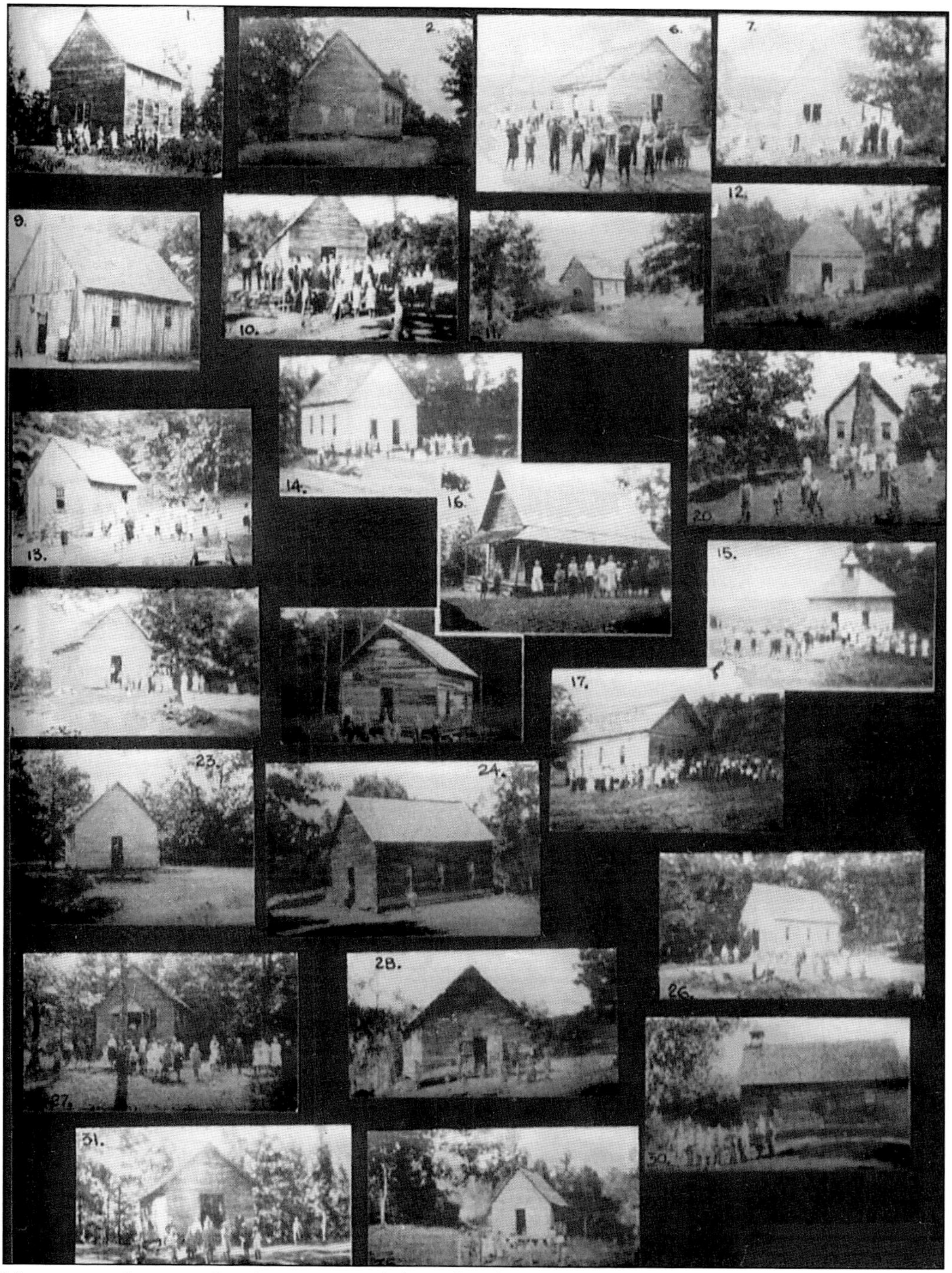

Numerous photographs show some of the schools from 1916. Seen above are the following: (first row) Bethany, Ivy Log, Ebenezer, and Smyrna; (second row) Pleasant View, Pleasant Hill, Windy Hill, and Brasstown; (third row) Harmony Grove, Track Rock, New Liberty, Berry, and Old Berry; (fourth row) Coosa, Pine Top, and Choestoe; (fifth row) Coosa and Mt. Pleasant; (sixth row) Mt. Lebanon and Mt. Airy; (seventh row) Corinth, Timber Ridge, and Mt. Pleasant. (Courtesy of Union County Board of Education.)

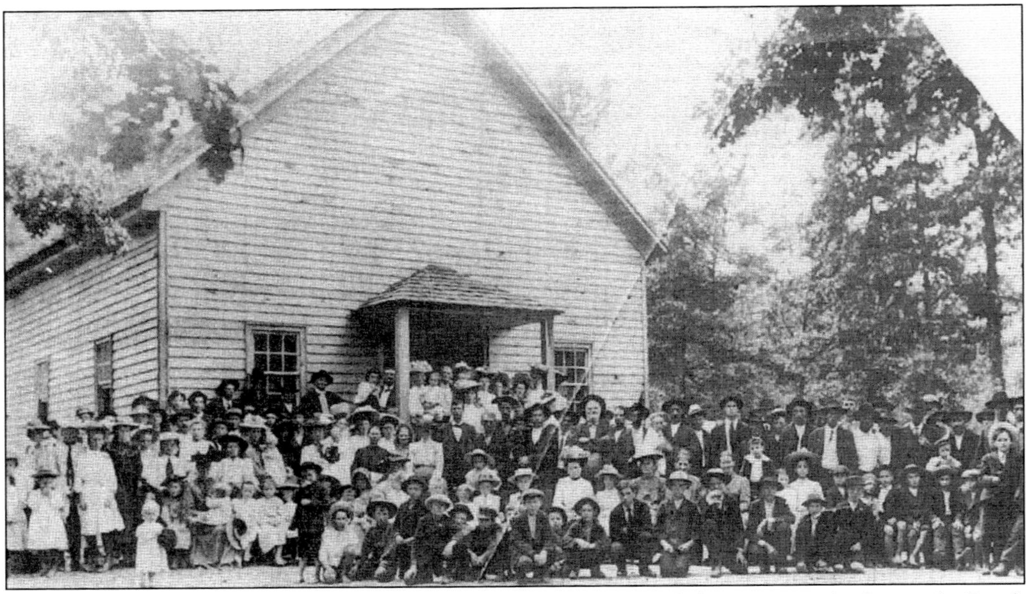

Cooper's Creek Baptist Church School is shown here around the year 1910. Cooper's Creek School existed from 1847 to 1955, located on Highway 60. (Photo as it appears in Coopers Creek Baptist Church 152nd anniversary commemorative booklet.)

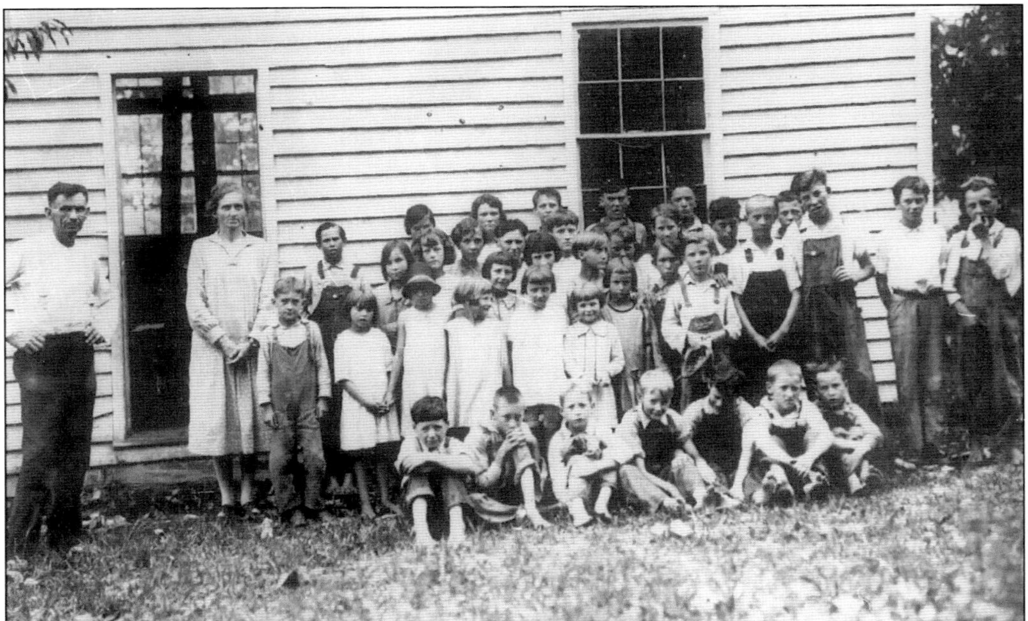

Members of the Ivy Log School, shown here in 1928, (from left to right) are (front row) Tom Elliott, Robert Martin, Luther Watts, Dale Elliott, Howell Ledford, ? Whitmore, and ? Whitmore; (middle row) unidentified, Ruby Anderson, Elway Ledford, Austine Elliott, Hazel Lance, Lavell Kirkendall, Carman Martin, two unidentified, Durane Burnett, three unidentified, Emory Walker, and two unidentified; (back row) Vester Anderson, two unidentified, Alice Whitmore, Earl Deaver, and two unidentified; (standing left at door) teacher Columbus F. Conley and teacher Bessie Mauney Lance. (Courtesy of Dale Elliott.)

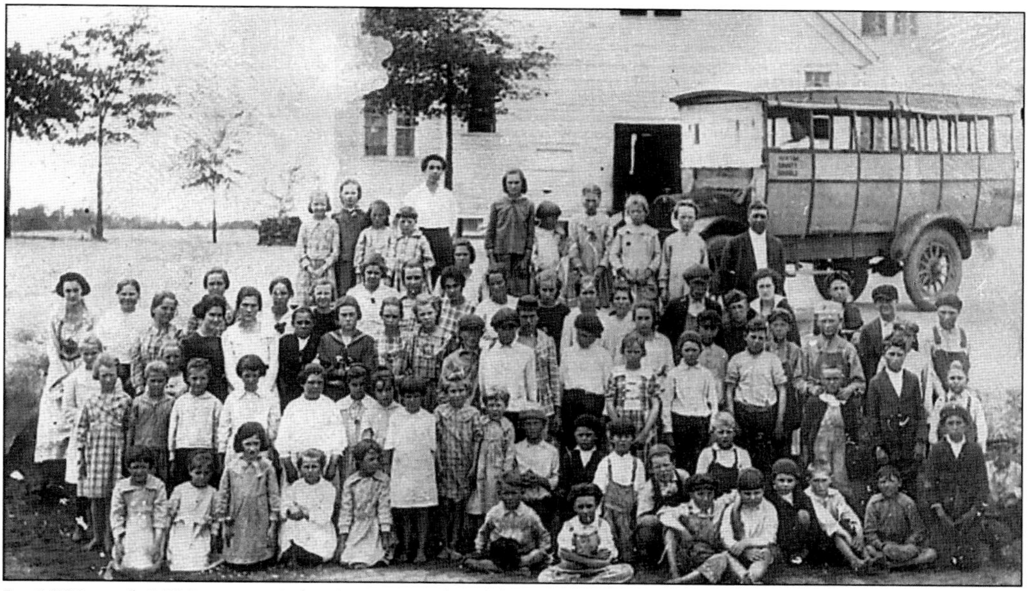

In 1932 and 1933, one of the longest school bus routes in the United States was operated in Union County. Students in the Suches area were brought to high school in Blairsville through Woody Gap via Turner's Corner. Students from the Hatchet Creek area walked over four miles down the Old Logan Turnpike to Route 129 to catch the bus to school in Blairsville. The mode of bus transportation was a Model T Ford Truck with handmade benches on the back. (Courtesy of Union County Historical Society.)

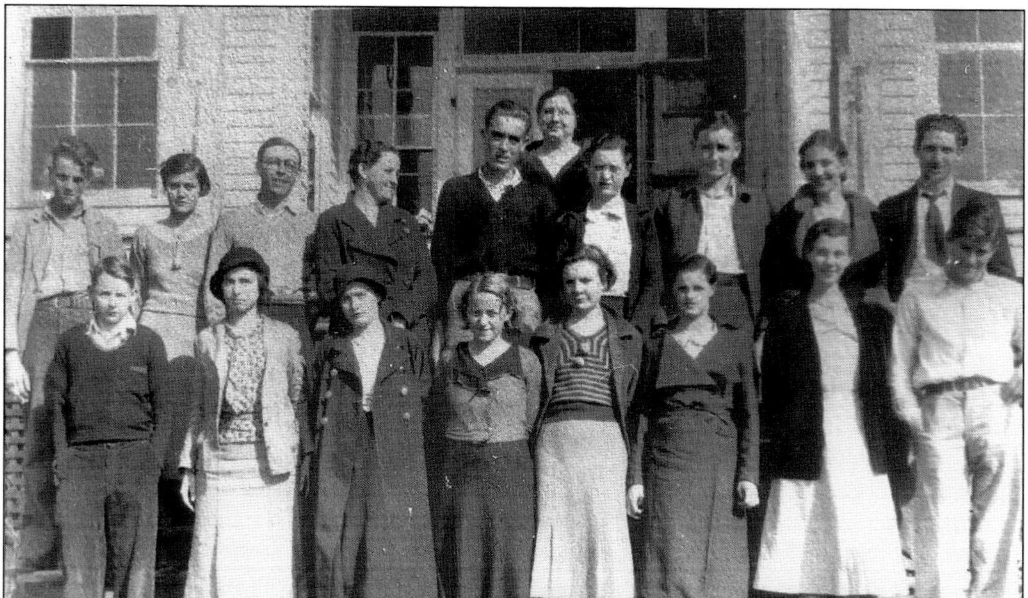

Union County High Junior Class of 1935 is pictured here. Members, left to right, include the following: (front row) Dale Elliott, Thelma Woodring, Leslie Akins, Madge Jones, Thelma Rogers, Hazel Hunter, unidentified, and Byron Herbert Reece; (back row) Garnet Morgan, Mary Berry, Wade Chastain, Georgia Erwin, Lenord Cagle, Eula Mae Scruggs, Ernest Martin, Loreen Jarrett, and George Watts. Teacher Geneva Hughes is pictured in the far rear of the photograph. (Courtesy of Dale Elliott.)

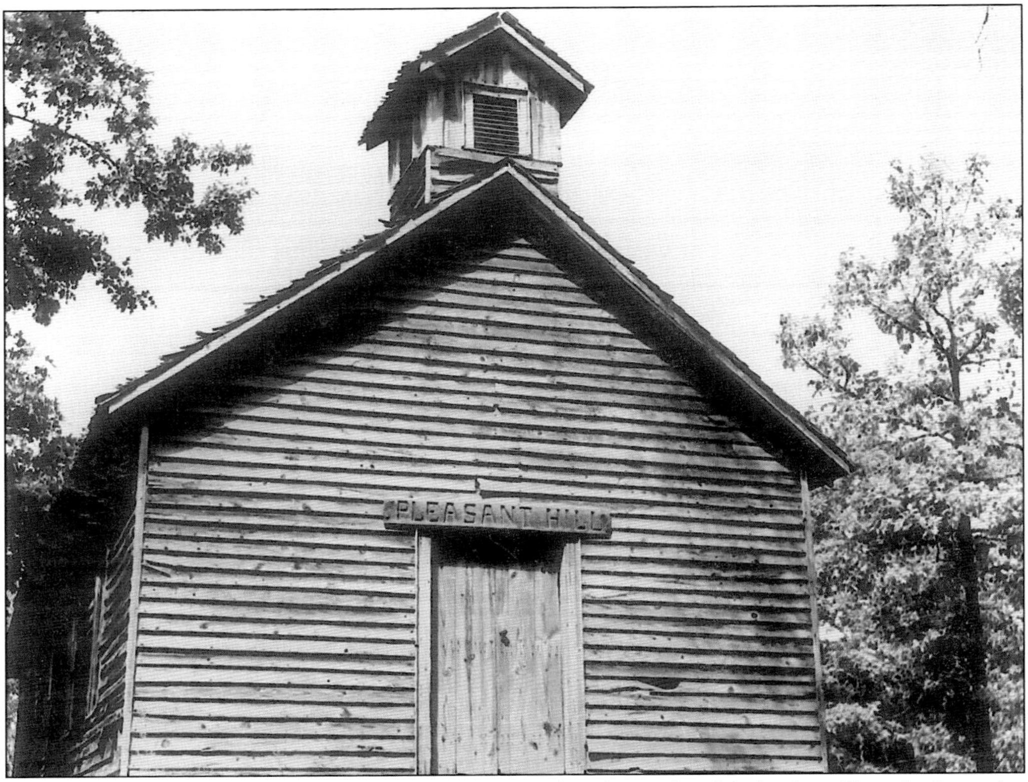

The Pleasant Hill School, also known as Pea Ridge, housed a Methodist Church from the late 1800s until 1927 and 1928 when it became a county school. (Courtesy of Union County Historical Society.)

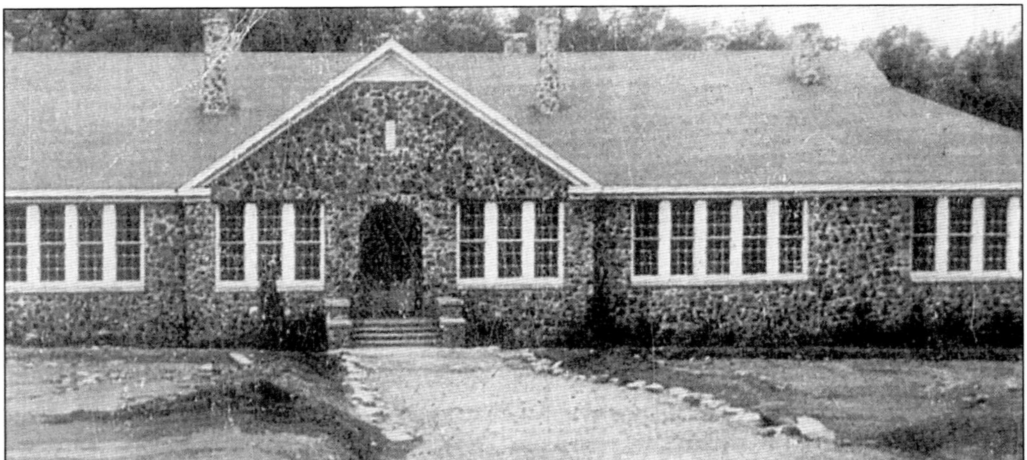

Woody Gap School, pending the National Register of Historic Places, began serving students in 1940. The original historic rock building still exists today. While renovations have taken place inside, the exterior of the structure has remained unchanged through the years. This photo was taken during the 1940s. Arthur Woody and Walter Woody purchased a 20-acre plot and presented it to the county for the new school. County Ordinary Frank Allison allotted $5,000 of county funds toward the building fund and Frank Shuler, School Superintendent, cashed a $10,000 bond to be used toward the cost of construction.

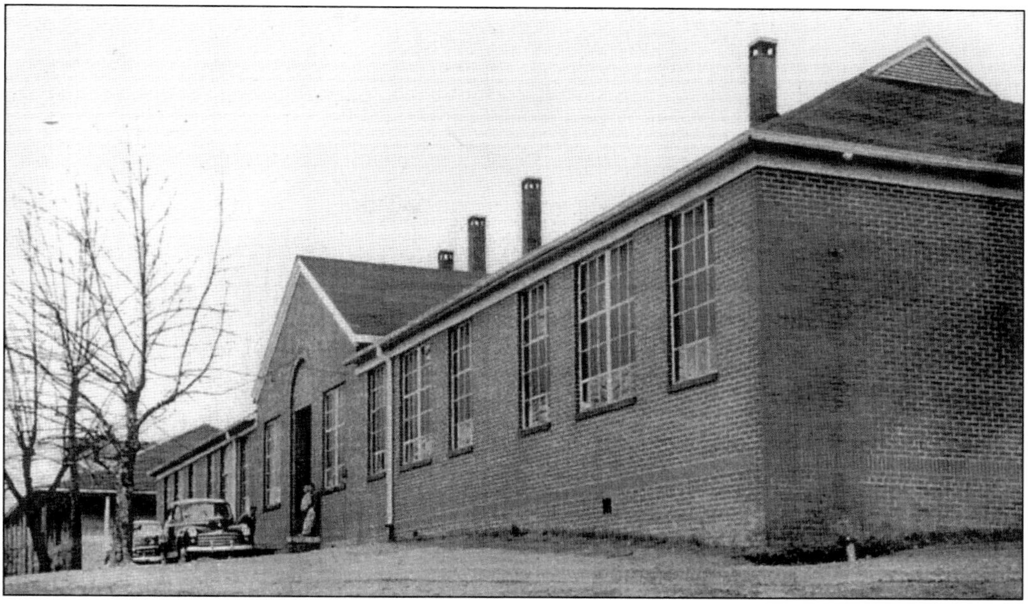

The first Union County High School, built in 1938, burned down Easter Sunday, April 19, 1949. The elementary school building in the back of this structure met the same fate. (Photo from *Treasured Memories*, 1949.)

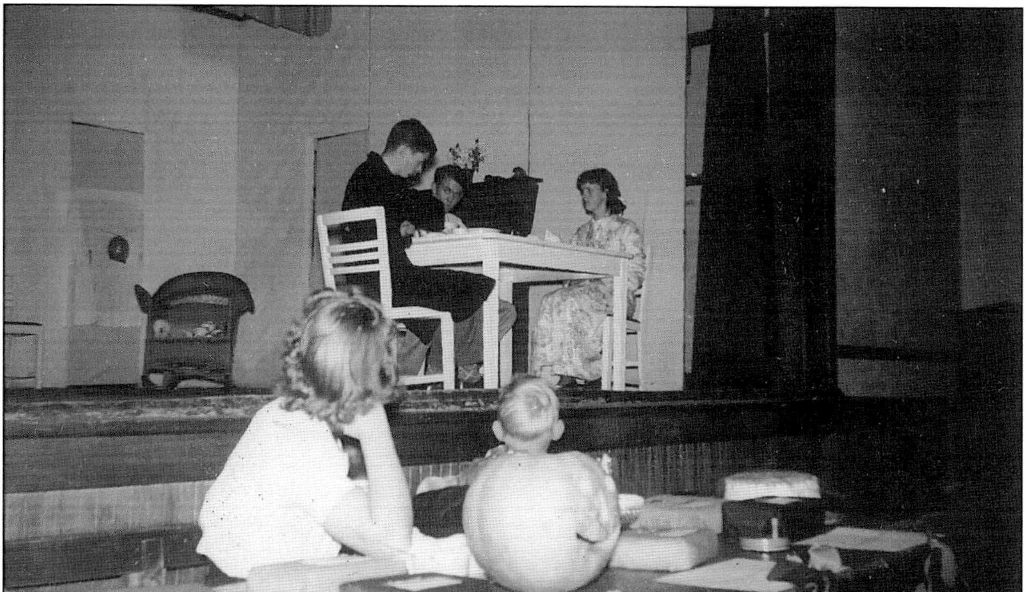

A school play takes place on the school stage that later burned in 1949. Seen around the table on stage are Emory Dockery, Barbara Ledford, and Coolidge Mason. Teacher Lizzie Mae Cooley and her son Jimmy sit with backs to the camera. (Courtesy of Union County Historical Society.)

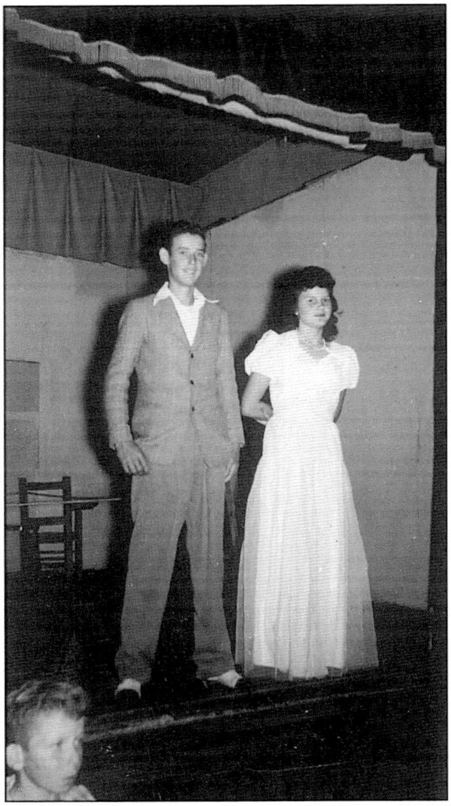

On stage at the Union County High Halloween Carnival in 1948 are King Bill Foster and Queen Betty Brown. The curtains on stage were a deep purple with bright gold fringe. Many remember the curtains as majestic. (Courtesy of Union County Historical Society.)

Pictured below is one of the last classes to graduate in the auditorium before the school burned down in 1949. (Courtesy of David Friedly.)

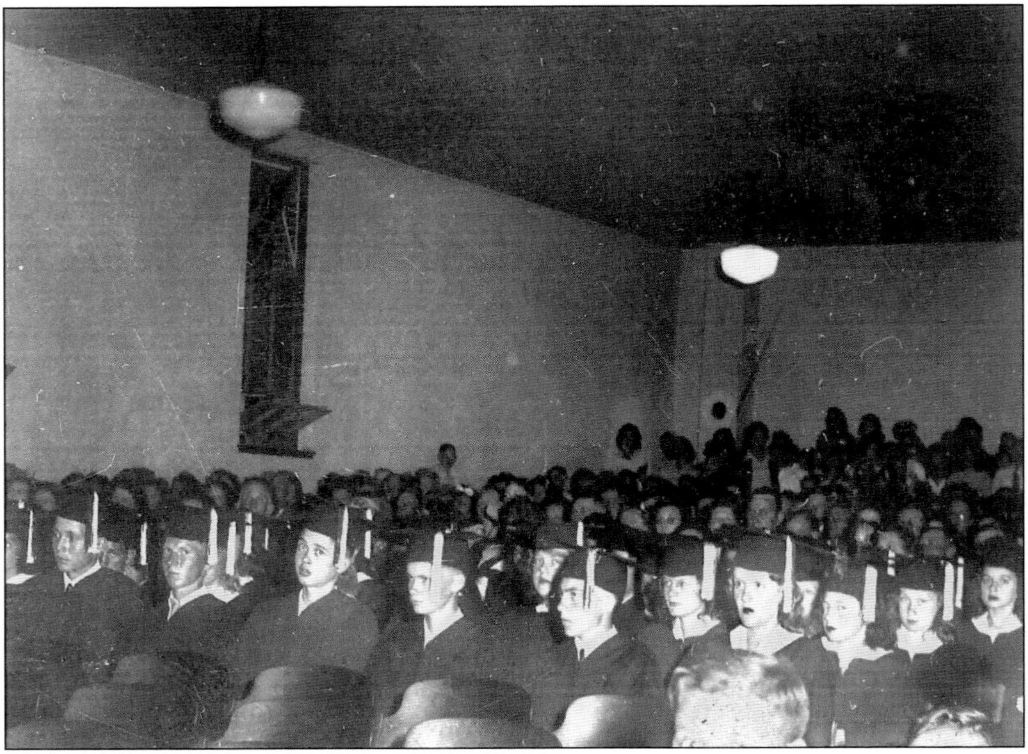

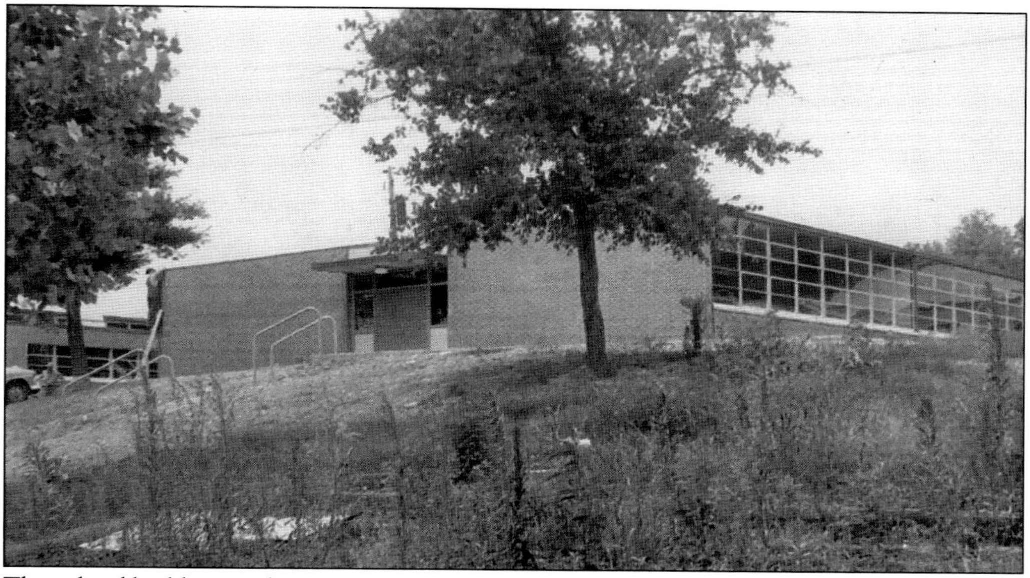

This school building, with construction complete in 1950, replaced the high school that burned. In 1951 and 1952 Union County High School graduation requirements changed from eleven years to twelve years. The last class to graduate from these buildings occurred in May 1969. (Courtesy of Union County Historical Society.)

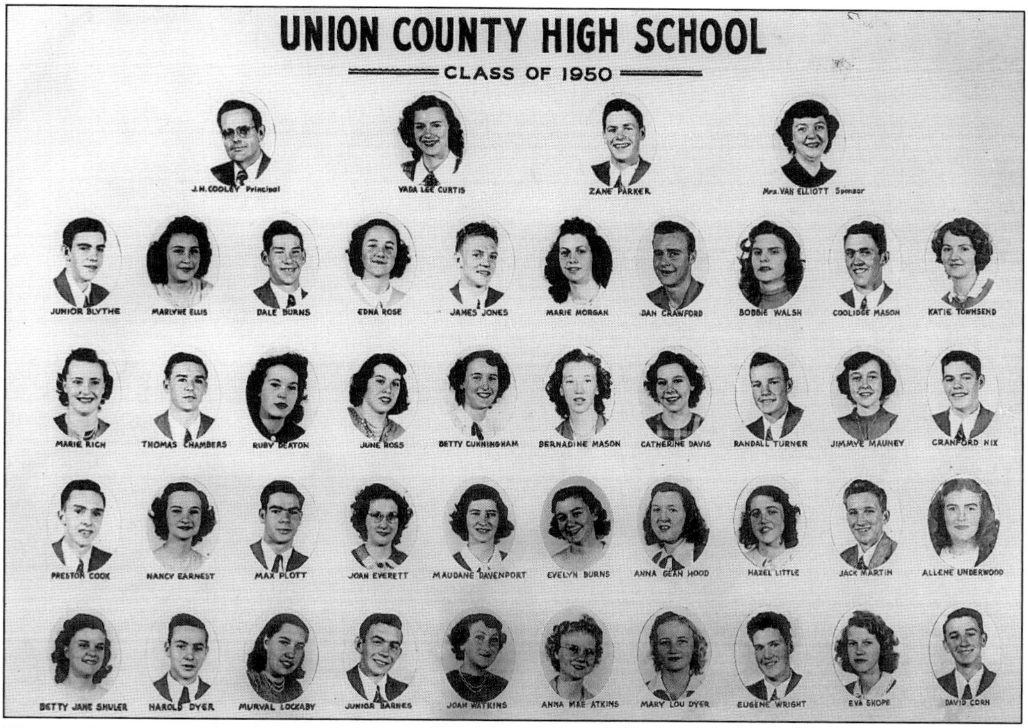

Union County High School senior class is shown here in 1950. When the school burned in 1949, all records, all photos, and memorabilia were lost. There was not enough time for the 1950 seniors to acquire or collect anything and thus no material for a yearbook. The only thing the seniors of 1950 have from their years in school is the above photograph. (Courtesy of Union County Historical Society.)

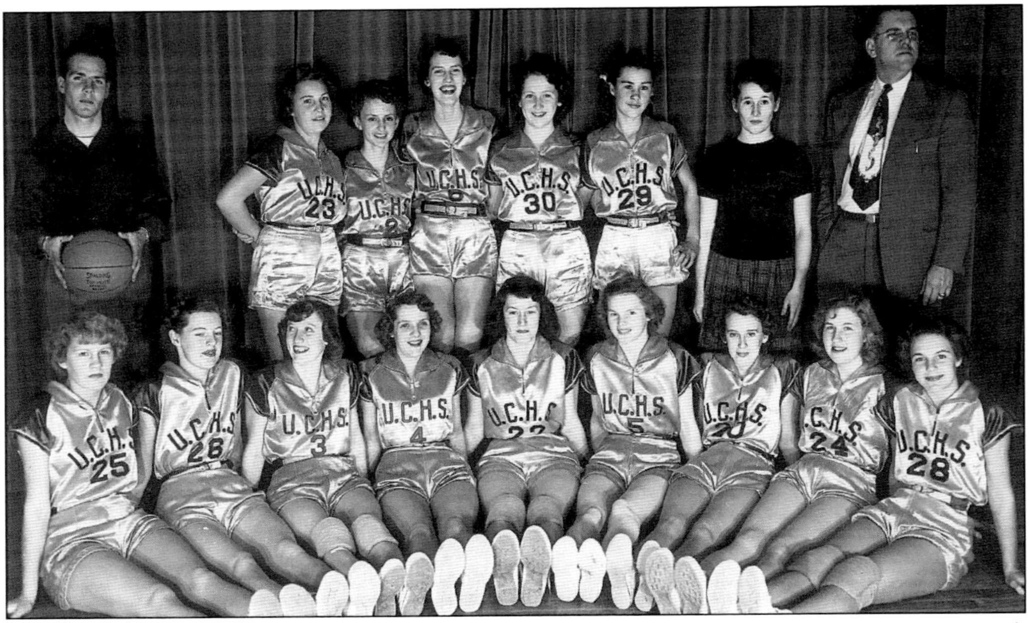

Union County High School 1953–1954 girls basketball team is shown here. Members pictured, from left to right, are (front row) Sarah Jo Ballew, Mary Ann Payne, Louise Whitmore, Betty Ann Kelley, Melva Lynn McAfee, Sarah Brown, Bennie Jo Conley, Betty Laura Killian, and Janie Berry; (back row) Coach James Butterworth, Joyce Lockaby, Marilyn Jenkins, Sue Henderson, Geraldine Payne, Maurine Ellis, Austelle Mason (manager), and Principal C.R. Collins. (Courtesy of Melva Lynn McAfee Drake.)

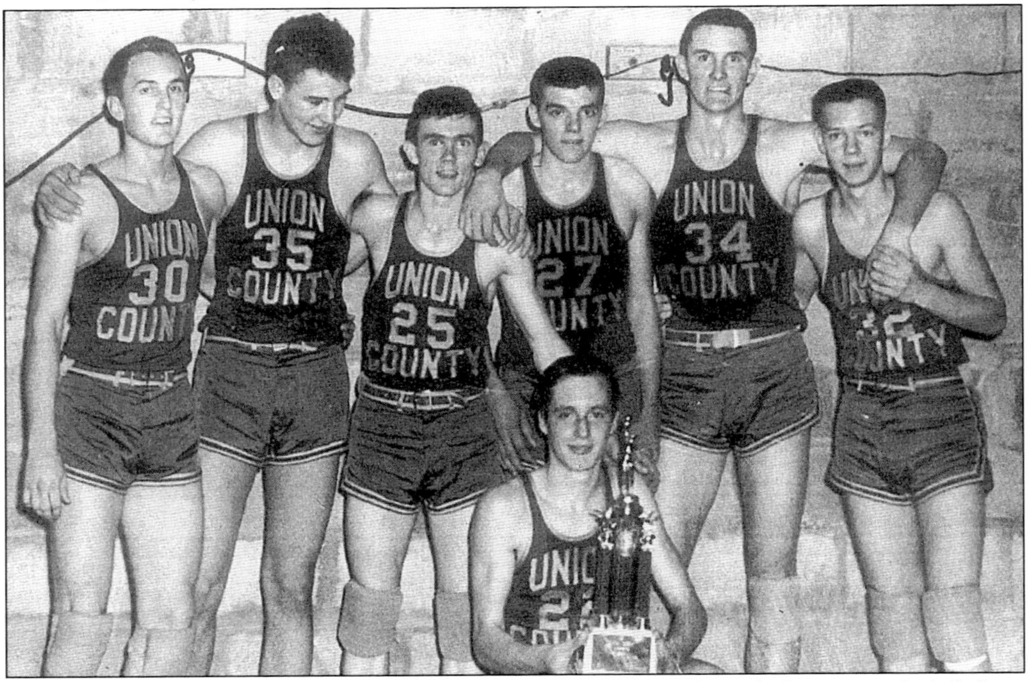

The Union County High School 1955 Basketball Champions of North Georgia included, from left to right, Bud Hill, George Berry, Bud Akins, Tommy Wilson, Jack Lance, and Charles Hill. Jackie Payne is kneeling in the picture. (Courtesy of Union County Historical Society.)

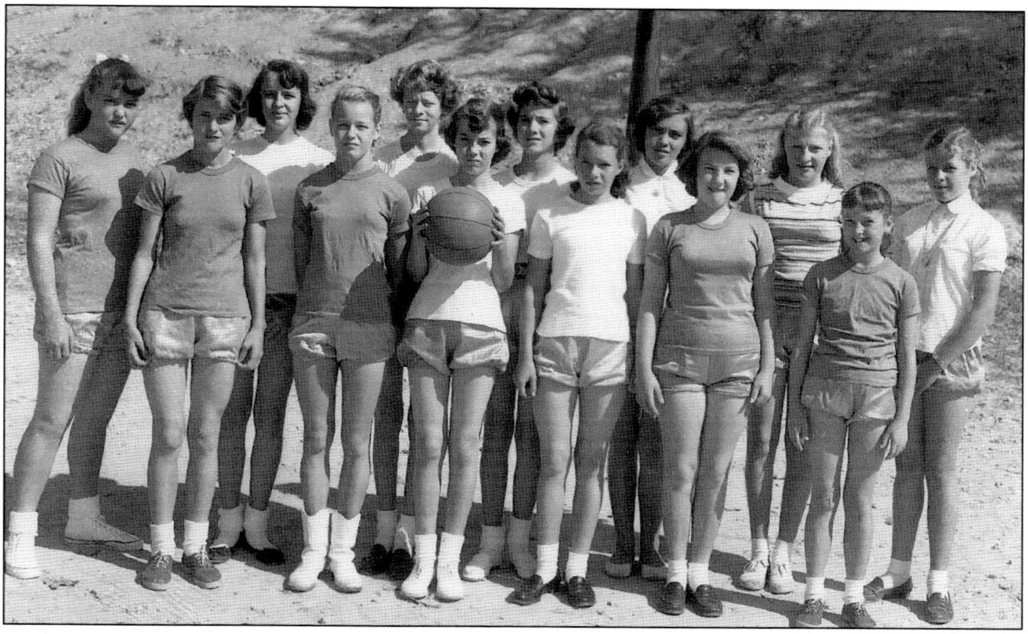

In this photograph c. 1956, the girls at Blairsville Elementary School play on a basketball court with a wooden backboard. The site they are playing on eventually became the Union County War Memorial. Note the footwear—the fourth girl from left is wearing white boots. Pictured from left to right are (front row) Grapelle Townsend, Myrtice Blalock, Carol Hutson, Mary Belle Plott, Patsy Young, and Janie Parker; (back row) Pattie Jenkins, Claudene Cook, Daisy Bowers, Sara Ann Swain, Willene Brown, Carolyn Plott, and Mary Lou Chambers. (Courtesy of Union County Historical Society.)

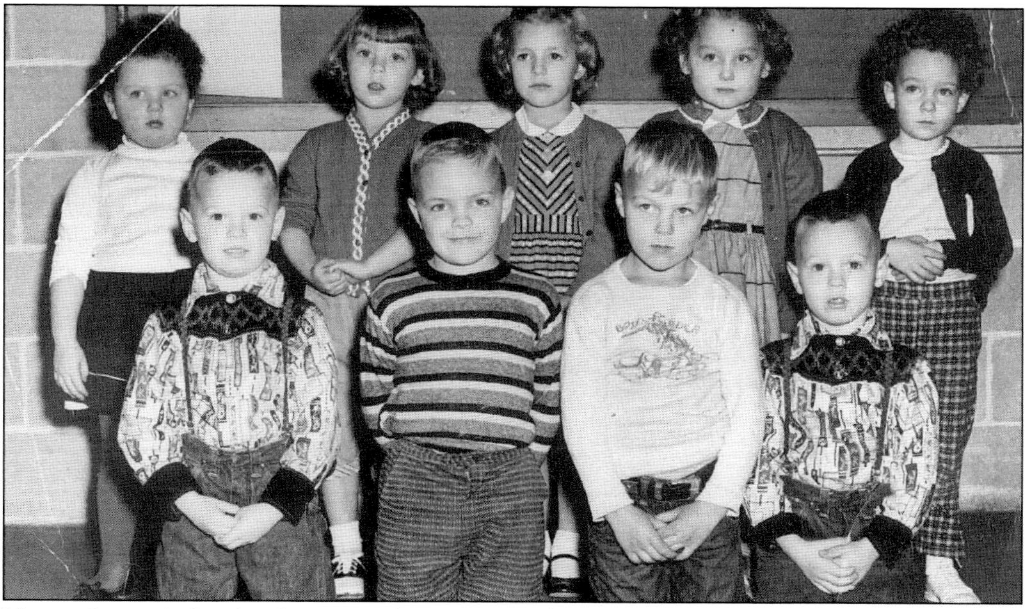

Union County's first kindergarten class is pictured in 1960. From left to right are (front row) Garry George, Barry Collins, Kent Foster, and Barry George; (back row) Cayce Davenport, Carolyn Seabolt, Ann Gowder, Donna West, and Grace Rollins. Teacher Mrs. Jo George is not pictured.

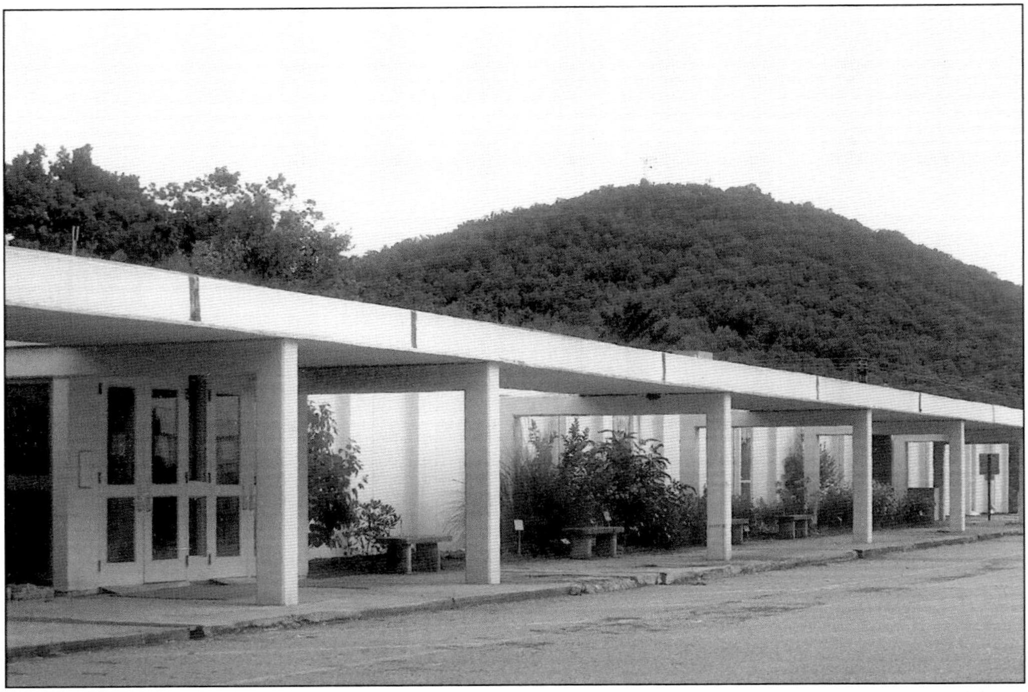

In the fall of 1969, the Union County High School students moved into the above building. The building sits atop one of the higher elevations in Blairsville. The parking lot gives a grand view of downtown Blairsville. (Photograph by Norman Cooper.)

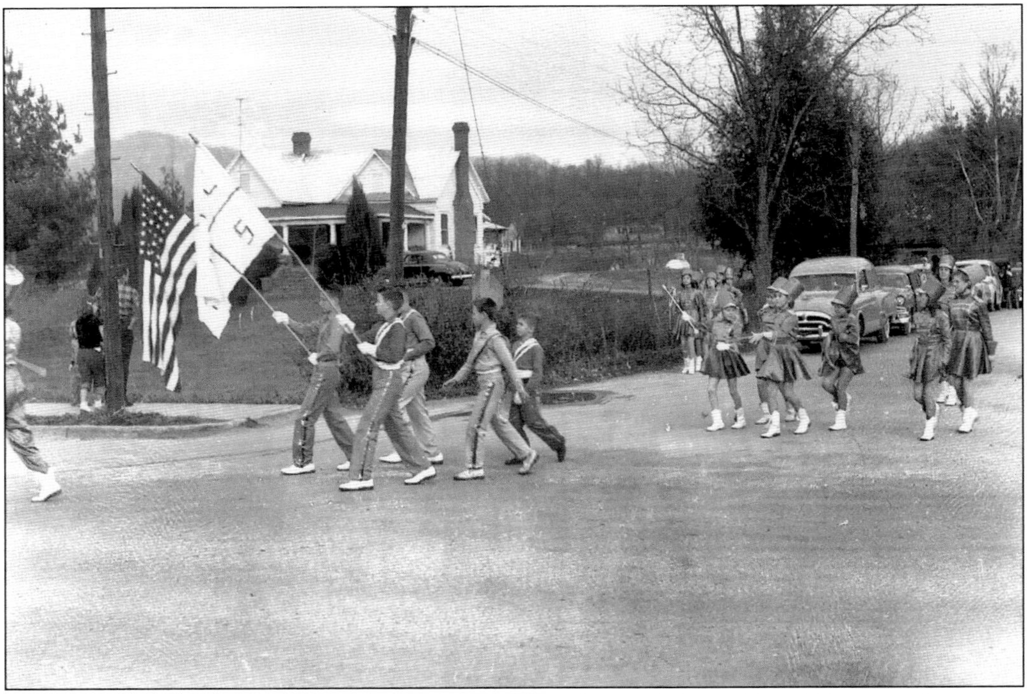

Shown here is the Union County Marching Band in 1956 at School Street. The white house seen is commonly known as the Butt-Mock House. (Courtesy of Union County Historical Society.)

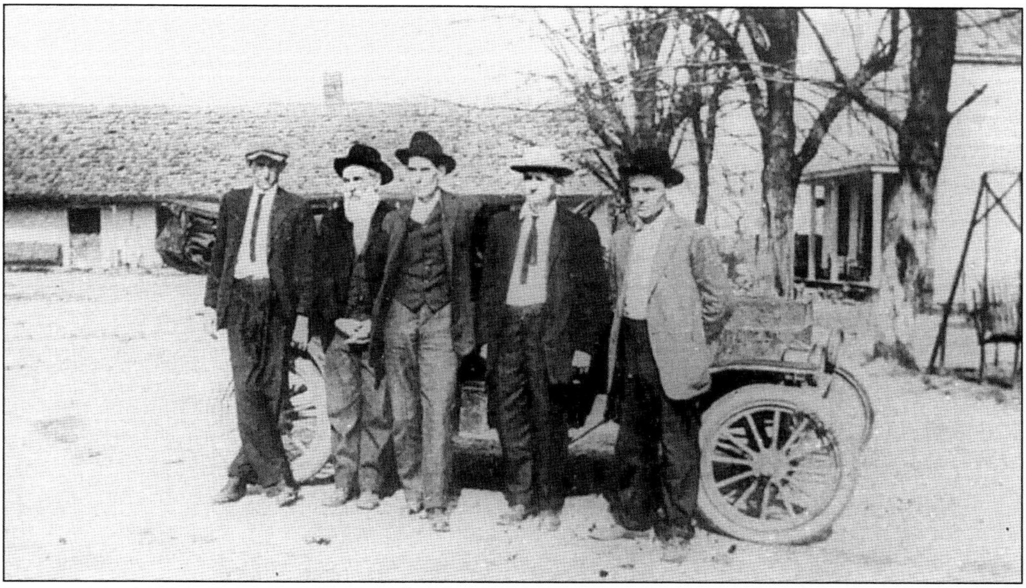

During 1916, M.L. Duggan, the Rural School Agent for Georgia, did an Educational Survey of the Union County School System. At this time, the Union County Board of Education included Superintendent T.E. Patterson, Bart Swanson, Chairman A.T. Sullivan, James Seabolt, and C.E. Rich. The taxable income of the county was $1,003,879. One-third of this income was owned by non-residents. The county had an area of 324 miles, a population of 6,918 people, and a school population of 2,114 white students and 19 black students.

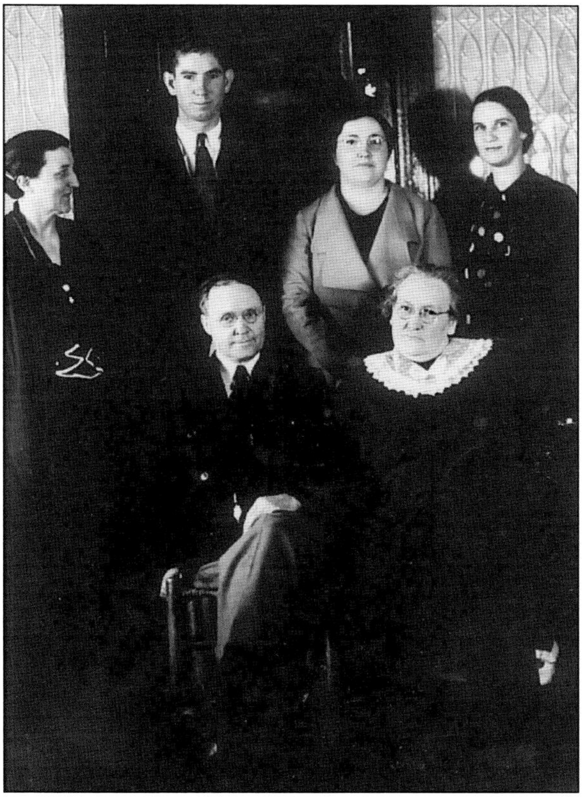

Pictured here is the first faculty of Union County High School in 1935. From left to right are (seated) Dr. J.M. Nicholson, Flora M. Nicholson, (standing) Gertrude W. Shuler, Clarence Shuler (Vocational Teacher), Geneva S. Hughes, and Dora H. Allison. Dr. James M. Nicholson, born in Union County, returned in 1929 after being away to become principal of Union County High School. He served until 1946. During his administration, the school became accredited, the alma mater was adopted and the panther was chosen as the school's mascot. (Courtesy of Union County Historical Society.)

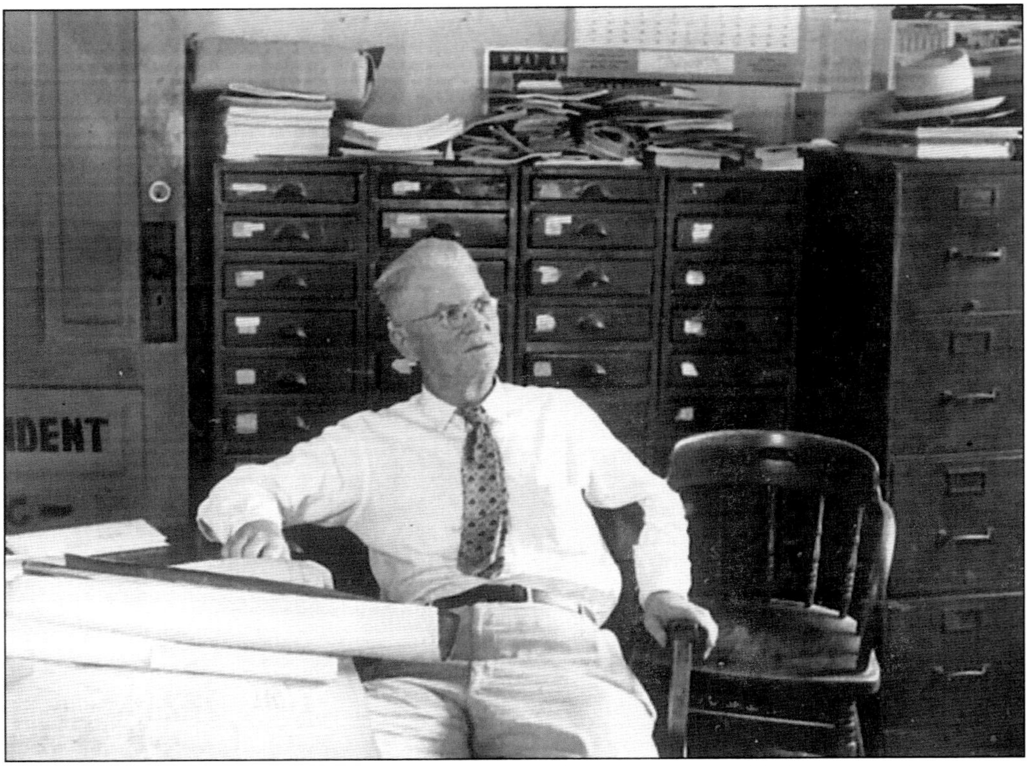

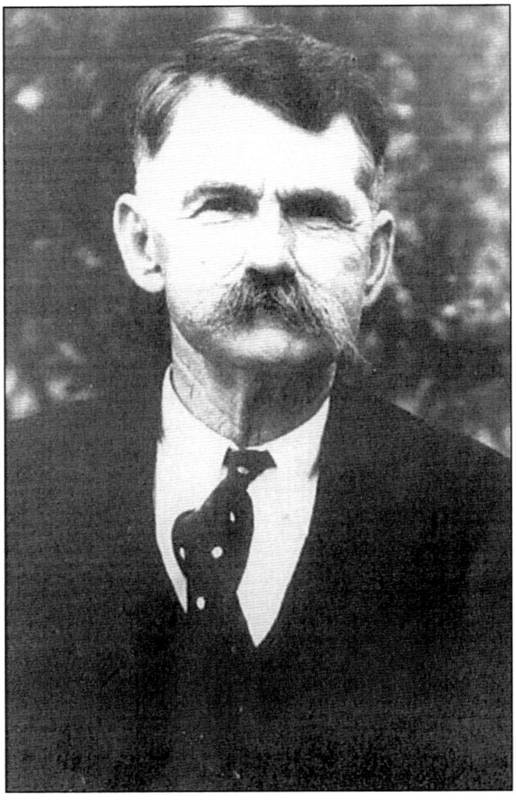

This photo of Frank Shuler was taken inside the old courthouse when he served as superintendent of Union County Schools. This was a position he held 1932 through 1948 and again in 1952 through 1956. Shuler led the system during the financially challenging years of 1930s and 1940s. A teacher's typical pay was $50 a month. Several times he went without his salary so the teachers could be paid. Prior to taking this post, Shuler was a World War I veteran and school teacher. (Courtesy of Union County Historical Society.)

Charles S. Mauney was born in 1868 and died in 1950. He served as county School Commissioner from 1900 to 1912. He was a teacher for 12 years from 1889 to 1900 and later 1913. He was a member and chairman of the Board of Education for many years. (Courtesy of Blanche Mauney via Union County Historical Society)

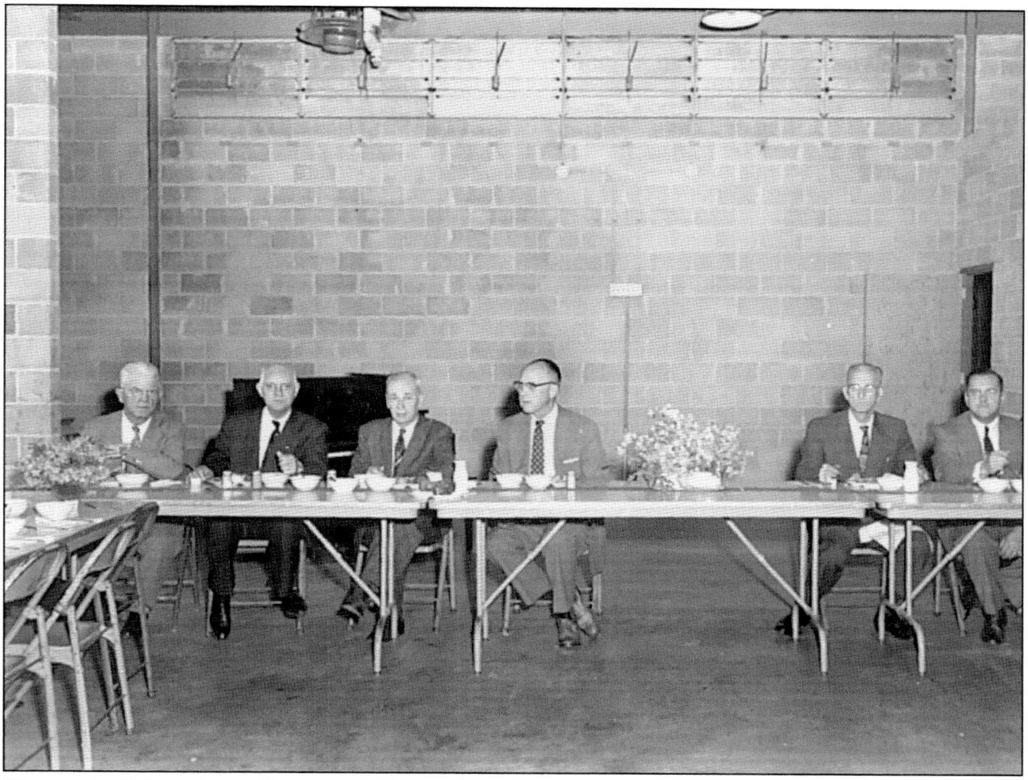

This early 1950s photo shows a meeting of educators. Pictured above are Frank Shuler, M.D. Collins, Jack Lance, Juan Jarrad, unidentified, and C.R. Collins. All known persons in the photo were native-born citizens of Union County. (Courtesy of Union County Historical Society.)

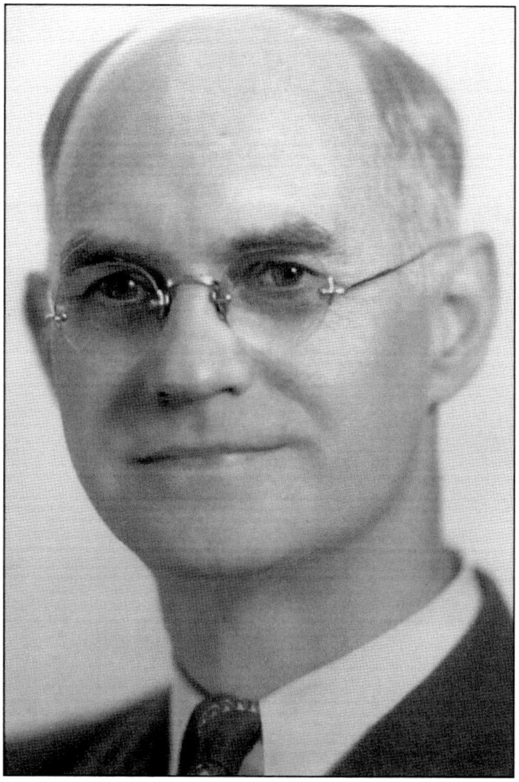

Mauney Douglas Collins, Ph.D., was a native of Union County. He attended school in a one-room, one-teacher schoolhouse in Choestoe prior to advancing on to higher education. Collins served as Georgia State Superintendent of Schools from 1933 until 1958. He was later named as Georgia State School Superintendent Emeritus. Collins has been described as the "architect and engineer" of the public school system in the state of Georgia. (Courtesy of Union County Historical Society.)

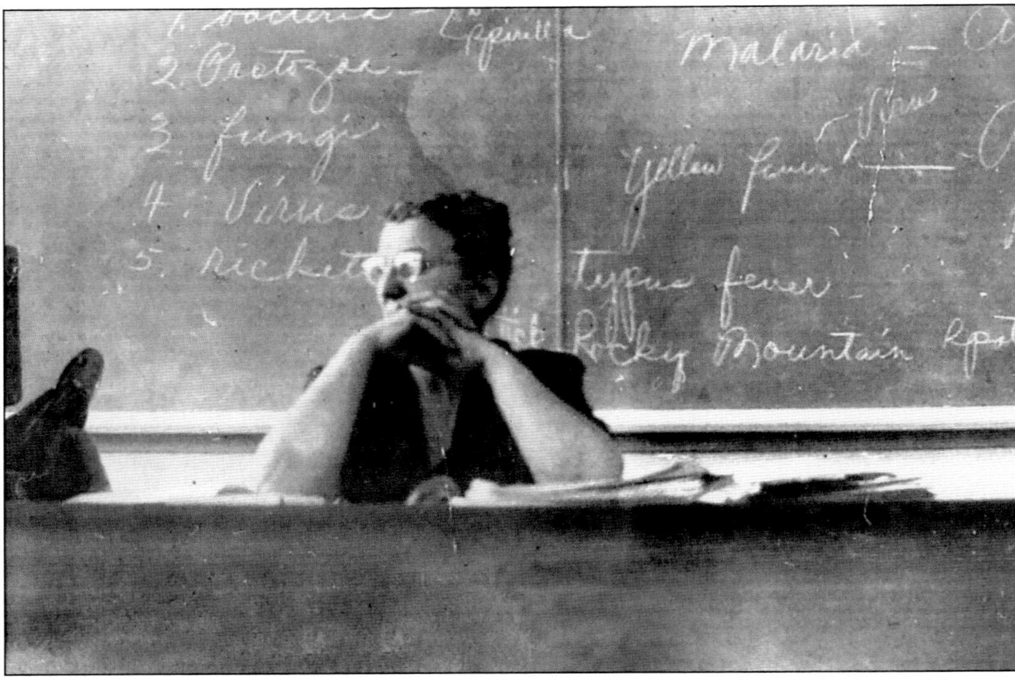

High school teacher Gertrude W. Shuler is shown here in 1952. She taught from 1931 until 1956. (Courtesy of Union County Historical Society.)

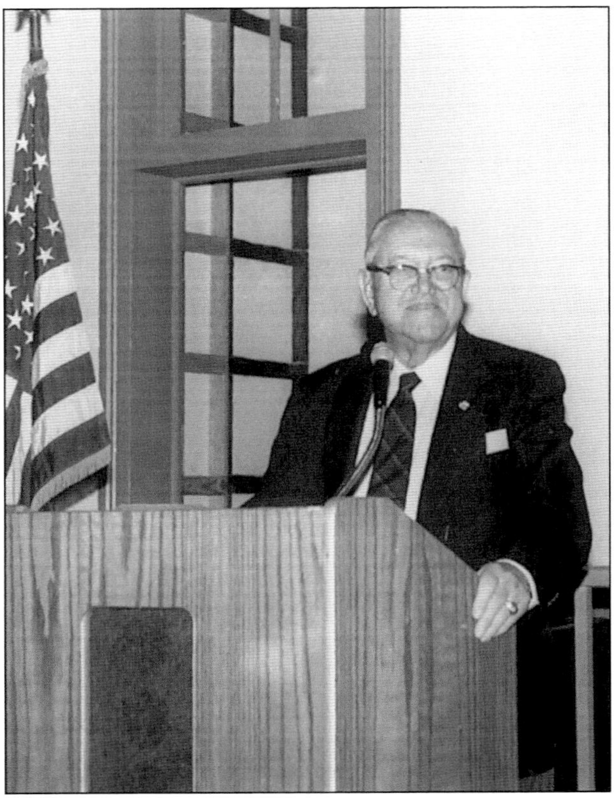

C.R. Collins attended public school in Union County and graduated from Blairsville Collegiate Institute in 1927. He later completed two years at Mercer University and began a long and successful career as an educator in the area. He served in schools around the state and in Union County, finally retiring from Woody Gap School in 1972 after 42 years of service. After the death of C.R. Collins, a road at the Blairsville campus was named in his honor. Georgia Representative Ralph Twiggs presented the resolution, designating Roscoe Collins Drive in Union County. (Photograph by Norman Cooper.)

Three

RELIGION

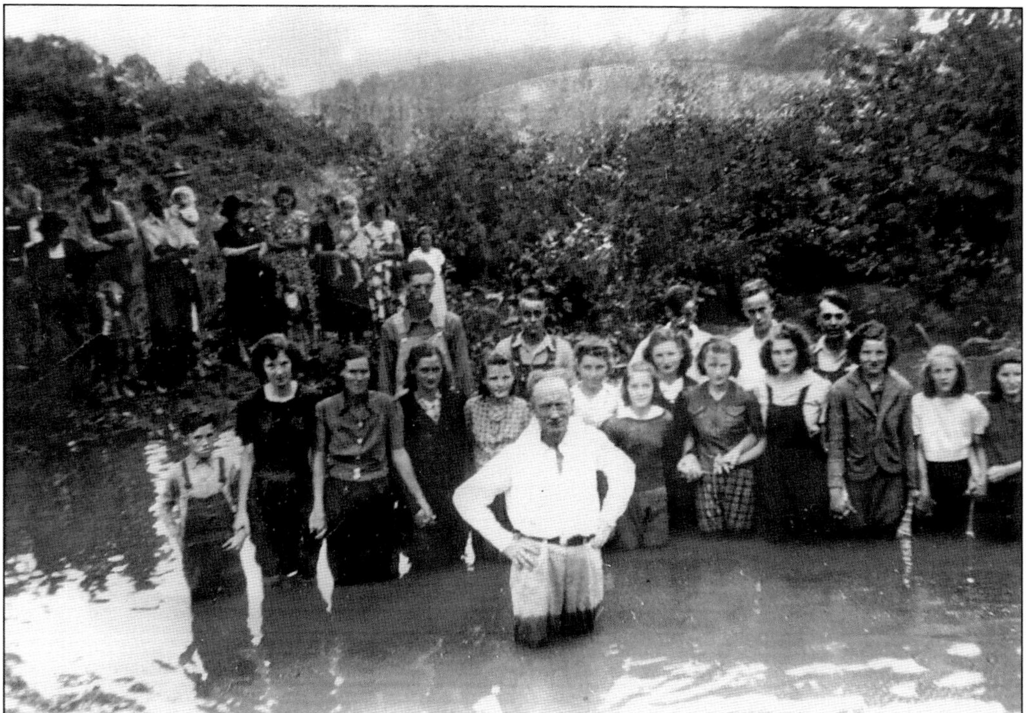

This picture shows an Ebenezer Baptist Church baptism in 1941. Pictured, from left to right, are the following: Ham Coffee, pastor; (front row) unidentified, Bonnie Thomas, Callie Mashburn, Mary Owenby, Mary Lee Mashburn, Nola Belle Lockaby, Betty Hemphill, Sue Plott, Susie Mae Hood, Ruby Henderson, Lois Plott, Geraldine Plott, and Christine Plott; (back row) Waymon Bradley, Oscar Henderson, Clyde Garrett, Cecil Thomas, and Cline Morgan. (Courtesy of W. Lake Stroud.)

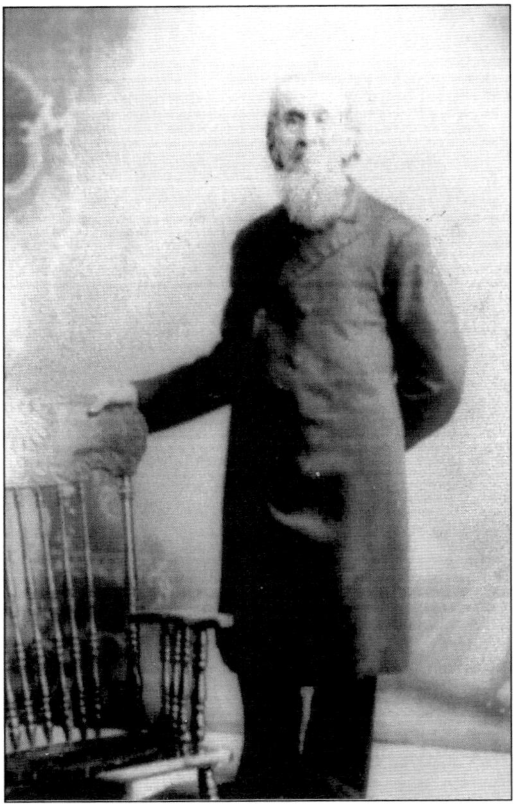

Alfred ("Pappy") Corn, born in 1817, lived in North Georgia as a missionary to the Indians through the use of an interpreter. He was ordained in 1850 by Elder Chastain, John Pruitt, and Rev. Adams Corn at Antioch Baptist Church in Union County. From that time on, he preached at many churches including Antioch, Zebulon, Brasstown, Old Union, Ivy Log, Macedonia, Martins Creek, and Tisquitty. He was the pastor of Ebenezer Baptist in 1857 at the time of its organization.

Pictured below is a baptism in the early 20th century. (Courtesy of Union County Historical Society.)

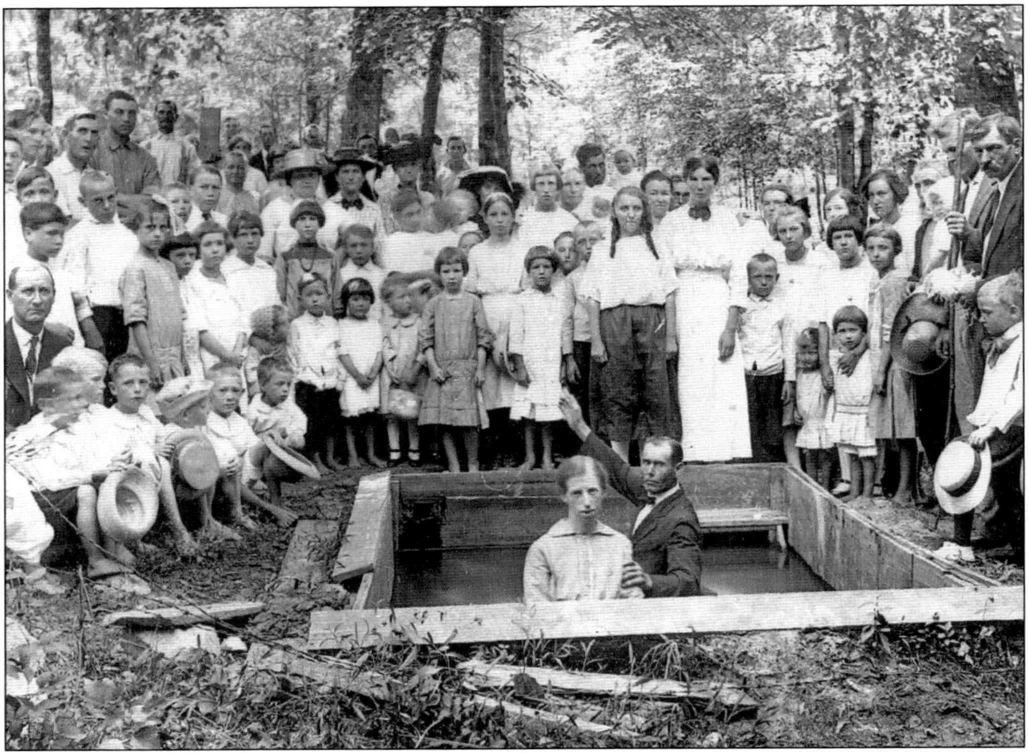

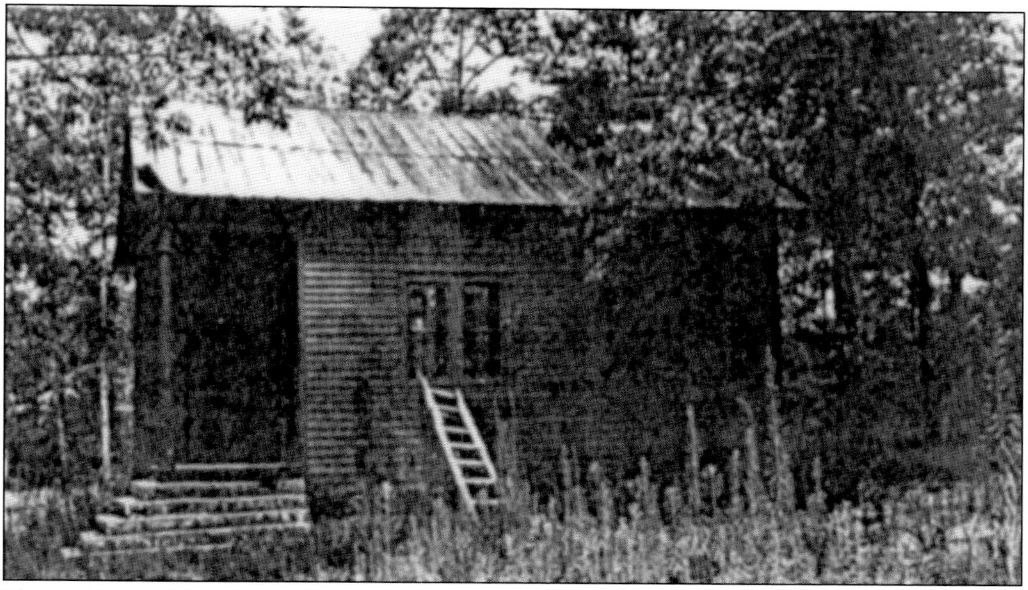

Shown here is Old Hood's Chapel School, established in the late 19th century. Many people gathered in the school for church service. Its location was on Logan Turnpike, which today is Russell Scenic Highway. It is believed that this is where Rev. John Lance preached. Lance left this location to travel back to his home in Wolf Creek. He took a route along a trail over a ridge near a place known as Cindy Cove. On the way home, he was waylaid and murdered by bootleggers. (Courtesy of Union County Historical Society.)

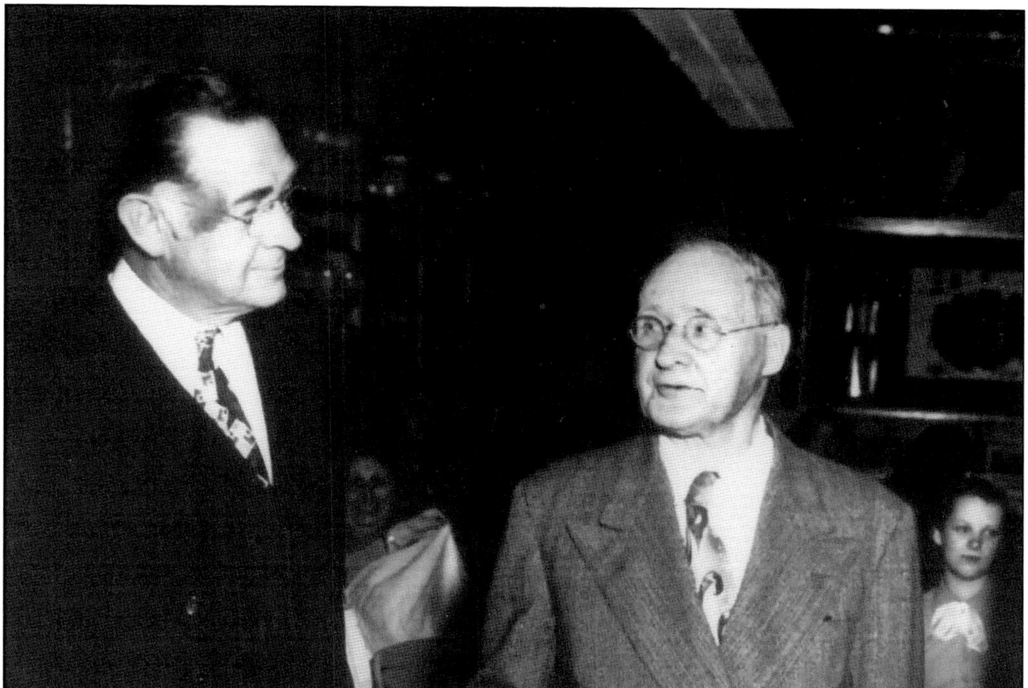

Shown here are the Rev. Claud Boynton and Prof. J.M. Nicholson. Reverend Boynton pastored churches at Zion, Choestoe, Union, and Blairsville in the 1930s, 1940s, and 1950s. (Courtesy of W. Lake Stroud.)

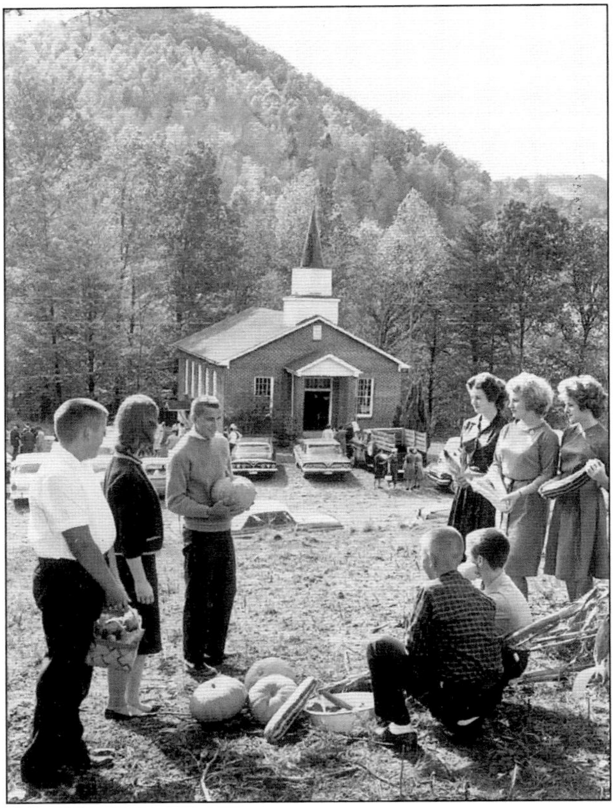

The Union Baptist Church Homecoming is pictured in 1960.

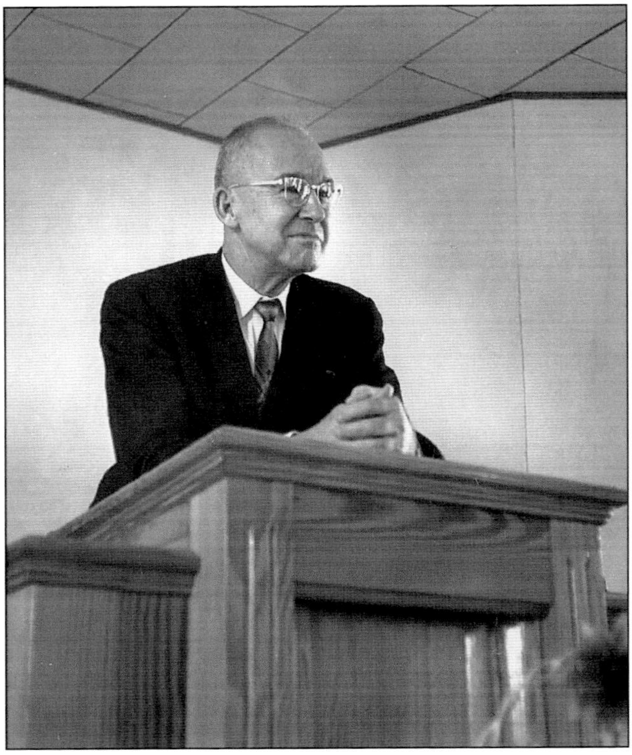

Harry Smith is pictured here at Union Baptist Church around 1960. He was also a teacher at Blairsville Collegiate Institute in the 1920s. (Courtesy of Union County Historical Society.)

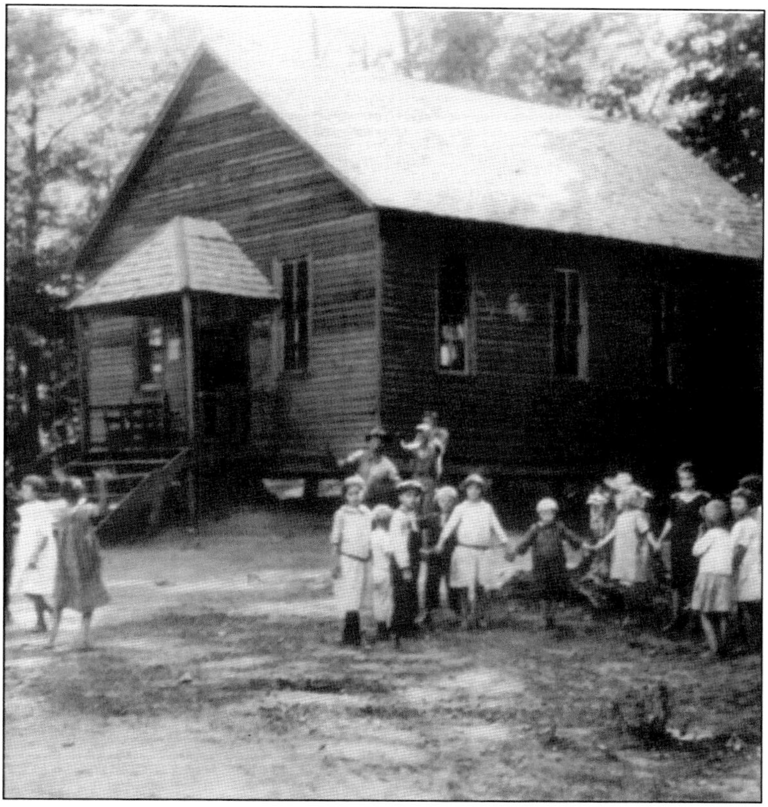

This picture shows Mt. Lebanon Church in the 1930s. (Courtesy of Ervin Gooch.)

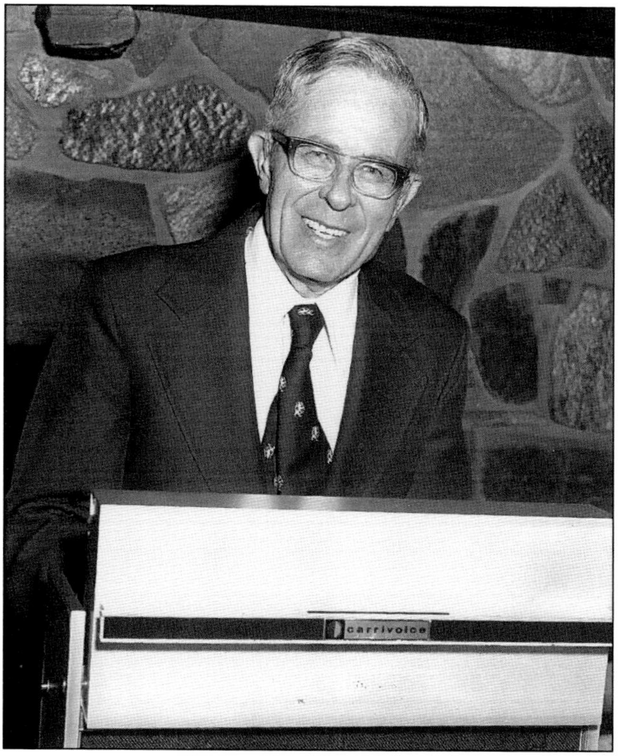

Rev. Jack Waldrip was a Methodist minister during the 1940s and 1950s in Union County. He organized many small churches in Union County and surrounding area and was named "Rural Minister of the Year" in Georgia. He was a member of the faculty at Young Harris College from 1947 to 1956. (Courtesy of Union County Historical Society.)

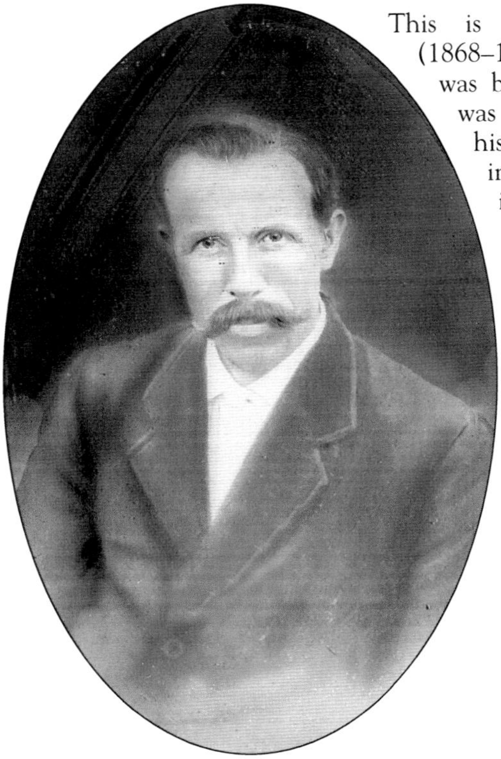

This is a photograph of Charles Edward Rich (1868–1919). Rich, a Baptist circuit riding preacher, was born in the mountains of Union County. He was schooled in the mountains and he felt it his spiritual duty and urge to preach to the people in the mountains. The churches he pastored included Choestoe, Harmony Grove, Union, and Zion. (Courtesy of Ann D. Rich.)

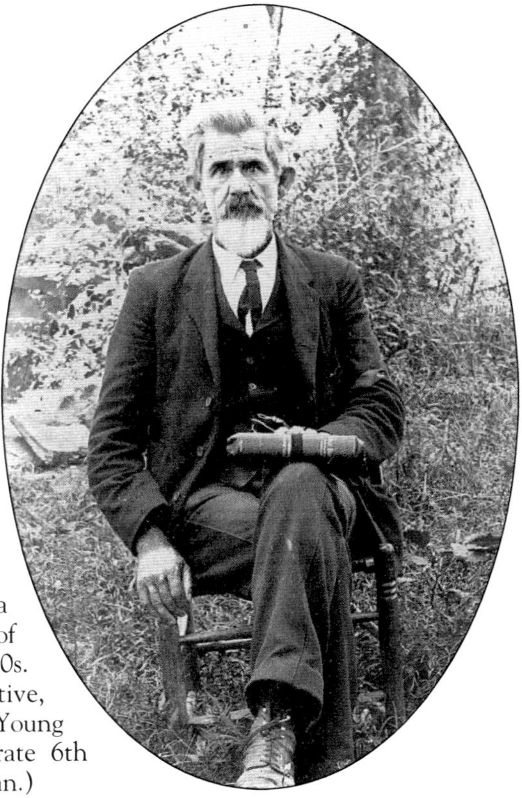

Rev. Thomas Coke Hughes (1844–1932) was a Methodist minister and known as "Minister of the Mountains." This photograph is c. late 1800s. In the early 1900s, he was a State Representative, clerk of the County Court, and Trustee of Young Harris College. He served in the Confederate 6th Calvary. (Courtesy of Carolyn Mauney Sullivan.)

Rev. Smith Loransey Brown, North Georgia Circuit Preacher, is shown here. Brown (1850–1931) was one of 10 children and was 11 years old when the Civil War began. The Confederates seized the horse that he used to plow the fields. When he was 15, he became a Christian and joined the Baptist church. He met Mary Elizabeth Souther (1853–1929) and they were married in just two months. They began housekeeping in a one-room log house in the Choestoe District of Union County. Smith was ordained a minister in 1903. Smith hitched up a team of bay mules to ride many miles to preach at churches all over North Georgia. When weather permitted, he would take the entire family in a covered wagon. It was part of grandson Emory Brown's responsibility to make sure that Smith's Bible was in the leather saddlebag thrown across the mule and the communion wine jug was tied to the other side. Both Reverend Smith and his wife are buried in New Liberty Baptist Church Cemetery, which is near their home place. (Courtesy of Evelyn Brown Lamar and Sarah Brown Partain.)

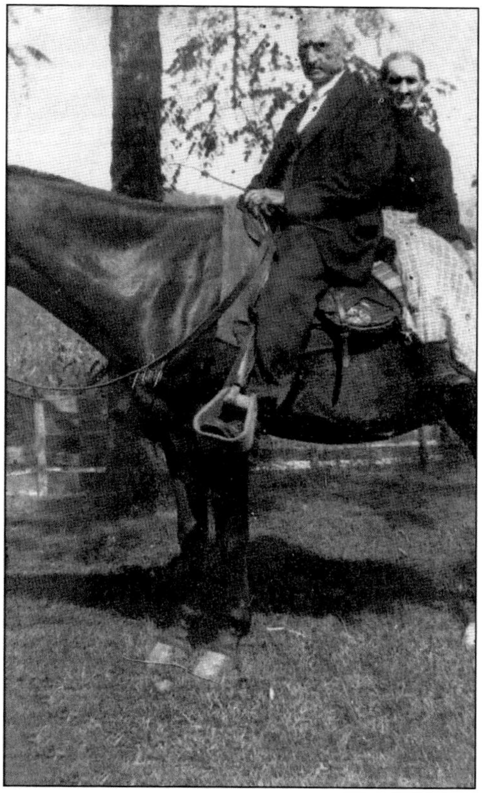

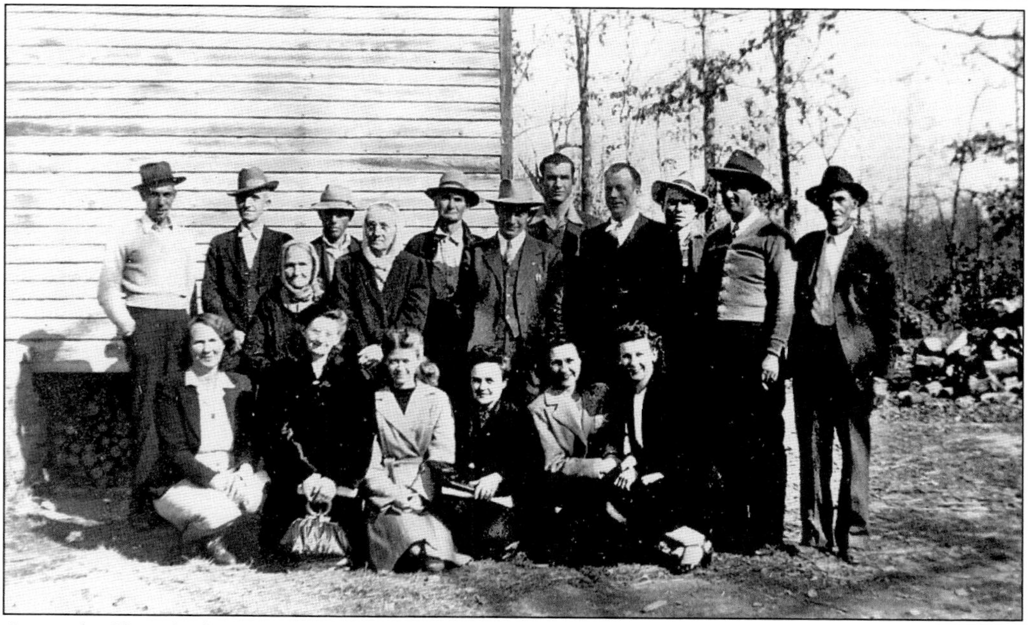

Antioch Church deacons and teachers, pictured c. 1940, are (from left to right) (front row) Evelyn Stepp, unidentified, Parelee Nation, Willie Drake, Lelia Metcalf, and Citter Colwell (back row) Ray Hemphill, Lee Truelove, two unidentified, Merzie Hemphill, Wilbur Nation, Bill Metcalf, Doc Nation, Frank Colwell, unidentified, Clyde Patterson, and Andy Colwell. (Courtesy of Melva Lynn Drake.)

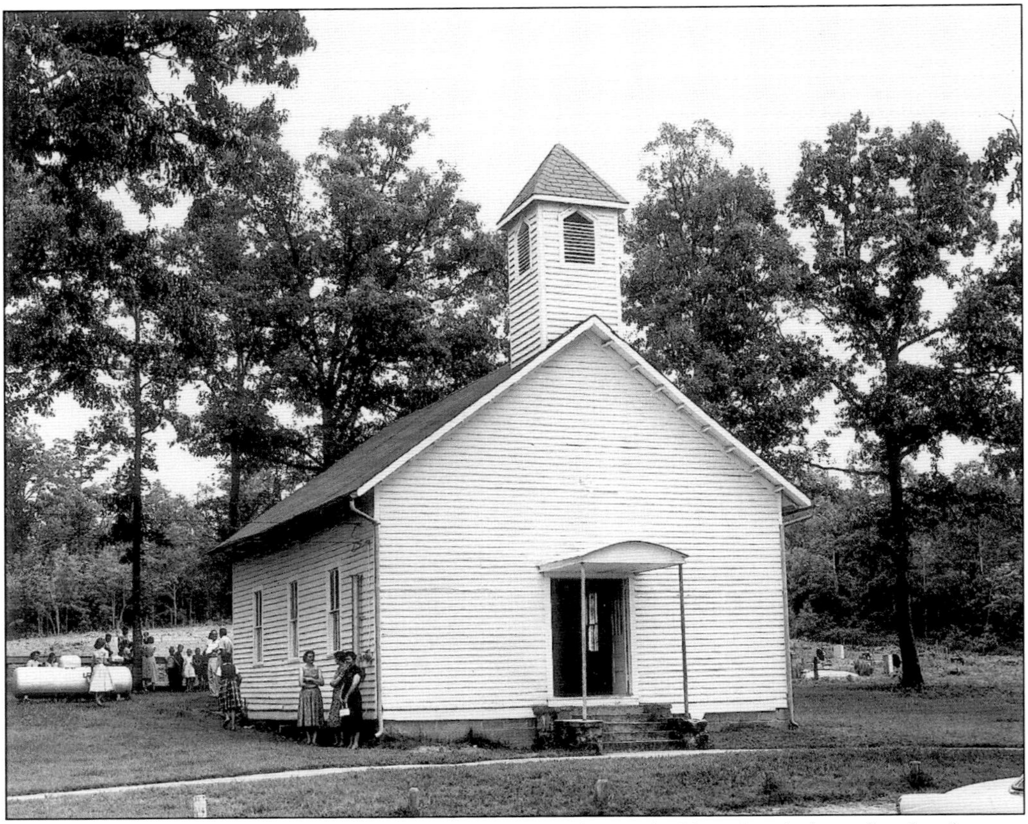

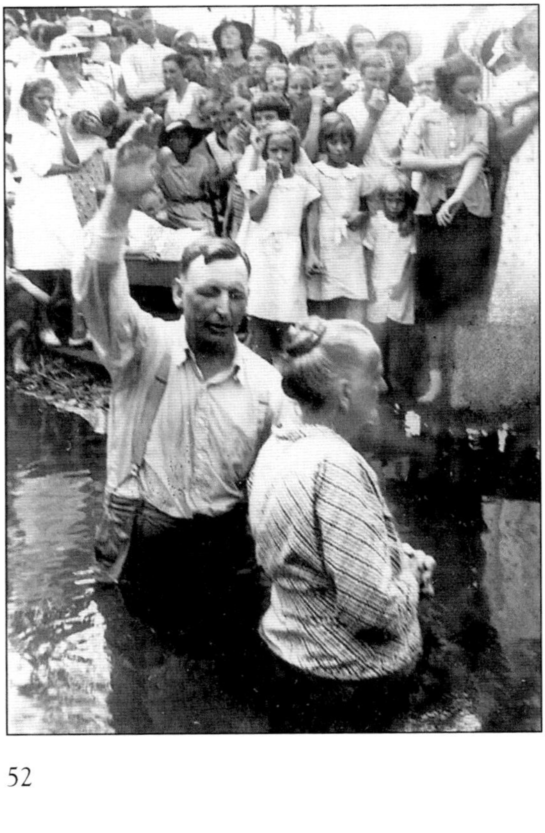

Antioch Church is believed to be the second oldest church in the county. This photograph was taken *c.* 1950s. (Courtesy of Melva Lynn Drake.)

Rev. Nando Stephens baptizes his mother Sarah Stephens. The date of this photograph is unknown.

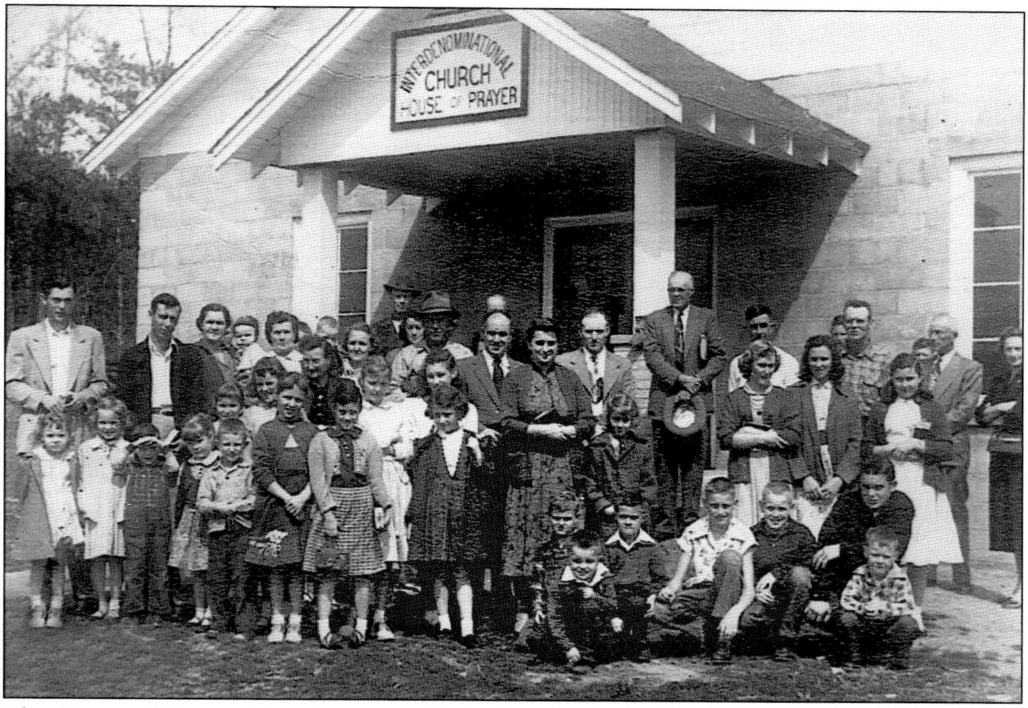

The House of Prayer Church was established in the 1950s. The doctrine of the church was founded on the Bible, love, and fellowship. A.M. McAfee, W.E. Kelley, Charlie Kelley, Clarence Helton, and Joe Brackett were the first Board of Trustees. In 1953, Rev. D.D. Kinnersley was asked to serve as the first pastor for the church. (Courtesy of House of Prayer.)

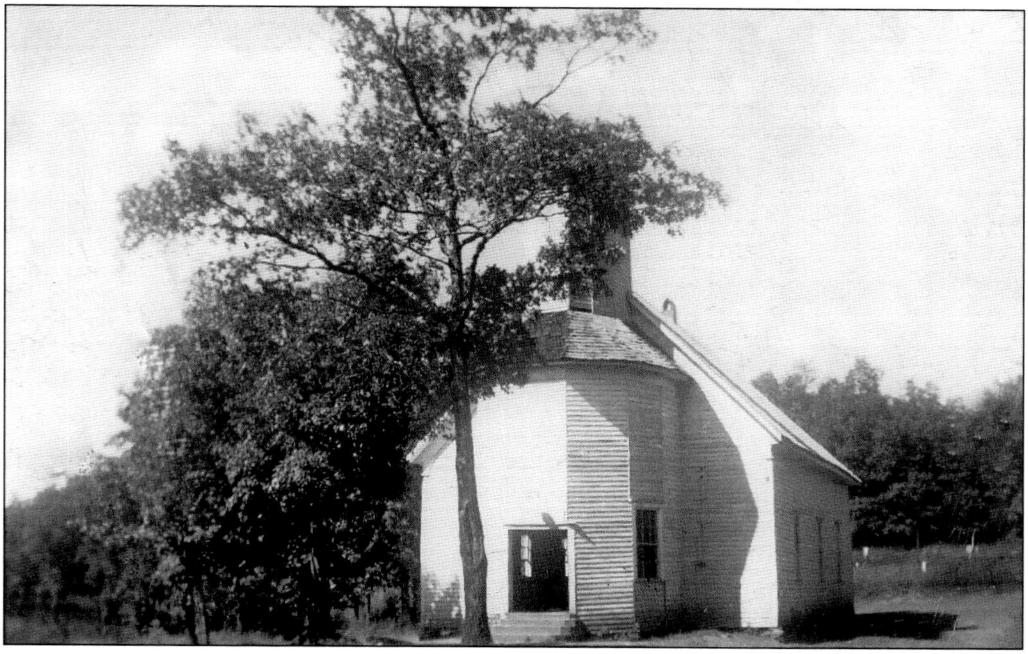

Choestoe Baptist Church, the oldest church in Union County, was established in 1832. This structure, the third church building, was built in 1917. Its records from 1834 are on file at the Georgia Archives. (Courtesy of Union County Historical Society.)

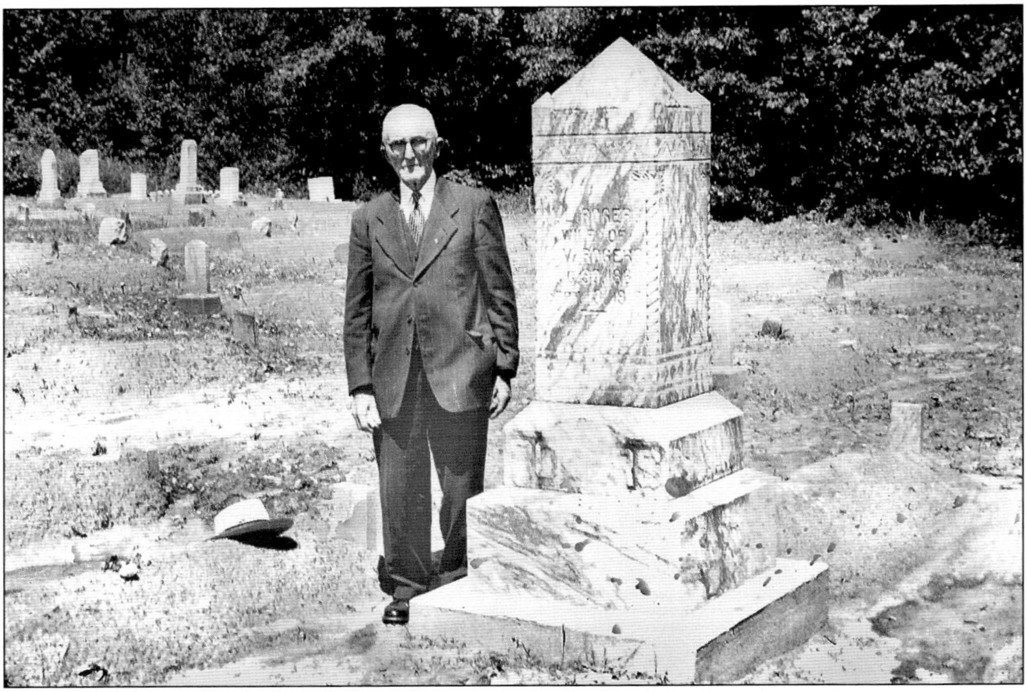

Throughout the decades from the 1800s until the late 1900s, churches and cemeteries were closely related. Those cemeteries that were not located on church property had a religious reverence associated with them. Shown here is Antioch Cemetery, with visitor Victor Rogers. (Courtesy of W. Lake Stroud.)

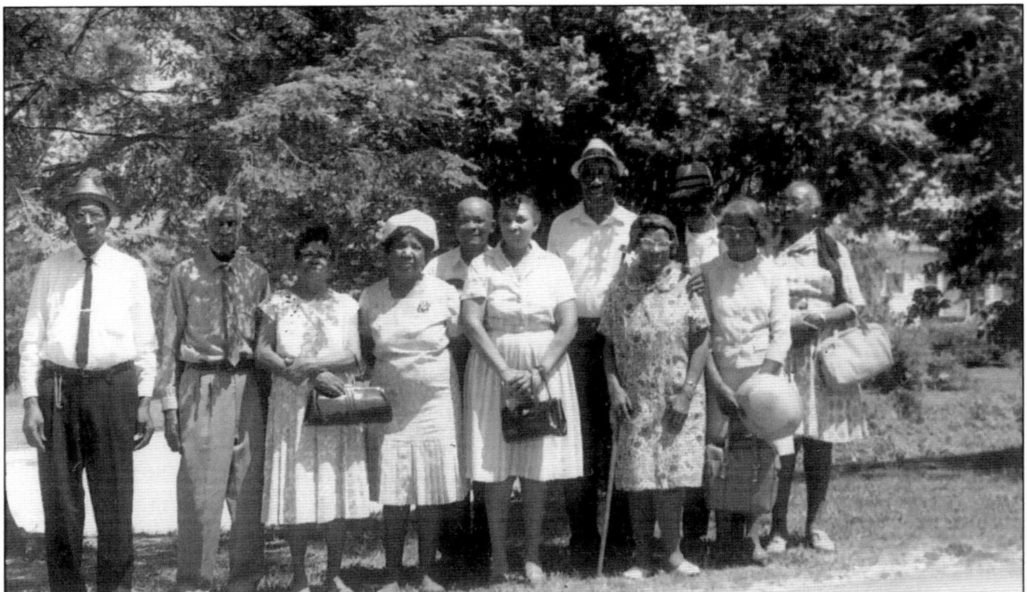

One of the oldest cemeteries in Union County is simply known as the "Negro Cemetery." This photo was taken in 1970 on Decoration Day at the cemetery. (Courtesy of Union County Historical Society.)

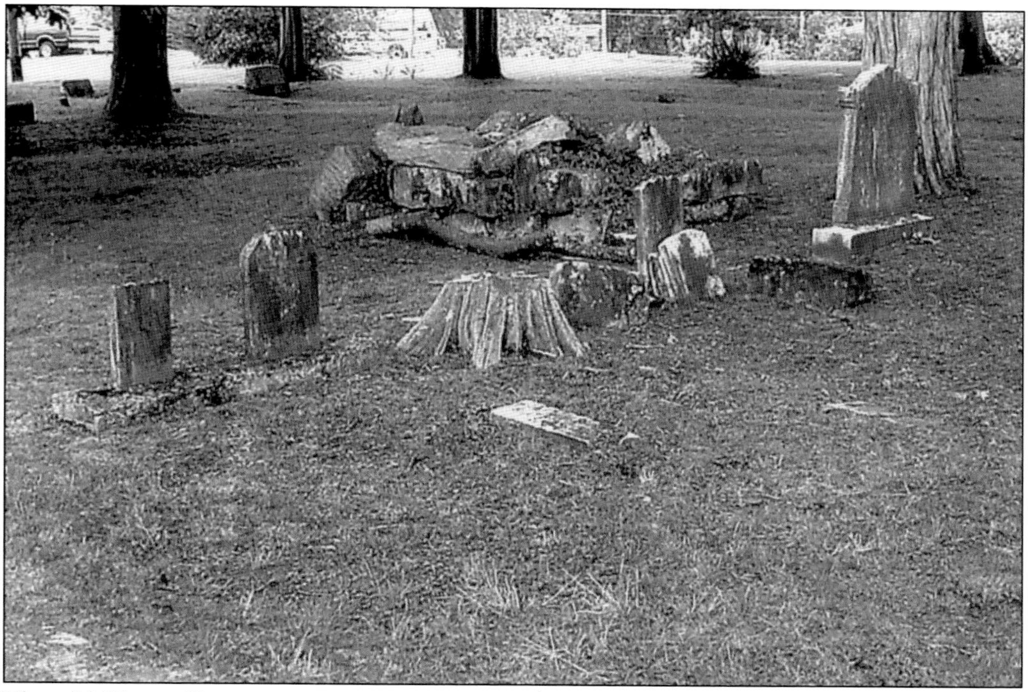

The old Blairsville cemetery contains graves of numerous people who were buried during the 1800s. The original stones and markers have been maintained. (Photograph by Norman Cooper.)

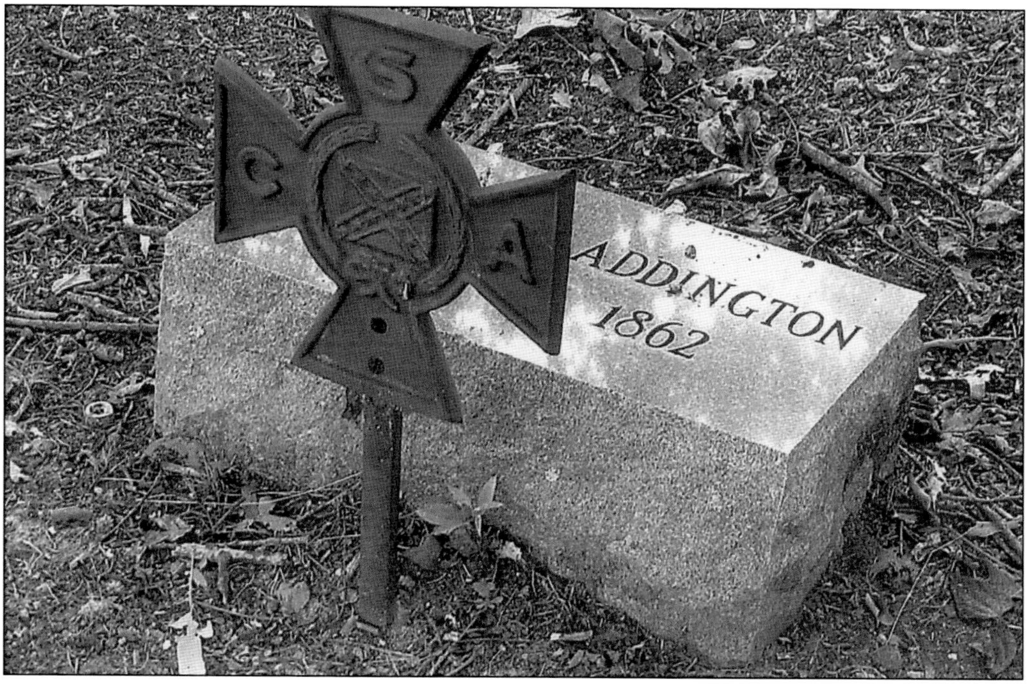

A rare Confederate States of America marker is pictured at this grave site. (Photograph by Norman Cooper.)

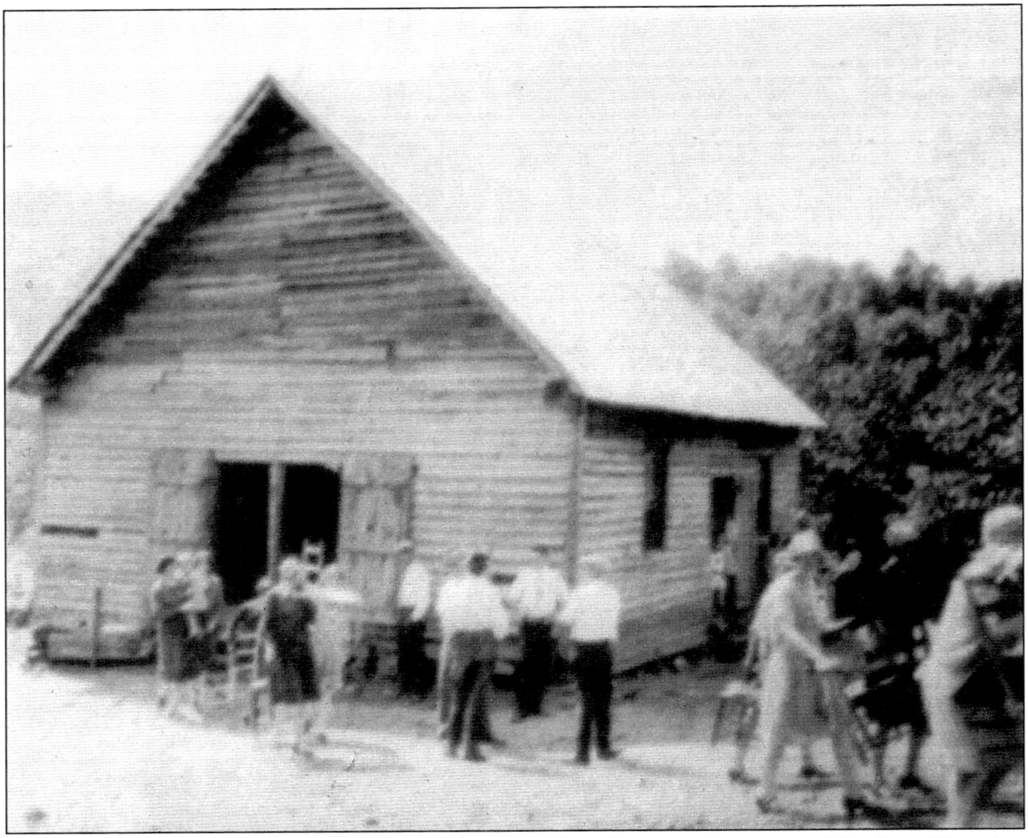

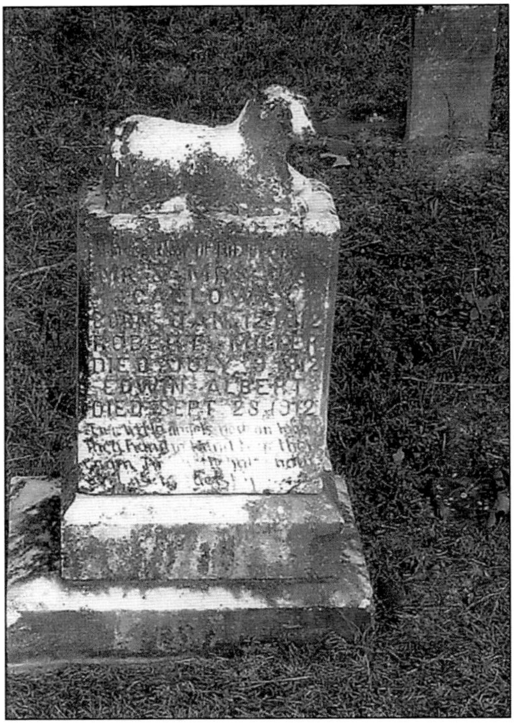

This photograph captures Mt. Airy Church and School in Suches. This structure was originally opened prior to the Civil War. After the war, it was reestablished in 1867. This building is where World War II–veteran and later County Commissioner Glenn Gooch was educated. This photo was taken sometime in the early part of the 20th century. Research among ledgers still in existence and based on markers in the cemetery, it is believed this church and school building is the oldest on the Suches side of the mountain in Union County. (Courtesy Ervin Gooch)

Around Union County, whether in cemeteries on church property or in private areas, religious symbols are very common. Lambs, angels, doves, crosses, and other symbols decorate the graves of children who died at birth, those who died at a young age, and adults of all ages. (Photograph by Norman Cooper.)

Four

OCCUPATIONS

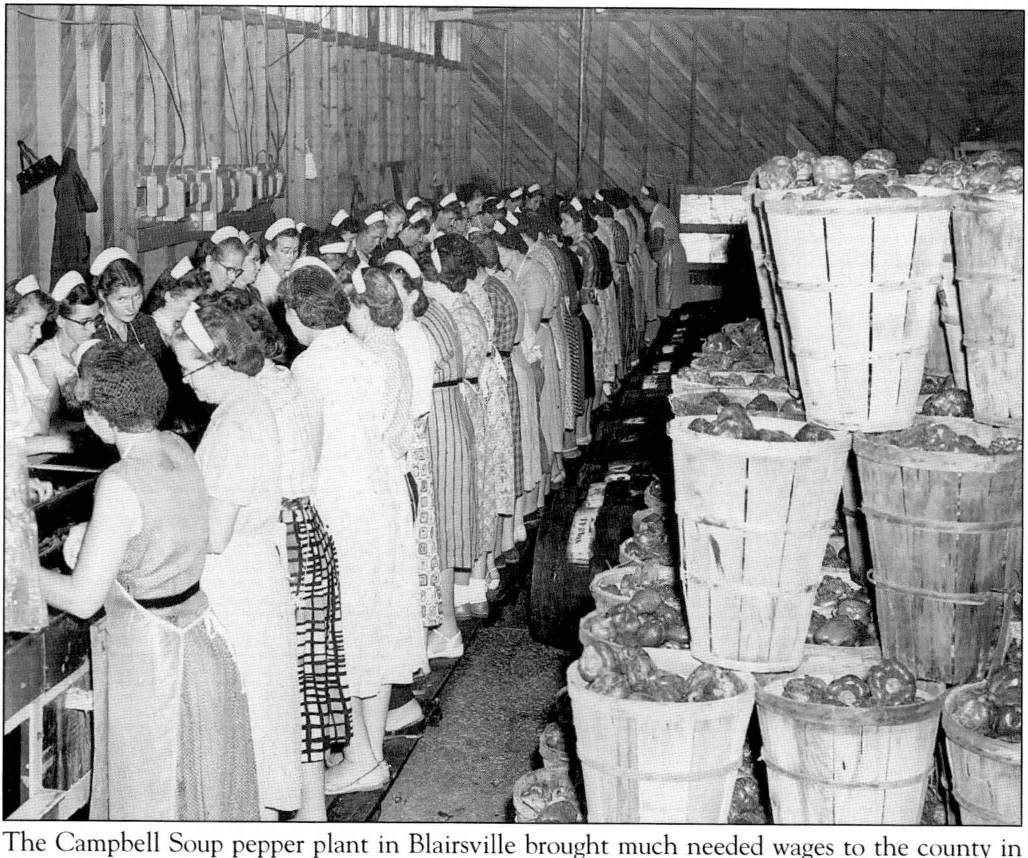

The Campbell Soup pepper plant in Blairsville brought much needed wages to the county in the early 1950s. (Courtesy of Frances Fair Partin.)

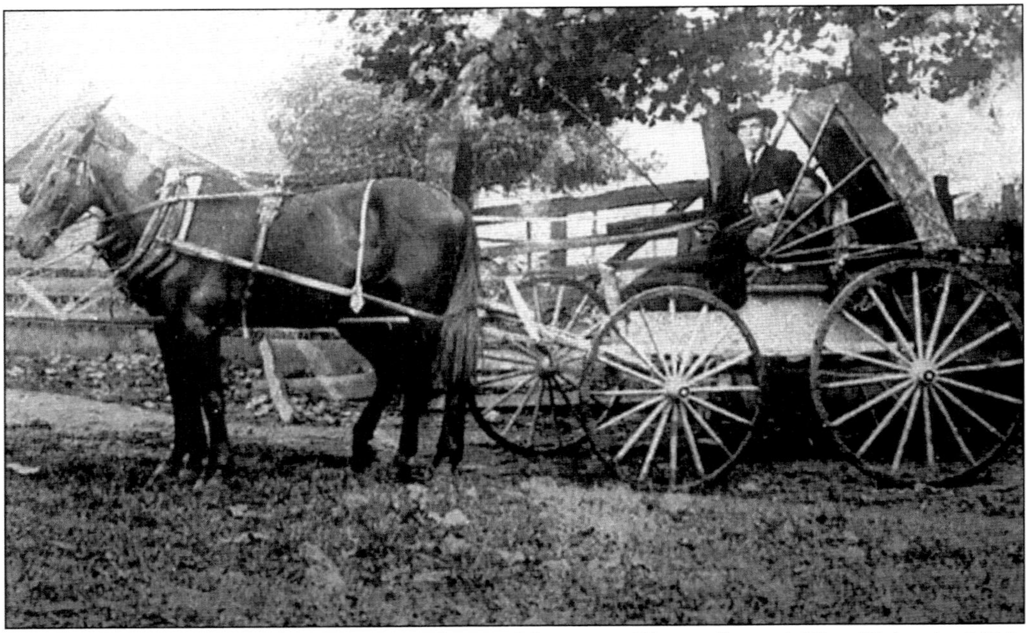

Marvin Akins is shown here carrying the mail between Blairsville and Blue Ridge in 1913. The trip usually required Marvin to spend the night in Blue Ridge. One time in particular, he chose to stay in order to witness a public hanging the following morning at the railway depot. (Courtesy of Pat Akins.)

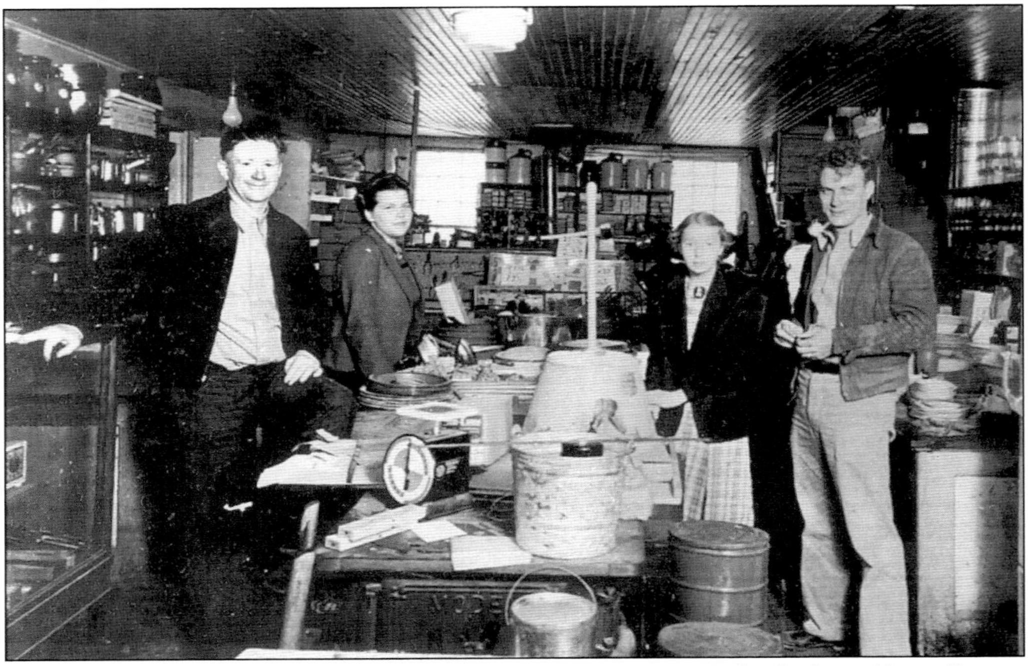

Meeks Hardware is pictured in 1941. Persons above are A.C. Colwell, Sara Akins, Francis Colwell, and Bill Meeks. The location of the store was on the corner, left of the main entrance to the 1899 courthouse. This photograph was taken as Bill Meeks was preparing to turn over operation of the store to Colwell. He was preparing to leave Union County to fight in World War II. (Courtesy of United Community Bank.)

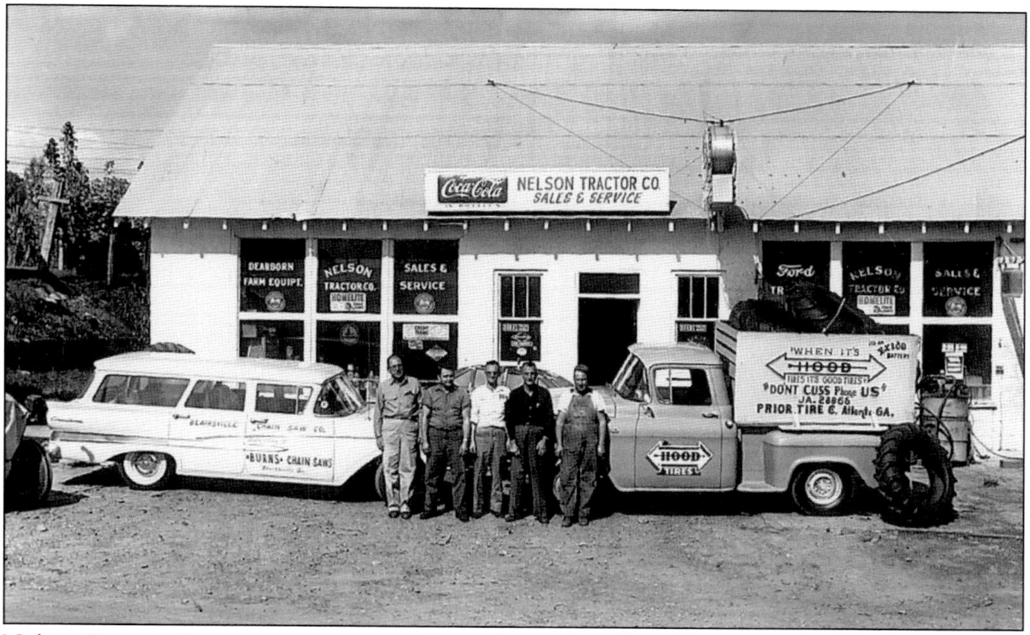

Nelson Tractor Company is seen in 1958, and era when diesel tractors were being introduced. The tractors would come into Atlanta on railroad and Nelson would go to Atlanta to pick them up at the distribution center. Seen in the photo are John Wade, J.C. Nelson, owner Cecil Nelson, Barney Owenby, and an unidentified man. (Courtesy of W.C. Nelson, Will Nelson.)

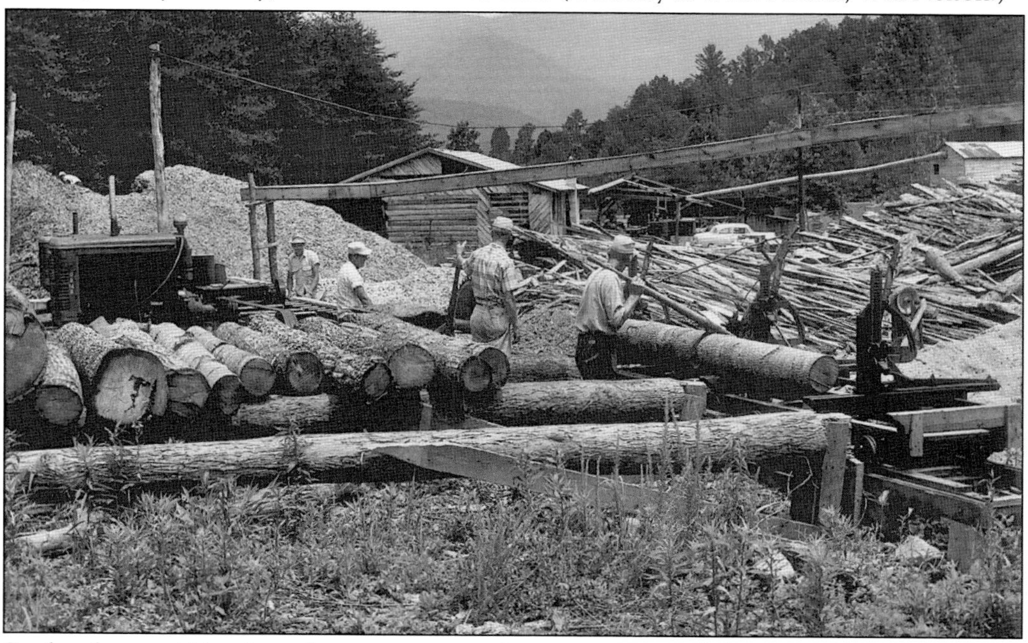

Settlers began sifting into the mountains and carving out small homesteads. Many of these settlers were of Scottish and English heritage. They sought out the remote coves and hidden valleys to reside in and lead solitary lives. Saw mills became a way of life in the mountains. Many mountainsides, once blanketed with trees, appeared as a virtual moonscape. Even then, the lumbering continued. It took less than 40 years to essentially destroy a large portion of the forests. (Courtesy of Union County Historical Society.)

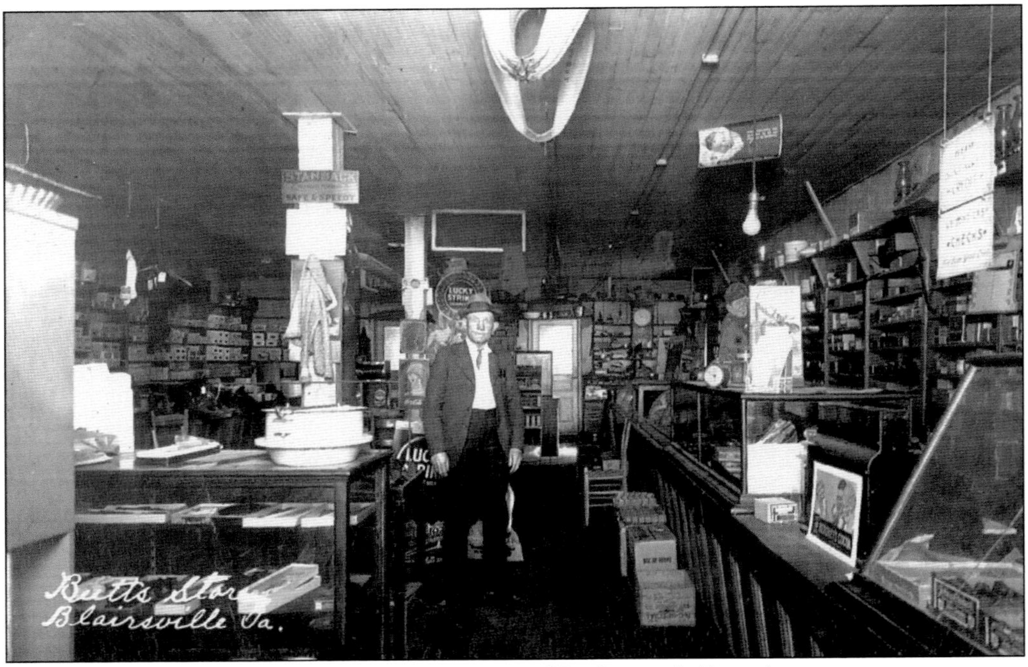

J.A. Butt Store is shown here *c.* 1930. (Courtesy of Dr. James A. Butts.)

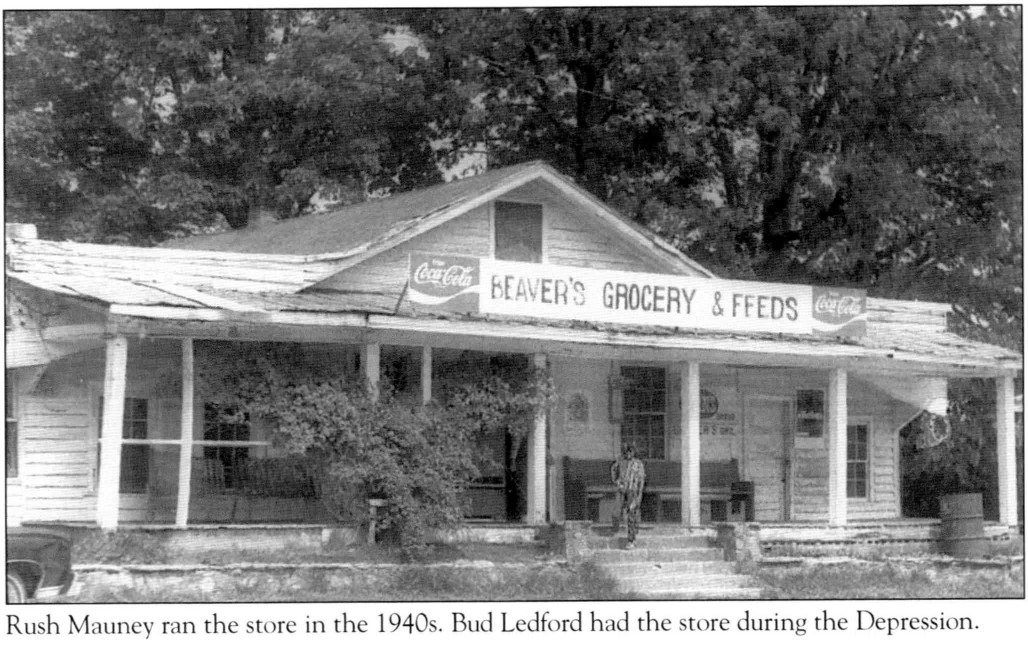

Rush Mauney ran the store in the 1940s. Bud Ledford had the store during the Depression.

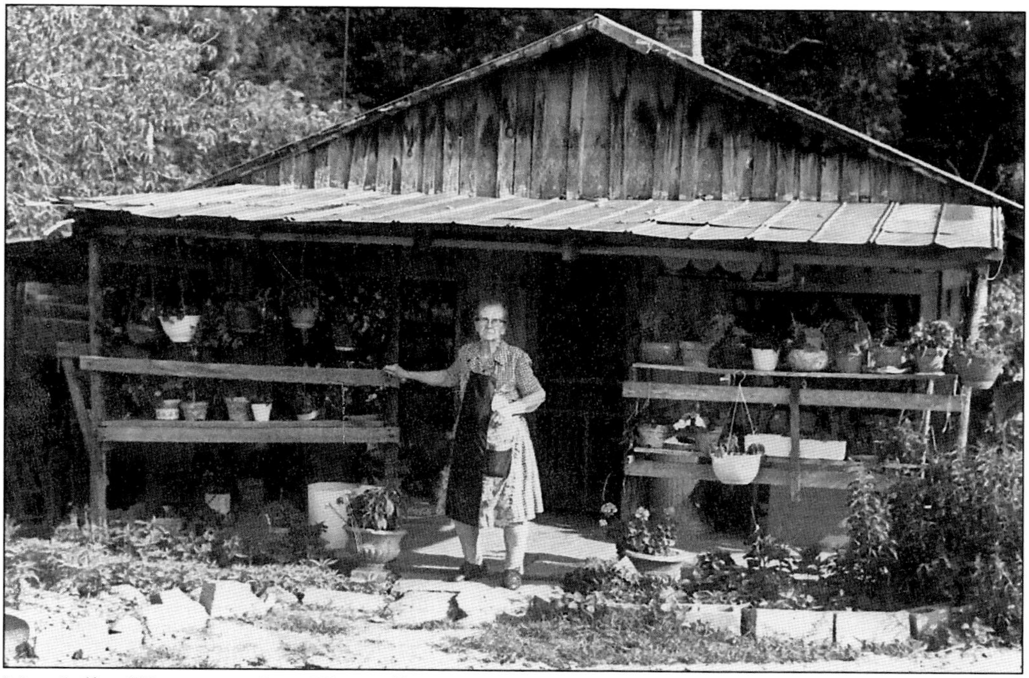

Mrs. Lillie West moved to Blairsville nine years after her husband James Oliver West died in 1939. She opened her store, West's Grocery, six days a week. It was not unusual for her to open up on Sunday if needed. Cigarettes, soft drinks, and ice cream were specialties. In 1948, soft drinks were five cents each. Mrs. West's spare time was spent singing the old ballads of the mountains—many of which had their roots in England, Scotland, and Ireland. She also played the banjo. (Courtesy of Kenneth West.)

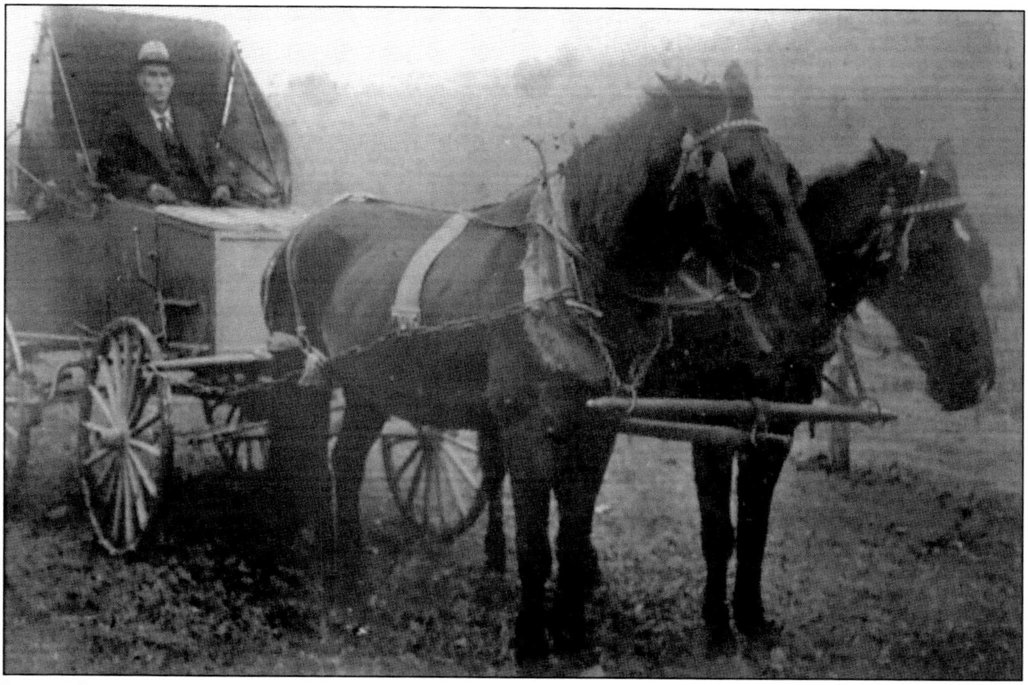

Lewis Queen is pictured with his Raleigh Products wagon c. 1920. (Courtesy of Dale Elliott.)

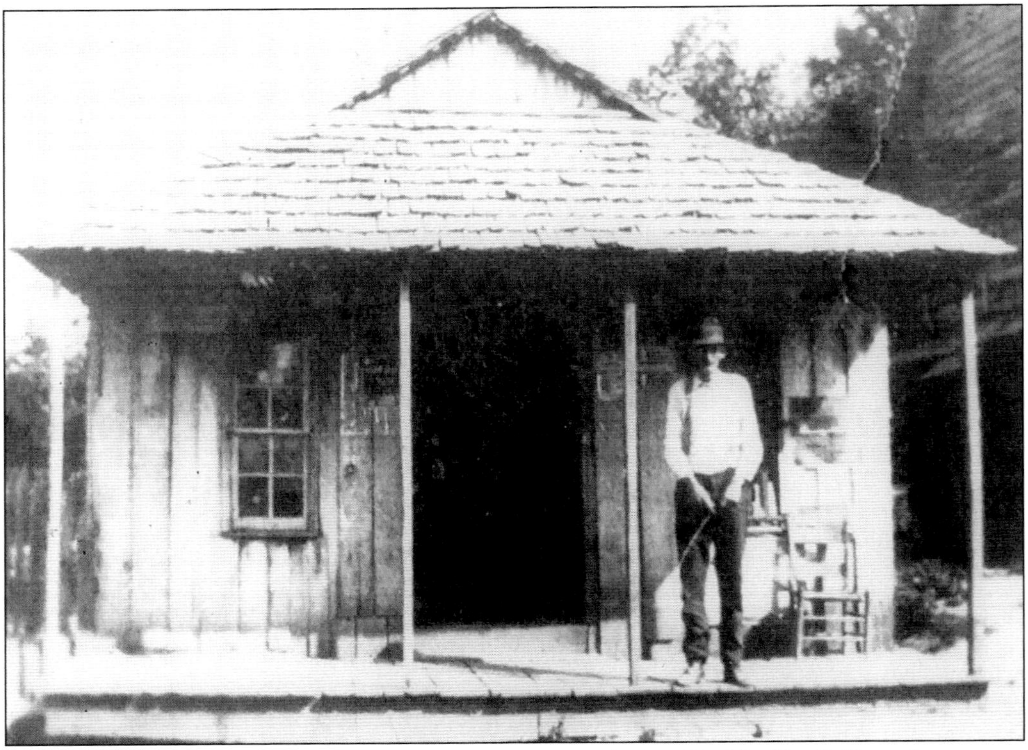

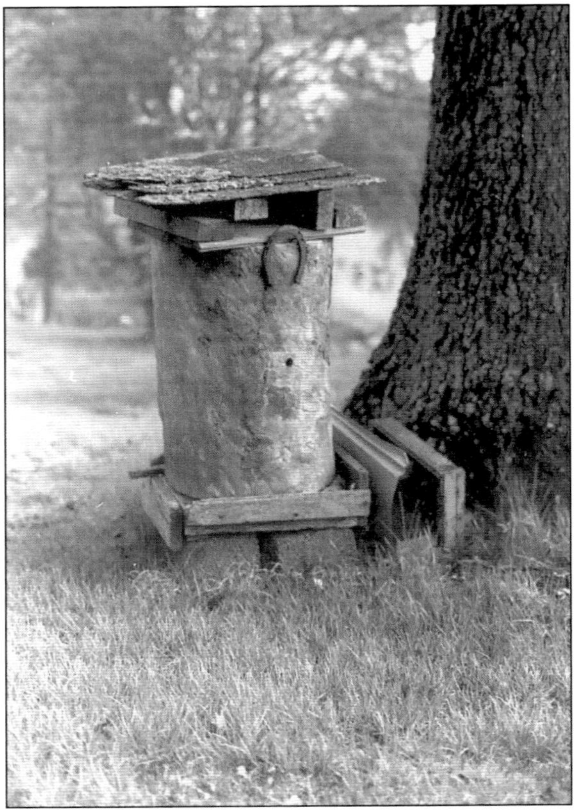

Arthur Paul Ledford's Store is displayed above. The date for this photograph is unknown.

Occupations such as bee-keeping were common for decades. This is an old bee hive device. (Courtesy of Union County Board of Education.)

Mrs. Bonnie Rich and her husband built boats for approximately two decades. They had their wood planed in Blue Ridge. Bonnie put the caulking compound in every joint. Boats sold for $1 a foot and they rented boats for $1.50 per day. (Courtesy of Union County Board of Education.)

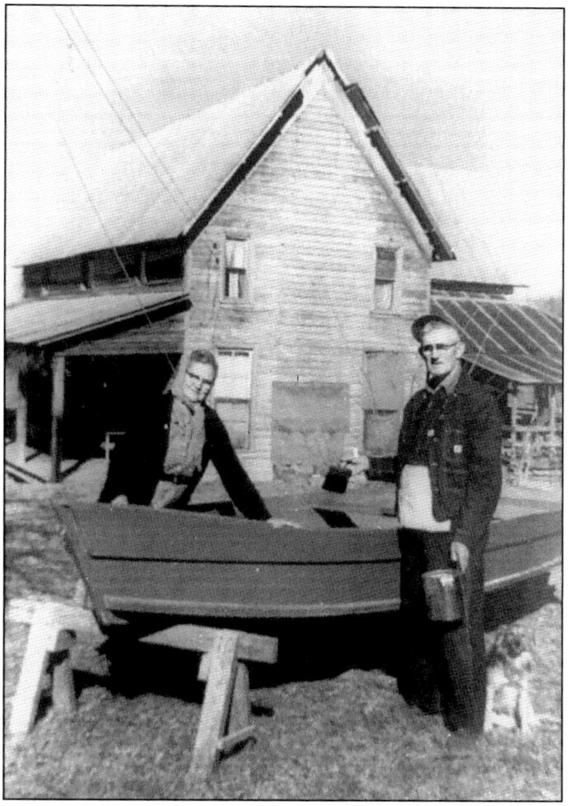

The North Georgia News is seen in the mid-1920s, on the Square in Blairsville with Press Davenport.

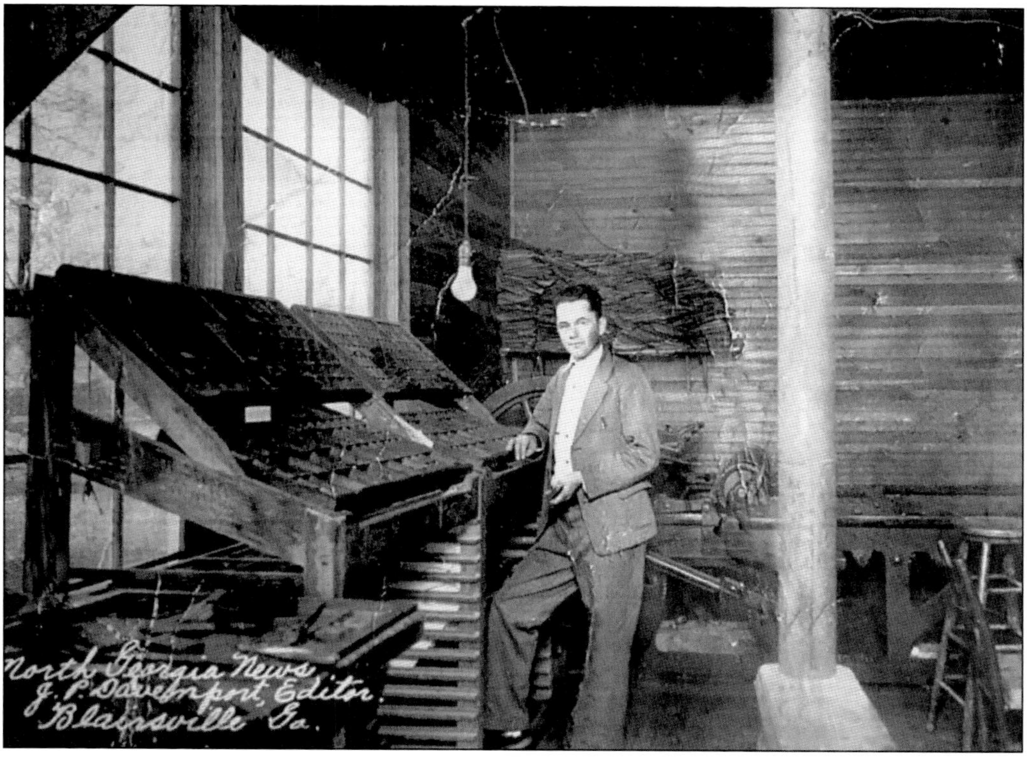

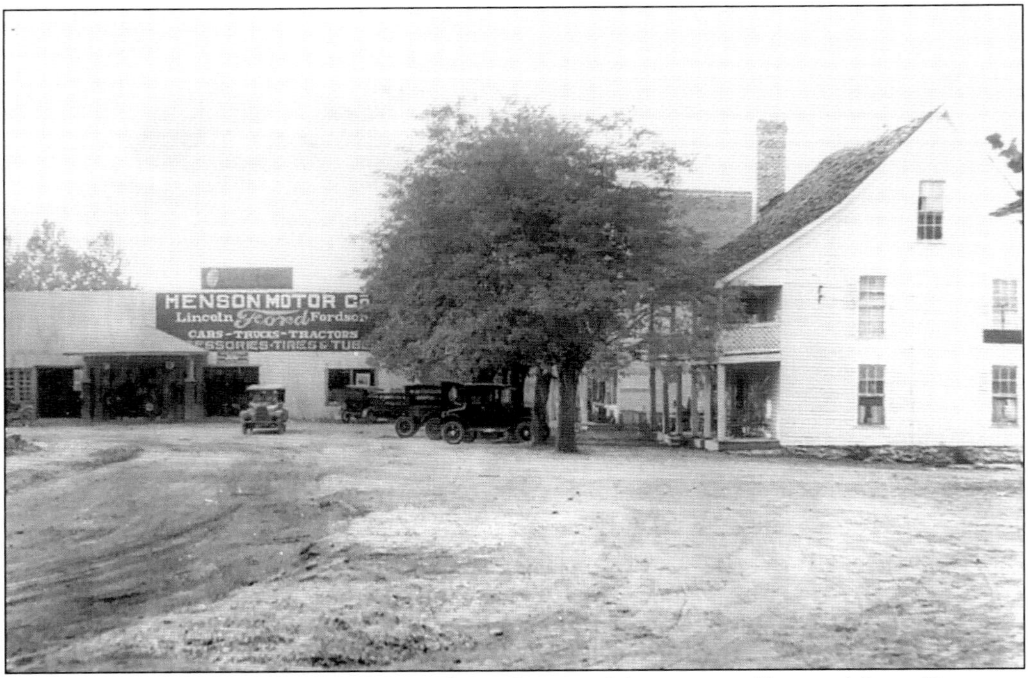

This photograph captures the Square in the early part of the century. Henson Motor Company is visible in the background. To the right is the Wellborn House, at the time, the oldest house in Blairsville. In the town, there was an assaying office. The house provided pegs for miners to hang their gold pouches.

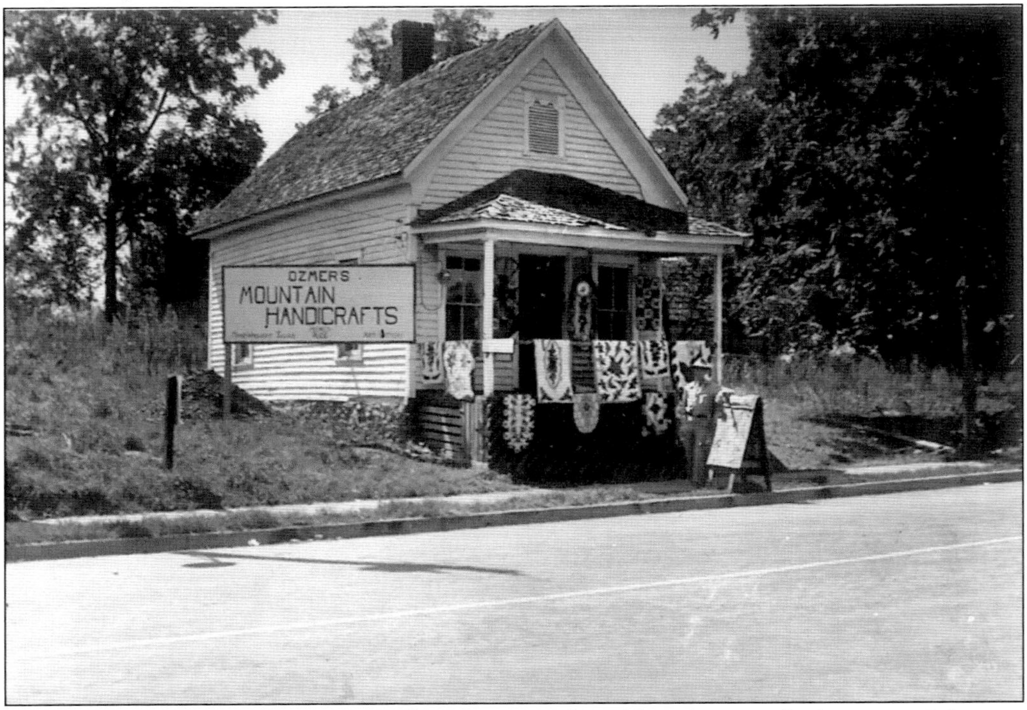

Ozmer's Gift Shop was located on Highway 129 South and later became the location of the post office. (Courtesy of W. Lake Stroud.)

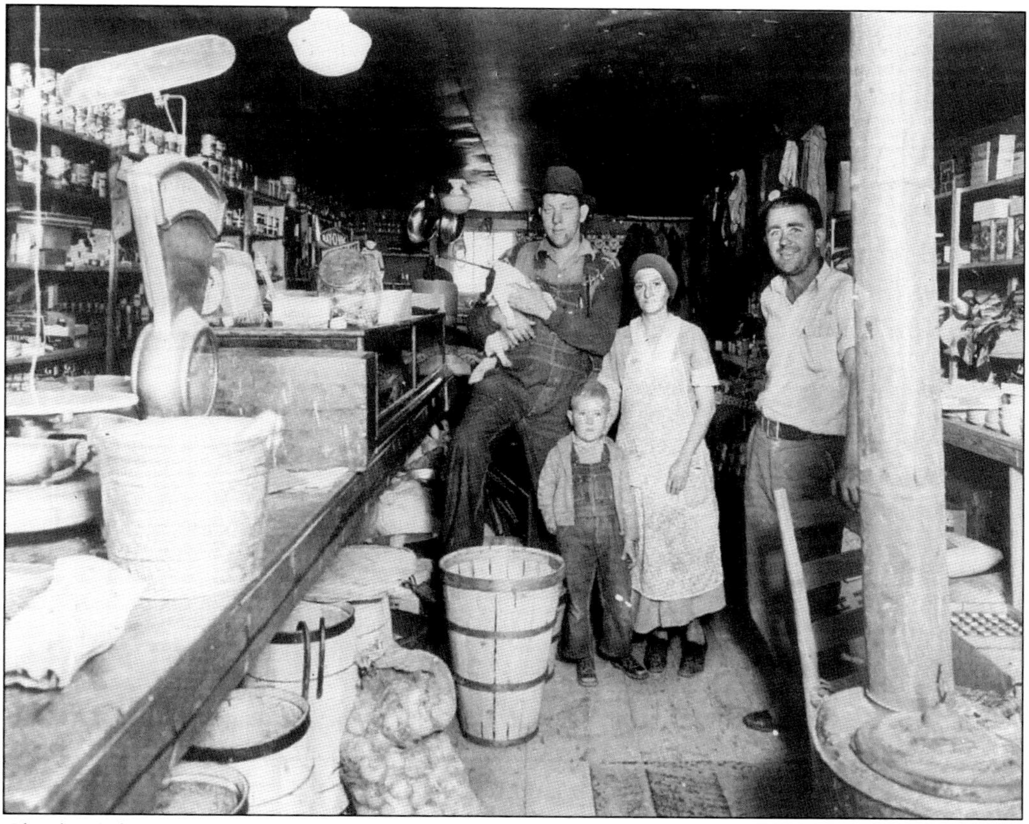

Charlie Odom's Store is shown in Youngstown about 1938. Pictured are Charlie Odom, Bertha Odom, Charles Partin, child, and Claude Partin. (Courtesy of Frances Fair Partin.)

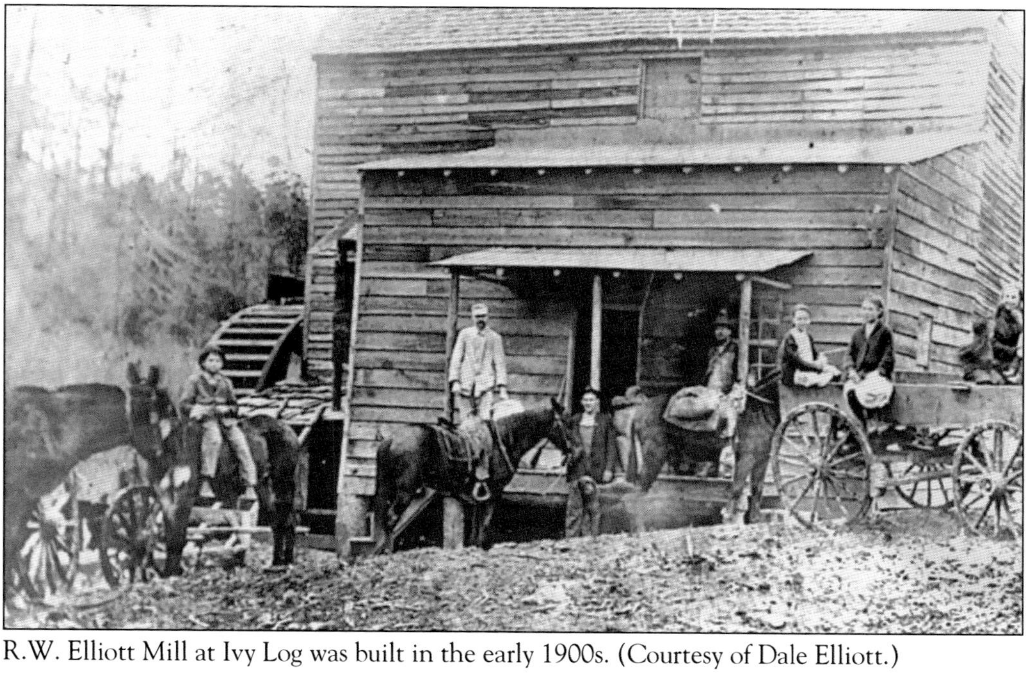

R.W. Elliott Mill at Ivy Log was built in the early 1900s. (Courtesy of Dale Elliott.)

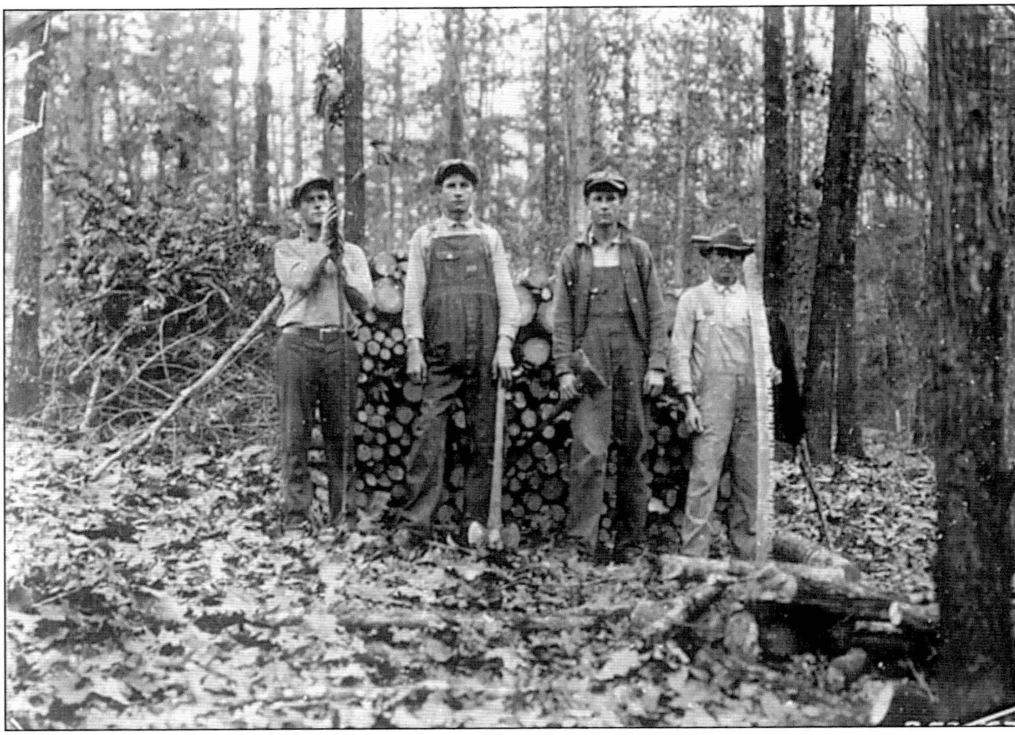

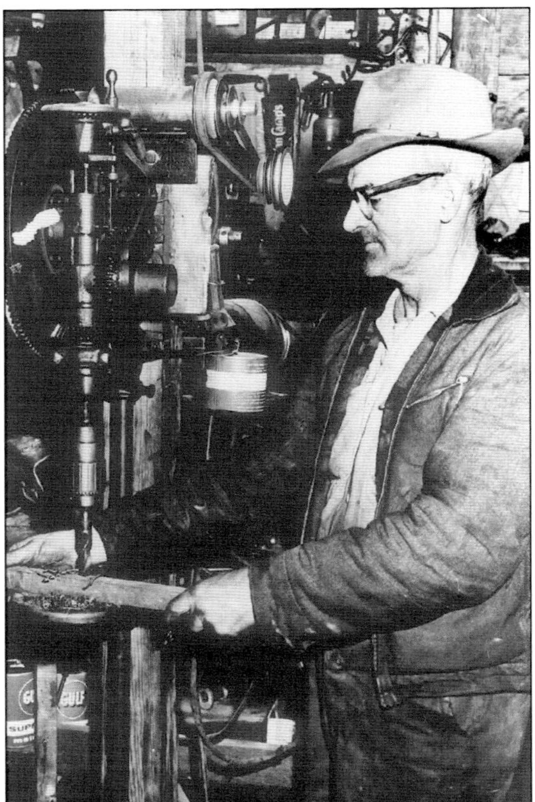

When everyone had wood burning stoves, cutting firewood was big business. Four cutters have two double-bit axes and two crosscut saws. Shown from left to right with their tools are unidentified, Henley Hamby, Manley Hamby, and Beulan Owenby. (Courtesy of Union County Historical Society.)

Jewell Twiggs was a machinist in the 1940s. (Courtesy of W. Lake Stroud.)

Horace Burns poses with his tobacco crop in the 1940s. Burns owned 3/10-acre tobacco allotment. Tobacco was taken to auction in Tennessee. (Courtesy of Jean Johnson.)

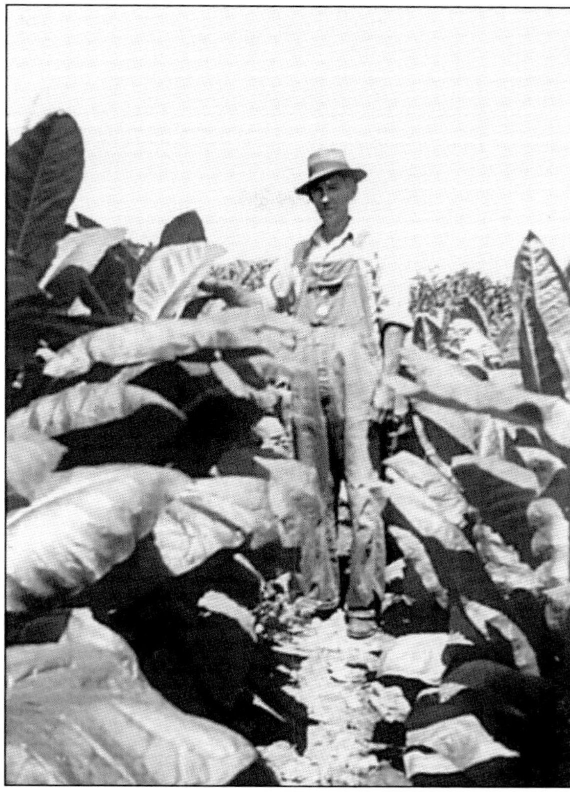

This store, located off the square, was built pre-1930s by Johnny Wimpey and Nell Duckworth Wimpey. (Courtesy of W. Lake Stroud.)

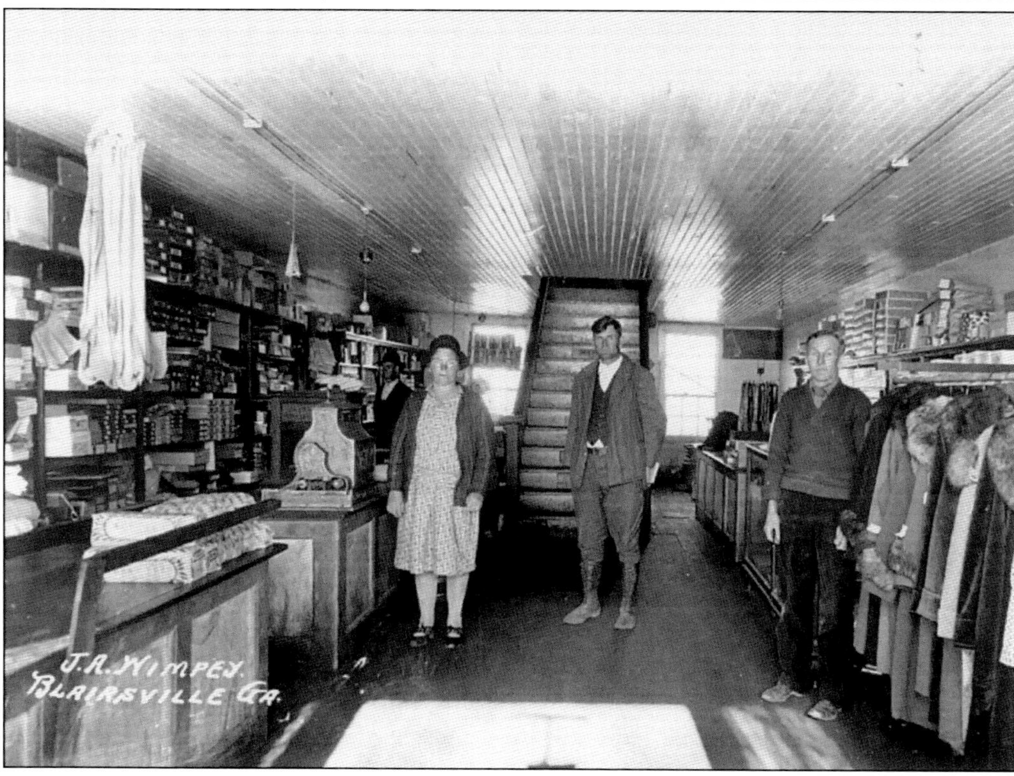

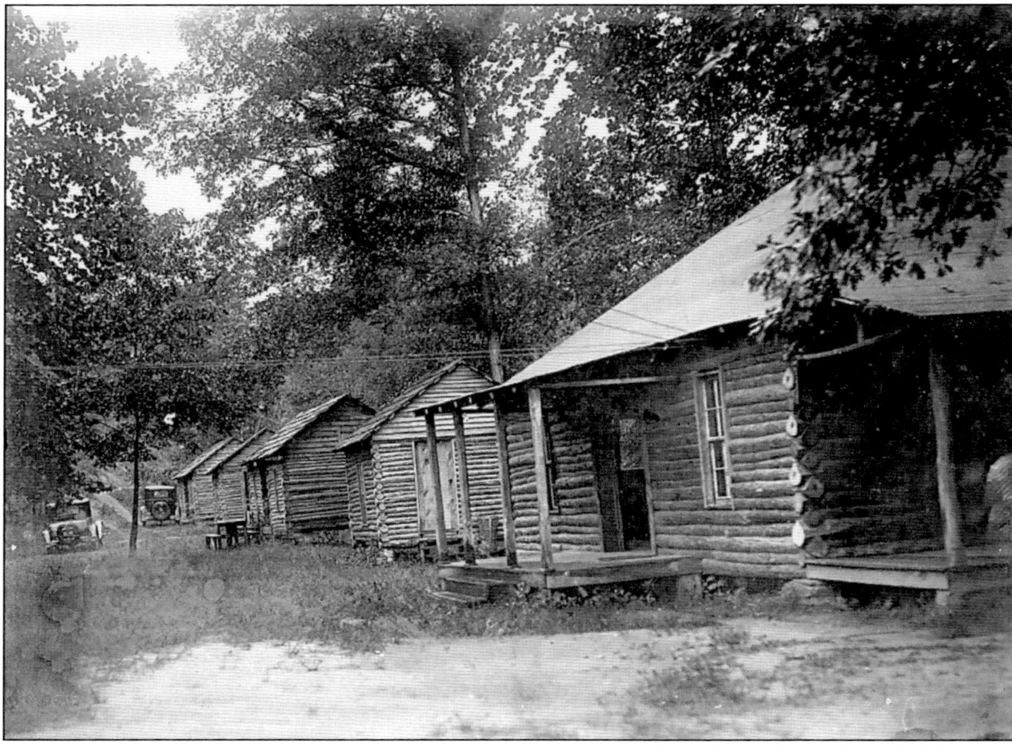

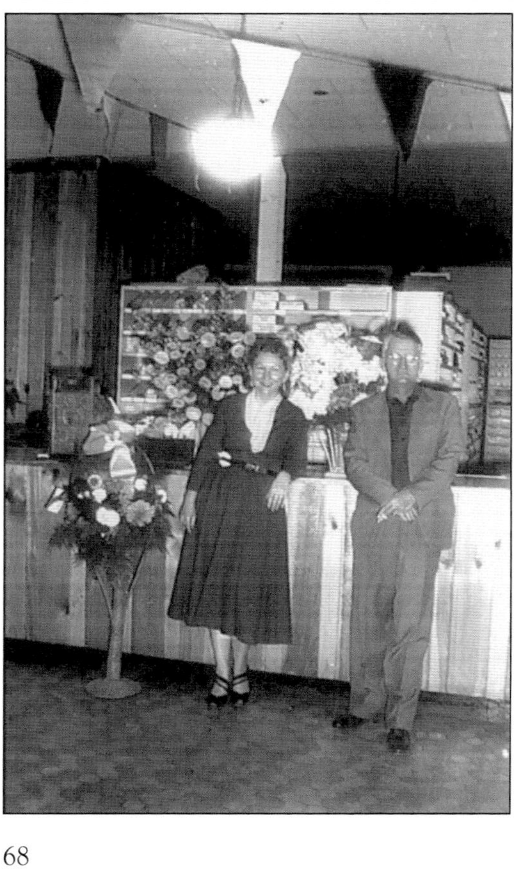

These cabins were near the Nottely River at Canal Lake. They were constructed before the lake was built by TVA in 1940. During this era, campgrounds were known as tourist camps. This photo was taken c. 1930s. (Courtesy of Melva Lynn Drake.)

Ralph J. Twiggs Sr. and Faye Hooper Twiggs pose at the opening of the Ford dealership at the new brick building on the square c. 1950. (Courtesy of David Friedly.)

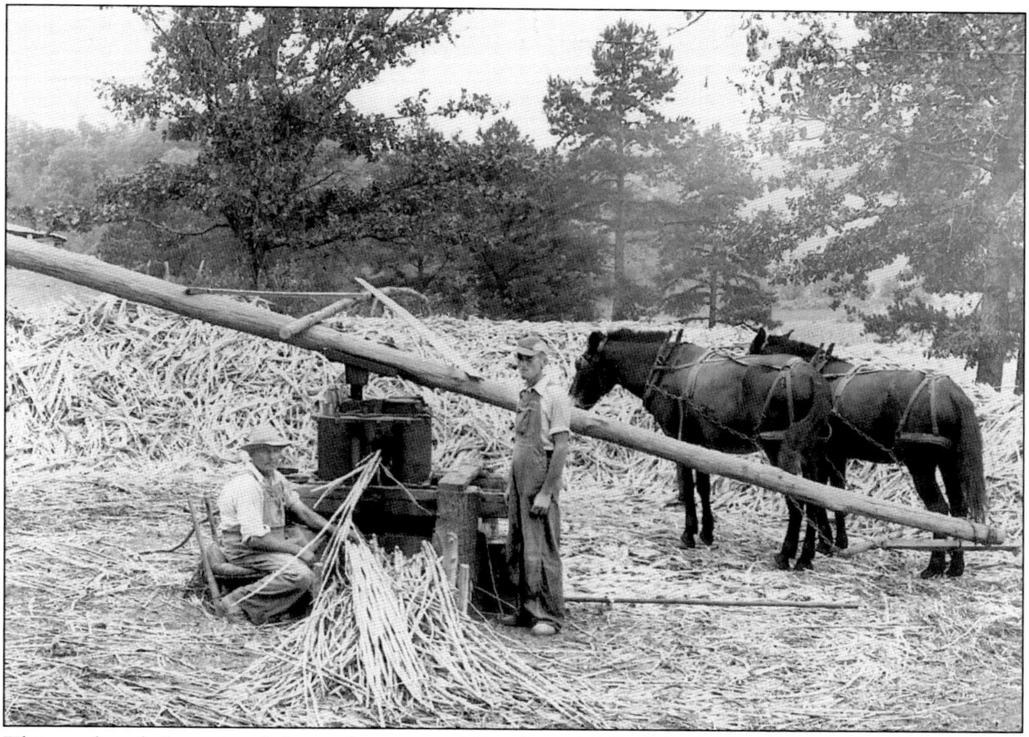

This undated photo is of the mule powered Sorghum Mill. (Courtesy of W. Lake Stroud.)

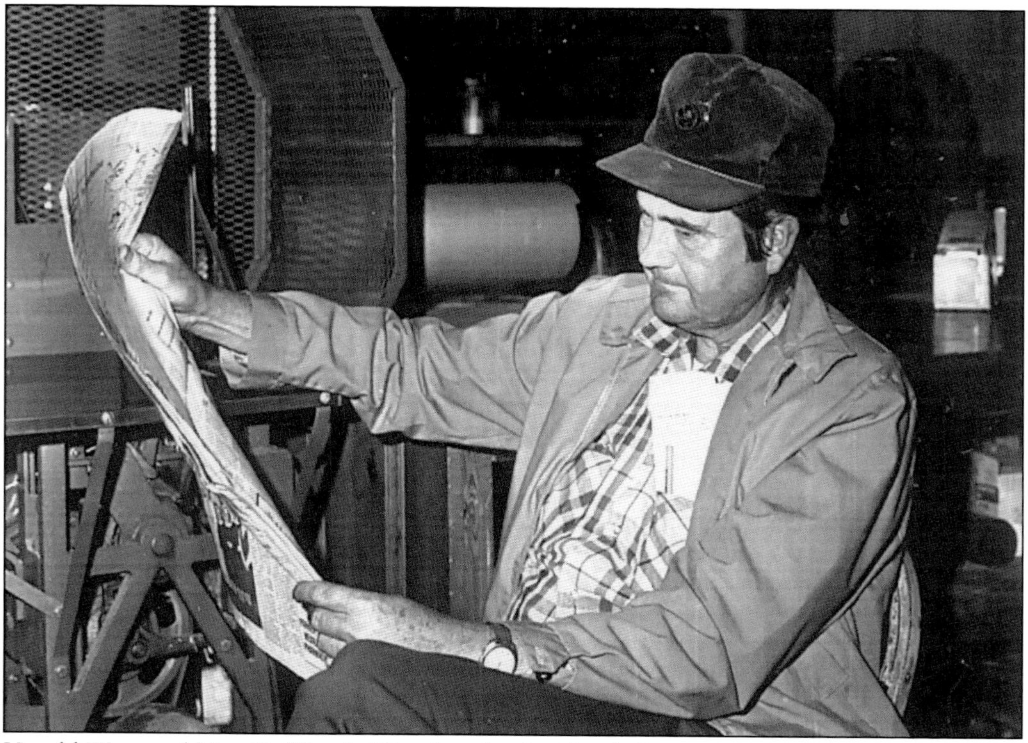

Harold West and his wife Wanda West bought the North Georgia News in 1953. (Courtesy of Kenneth West.)

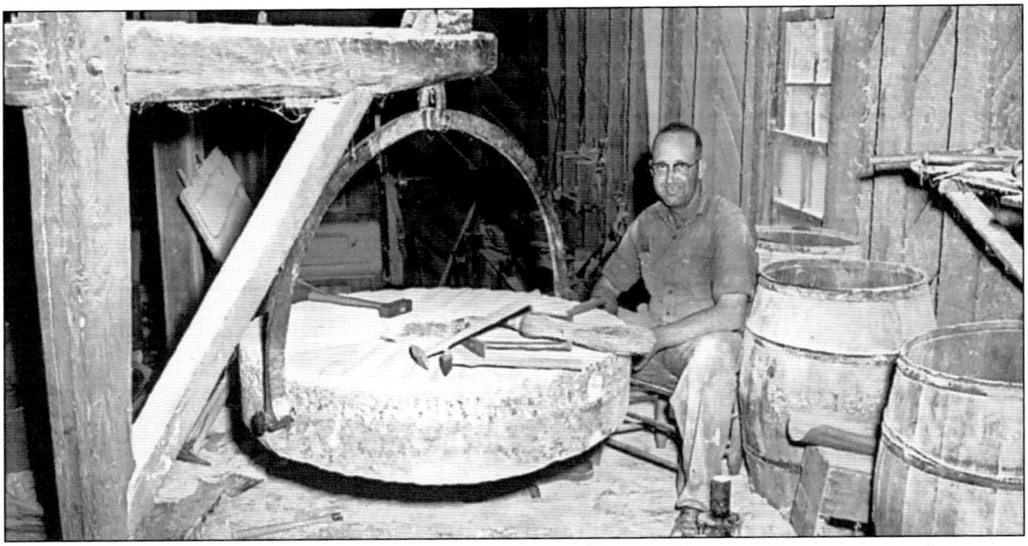

This photograph, *c.* 1960 shows that dressing the millstone deepens the groves in the stone, which grinds the corn. (Courtesy of Union County Historical Society.)

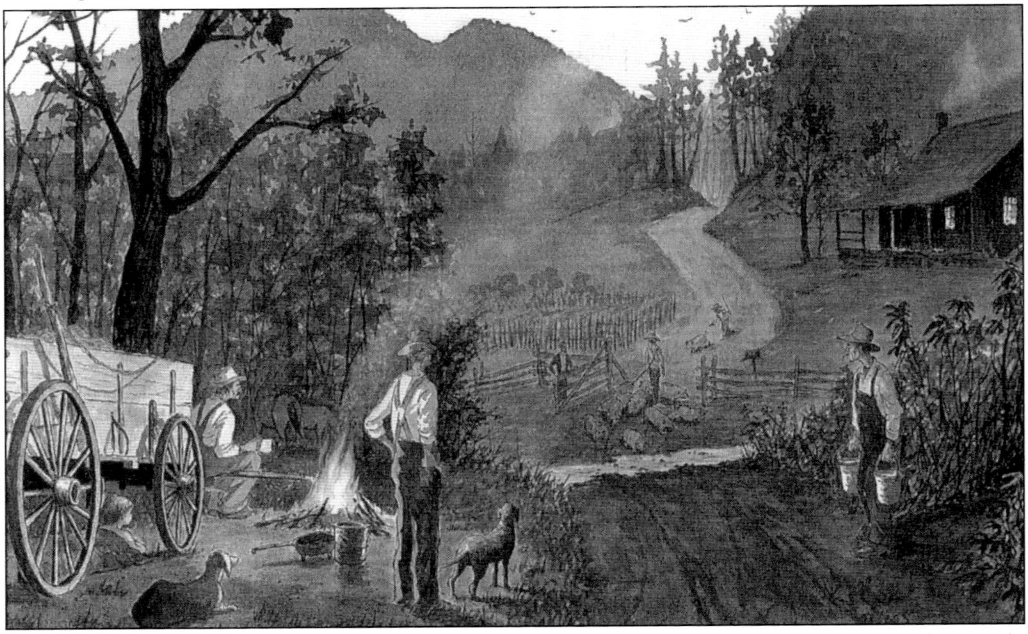

Shown here is Logan Turnpike 1920, as painted by John Kollock. Turnpikes provided an early way of building roads of any length. Those using the passage were charged a fee. The Union Turnpike Company was chartered in 1821. A portion of the road traveled through the Testnatee Gap to Blairsville. The main purpose of the road was to connect the mountain farmers with markets in Gainesville and to bring supplies over to merchants in the isolated communities. The road rose 3,138 feet. Often, a heavy wagon needed pushing on the way up the road. On the way down, logs were tied to the rear to keep the team from being overrun by the load. After the Civil War, Major Willis Logan bought extensive land on the south side of the Blue Ridge Mountains and in 1871 paid $3,000 for the rights to the toll road. The fee was two cents per mile for four-wheeled wagons with two or more horses or oxen, one cent per mile for each head of sheep or pigs. (Courtesy of John Kollock.)

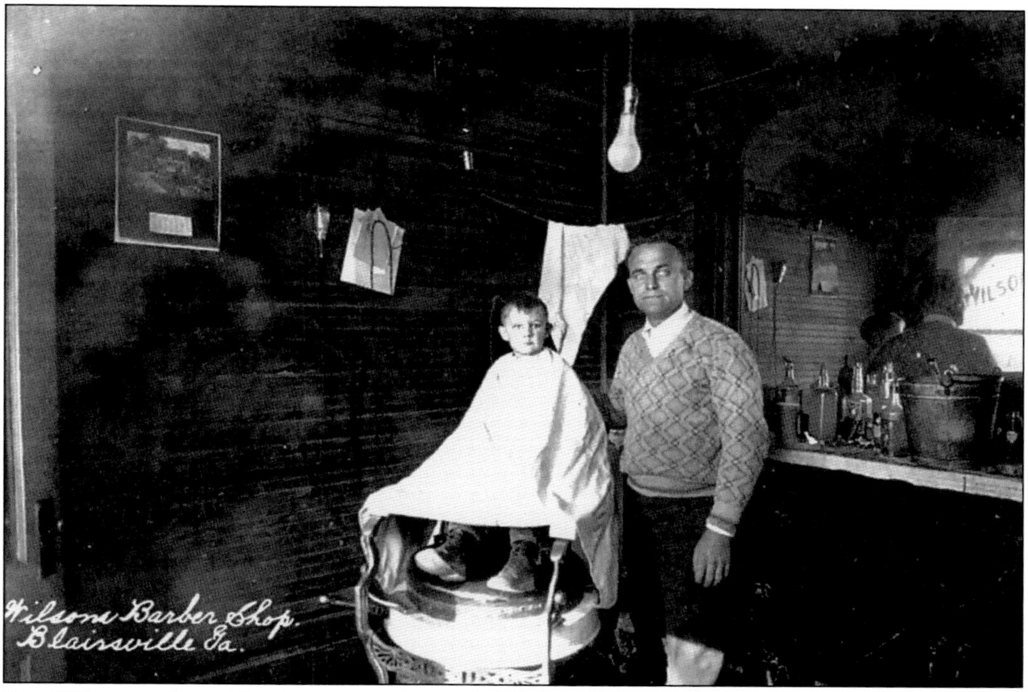

Ben Wilson and son Charles pose in the early 1930s at Wilson's Barber Shop in Blairsville, next to the Akins Hotel. (Courtesy of Union County Historical Society.)

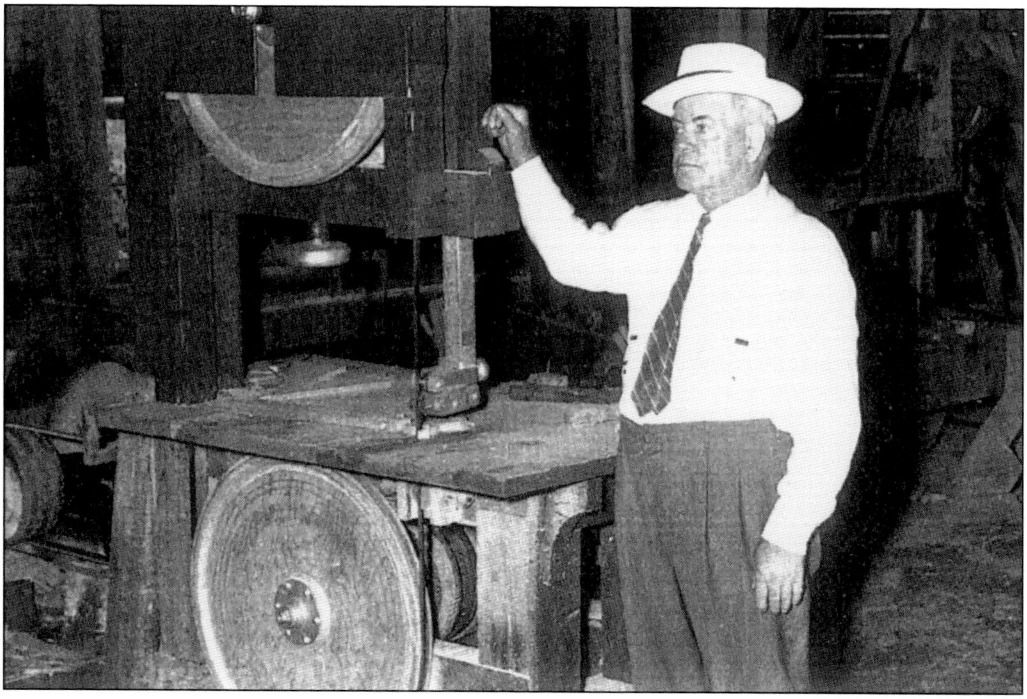

Rev. Jimmy Hood was a minister, carpenter, blacksmith, inventor, songwriter, and school teacher. This photograph is c. 1950. (Courtesy of Union County Historical Society.)

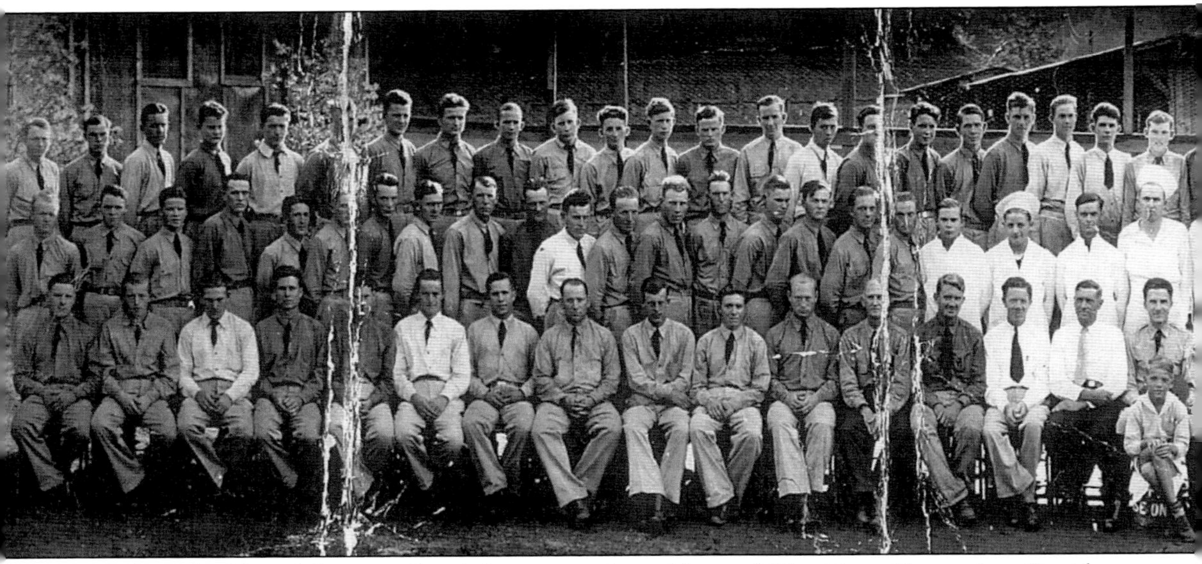

When the United States suffered the economic problems of The Great Depression, President Franklin D. Roosevelt extolled the virtues of hard work. It was in his acceptance of the Democratic nomination for president in July 1932 that FDR began his conservation movement, proposing putting men to work. It was a massive operation destined to become the most popular experiment of the New Deal. Americans were without work, banks were closed, there was no food on the table, and children and adults alike were aimlessly walking the streets of America in search of a better life that seemed out of reach. In March 1933, FDR summoned Congress to Washington. Congress heard his plan to enlist 250,000 men in an effort to "preserve the natural resources of these United States." From the initial crop of 250,000 boys, the Civilian Conservation Corps (CCC) grew to provide jobs for 2.5 million young men between the ages of 17 and 25. During its time, there were many nicknames for the CCC, but the most common by far was "Roosevelt's Tree Army." This name stuck because the recruits were young men (boys) who enrolled for a term of service, lived in camps, much like the soldiers in an army. Each camp

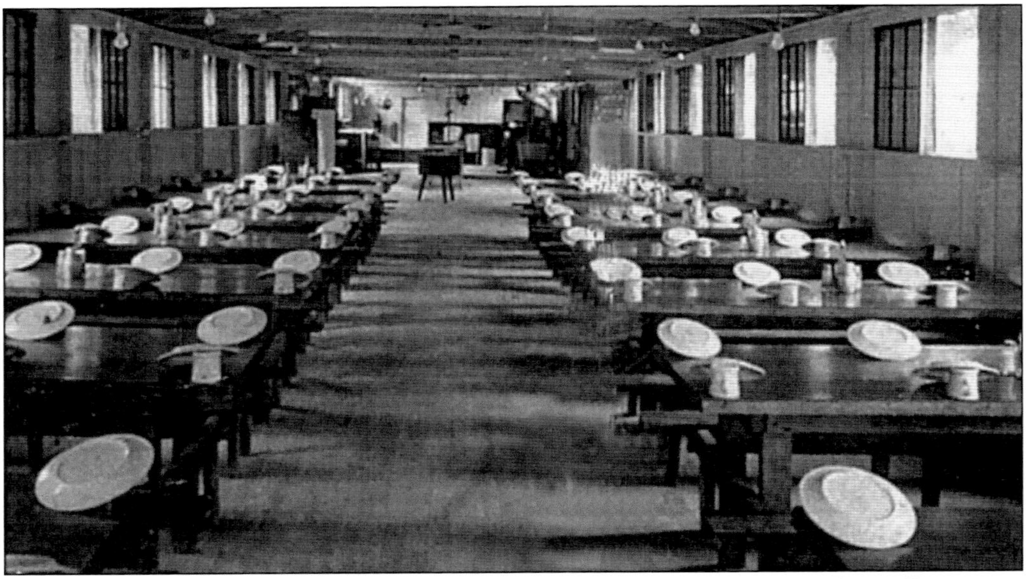

Shown here is the Mess Hall for the 431st Co CCC Camp Enotah, Georgia Blairsville.

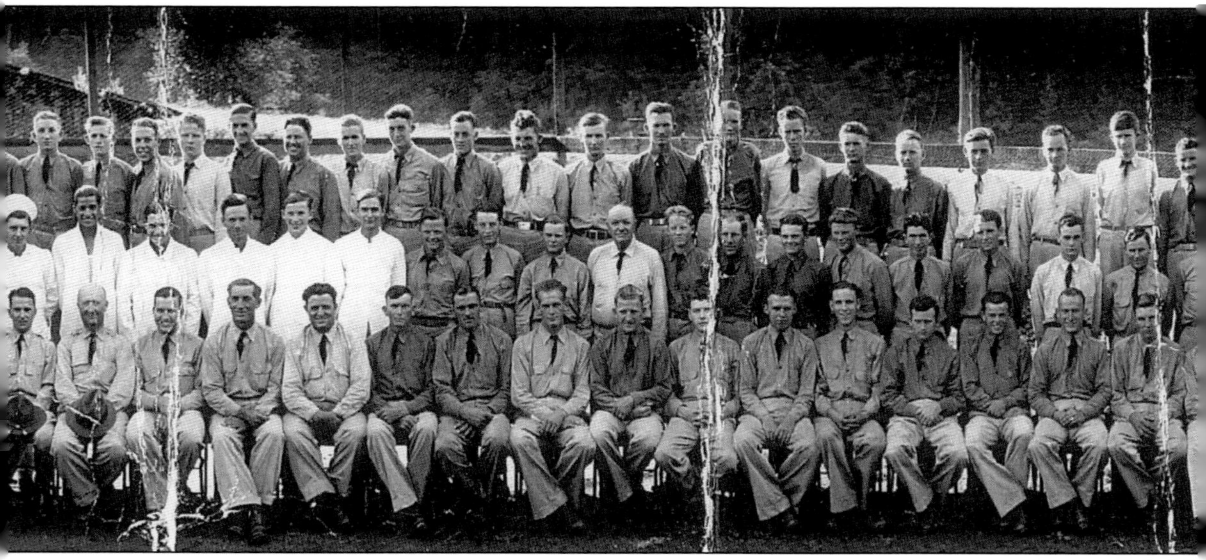

had a commanding officer (normally a lieutenant or colonel in the army), a mess hall, laundry, and tool house. Modular barracks made it easy to add to a camp or tear it down. Each CCC boy would receive $30 a month. The majority of this money would go to his wife or family and he would keep a bit for himself. One of the major tasks of the corps was reforestation. Much of the land in north Georgia and throughout the Southeast had been stripped bare and left as worthless. In addition to the reforestation, corps members would build roads and fire control trails, work on erosion control, or fight forest fires. Today's Chattahoochee National Forest was partially reforested with the help of the CCC. Completed in 1942, Lake Winfield Scott is the lasting legacy of the Civilian Conservation Corps in north Georgia. Named for General Winfield Scott, who led the United States Army for 40 years and ran for President in 1852. Vogel State Park is an example of CCC success. The CCC built the original dams, cabins, walkways, and the roads in Vogel State Park. Much of the rock work at Vogel and at Walasi-Yi Center was built by Chess Duckworth, a local and very talented rock mason.

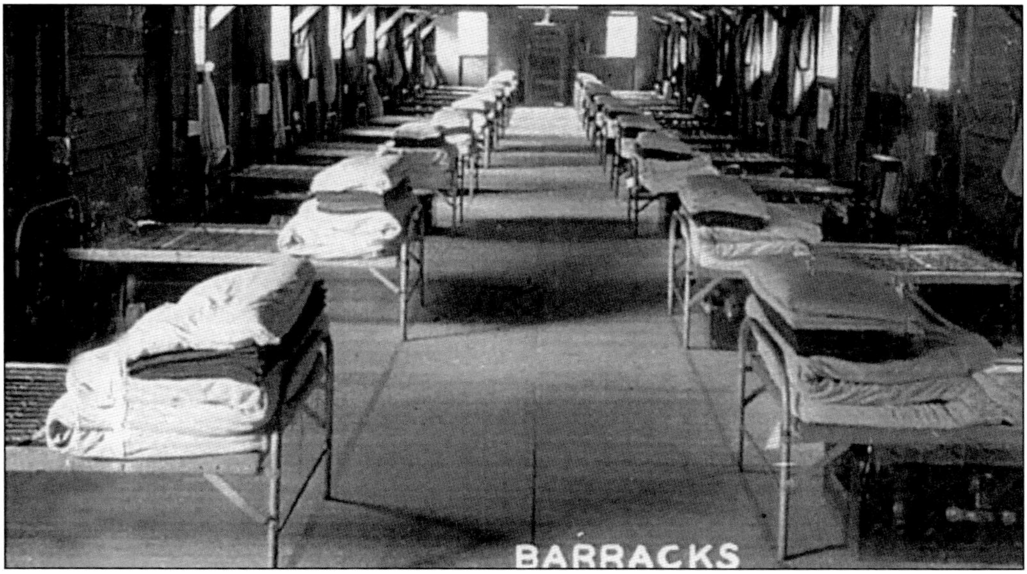

Shown here is the Barracks for the CCC 431st Co CCC Camp Enotah, Georgia in Blairsville.

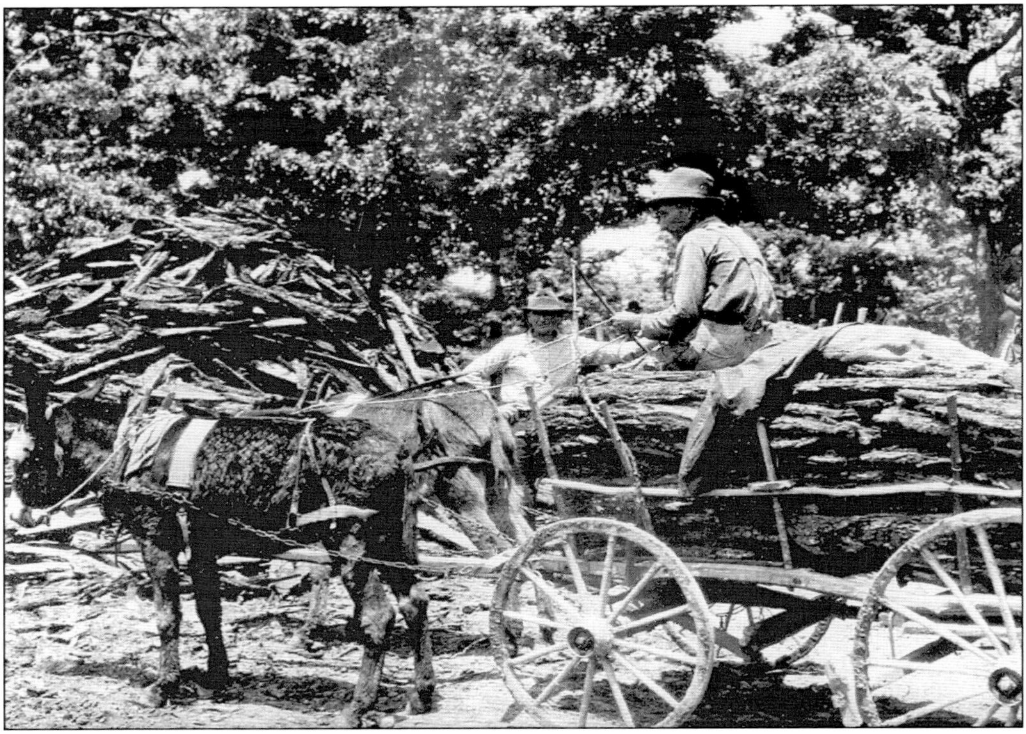

Getting Chestnut bark (*c.* 1920) to the market required a horse-drawn wagon. This bark was valued for its tannic acid, which was used to cure leather. The native chestnut tree is virtually extinct. (Courtesy of United Community Bank.)

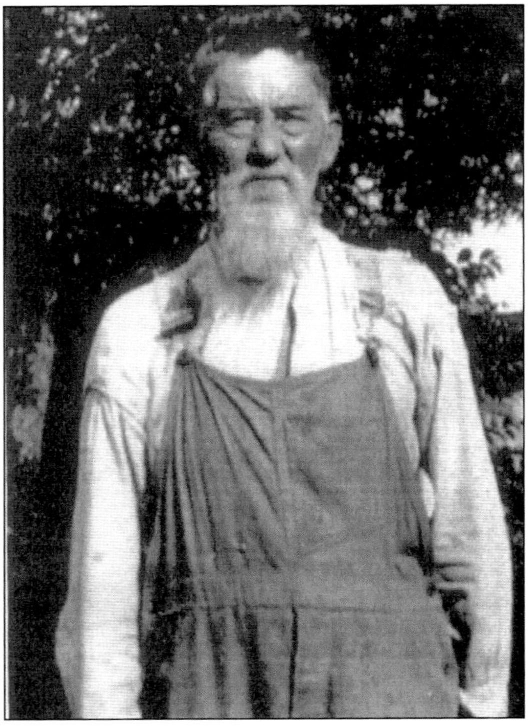

William Luther Chapman, farmer, was a typical wool hat farmer. This photograph is *c.* 1930. (Courtesy of Dale Elliott.)

Five

Community Life and Notable People

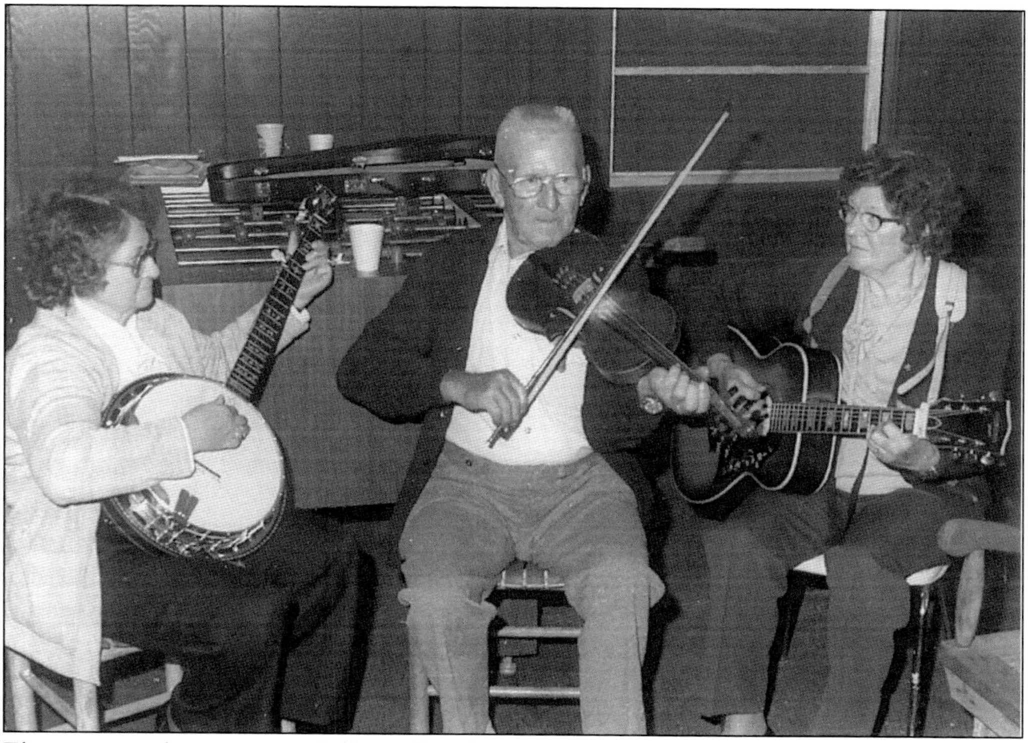

The common denominator of all people in Union County was the love of music. Regardless of one's occupation or call in life, music was something everyone enjoyed together without regard to social or economic status. Marie Rogers Cornwell (playing banjo), Walter Rogers (playing fiddle), and Fannie Rogers Akins (playing a guitar) join in a typical time of music making.

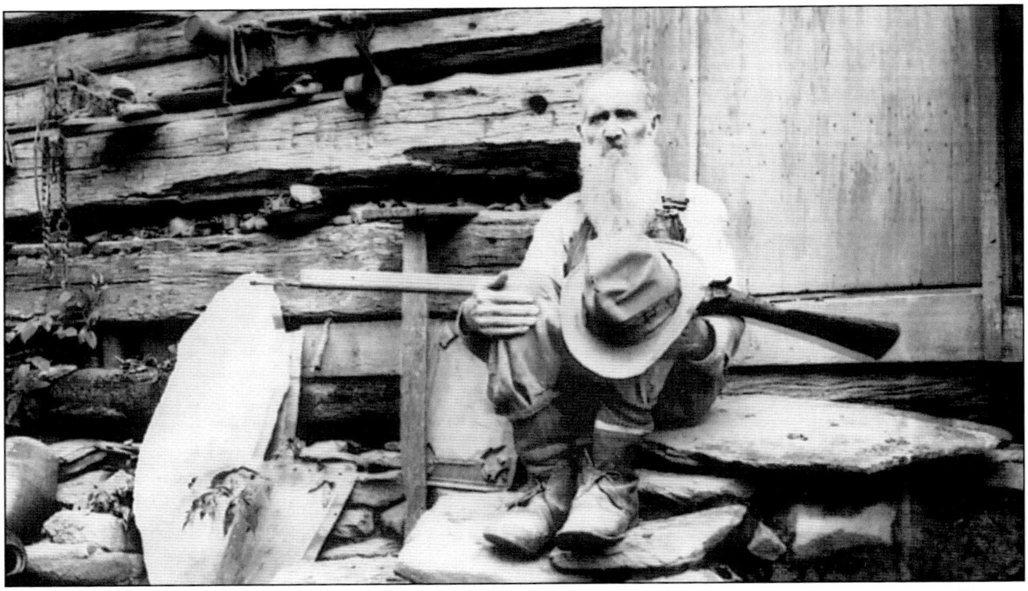

Peter Young was one of the original pioneers at the end of the 19th Century. He was a farmer and gold digger.

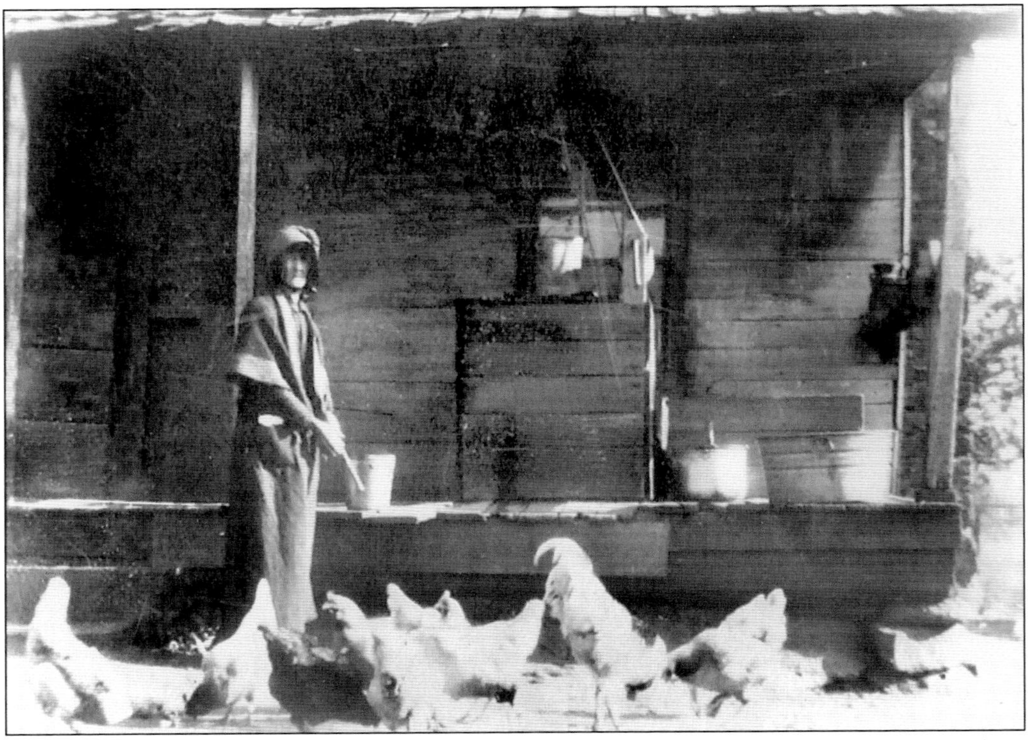

Eliza Logan Reece always had chickens and shelled corn for them by hand. She liked to knit and made socks and sweaters c. 1930. (Courtesy of Helen Wright.)

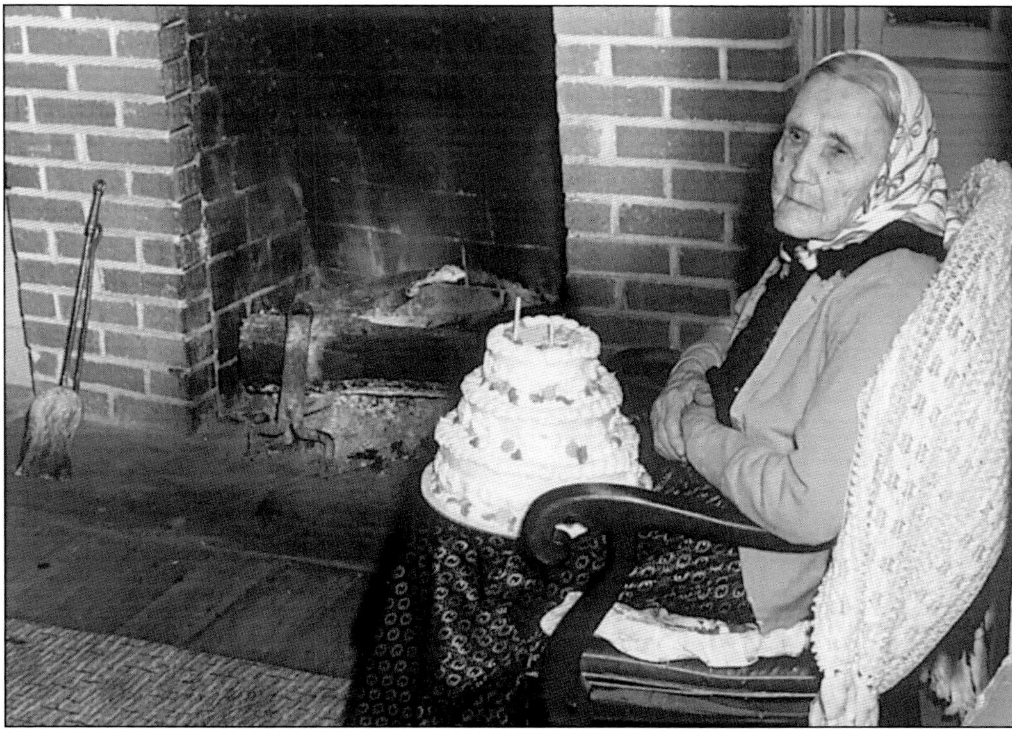

Mrs. Sarah Dyer celebrates her 100th birthday in 1958. (Courtesy of Union County Historical Society.)

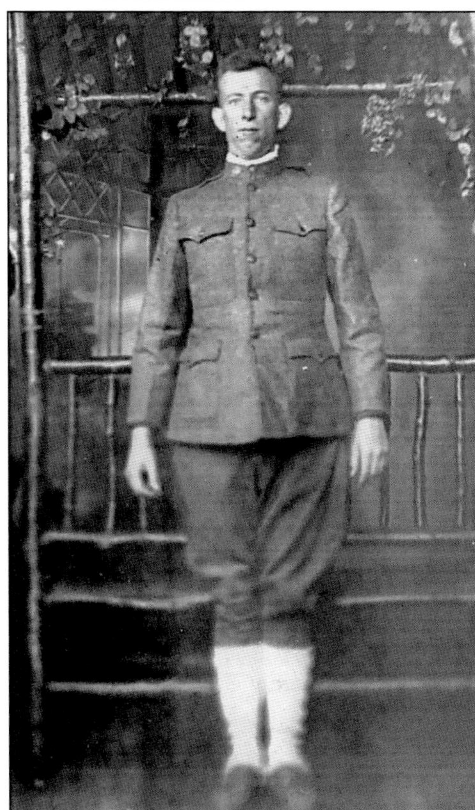

Arthur Burns, World War I soldier from Union County from the Ivy Log District is pictured here. He was born 1894 and died 1939. (Courtesy of Dale Elliott.)

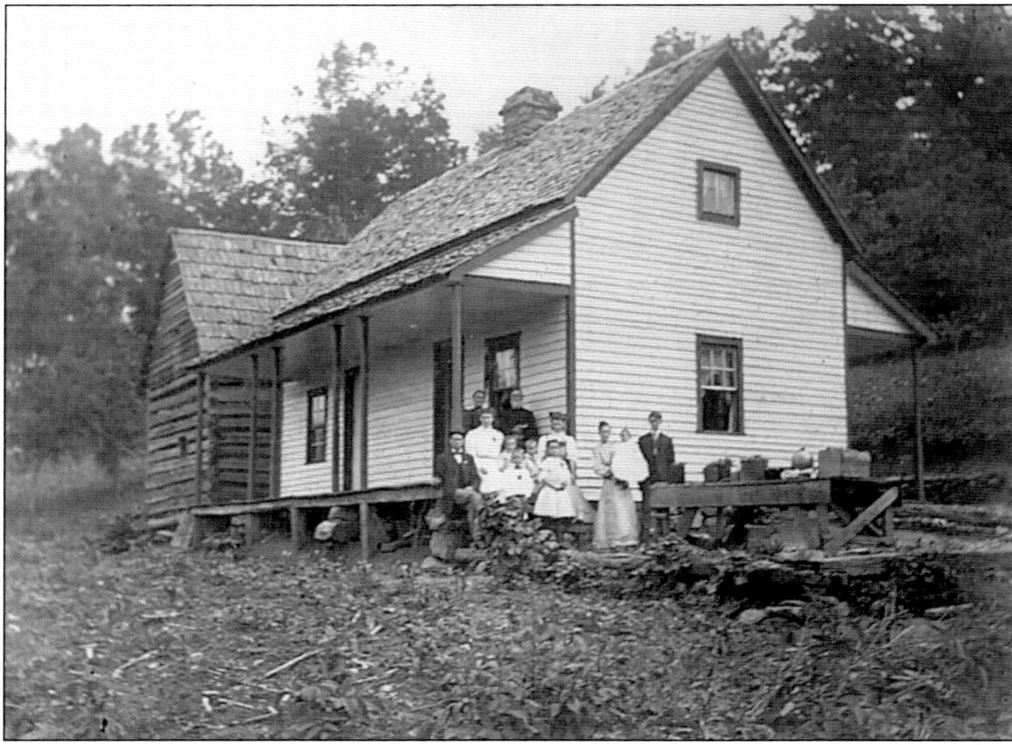

The home of George Dills appears on a postcard. The people and the date are unidentified. (Courtesy of Bertha Crisp.)

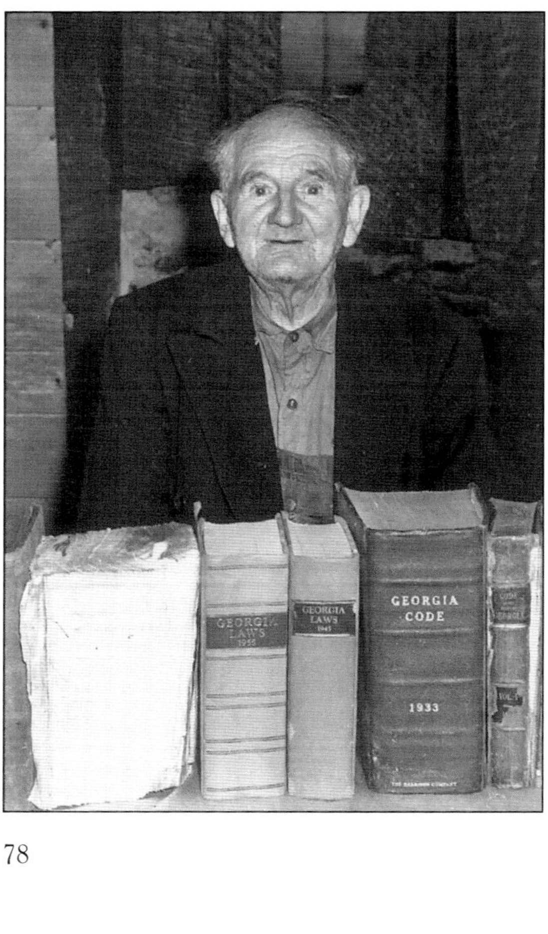

Robert Lee Nelson, Justice of the Peace for Brasstown Militia District, was first elected in 1920. He has been referred to as the "Judge Bean" of Union County. After Nelson lost his official title, he was told by the governor that he had no jurisdiction over the area. Nelson's response was, "You look after your side of the mountain and I'll look after mine."

The Rogers Family with dominickers (also known as Dominique Chickens) and turkeys are shown in this photograph, *c.* 1920. From left to right are the following: Dr. W.H. Rogers, George Shelton Rogers (father of W.H.), Nora Sullivan Rogers (daughter of Tom Sullivan), and Roy Rogers. (Courtesy Fran Collins Kent.)

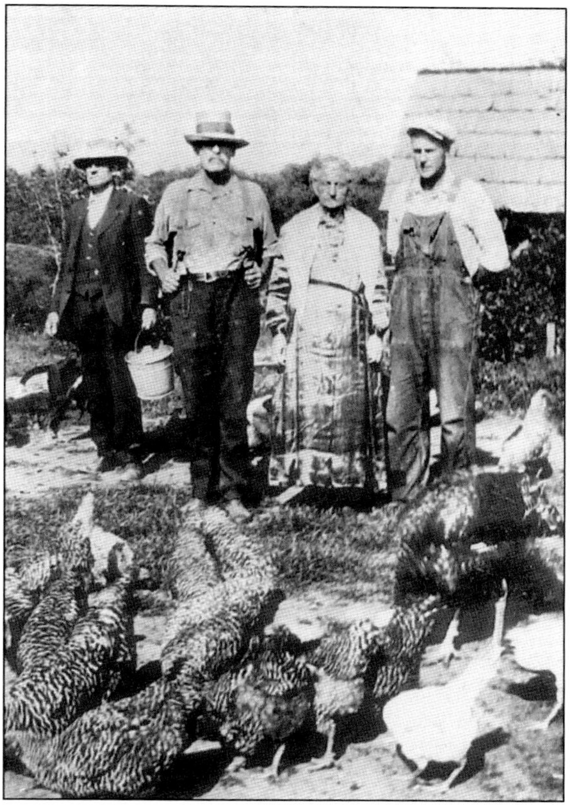

Leanna Elliott, Clyde Elliott, Ethel Elliott, and Pearl Elliott are shown at Neel Gap in 1929. (Courtesy of Dale Elliott.)

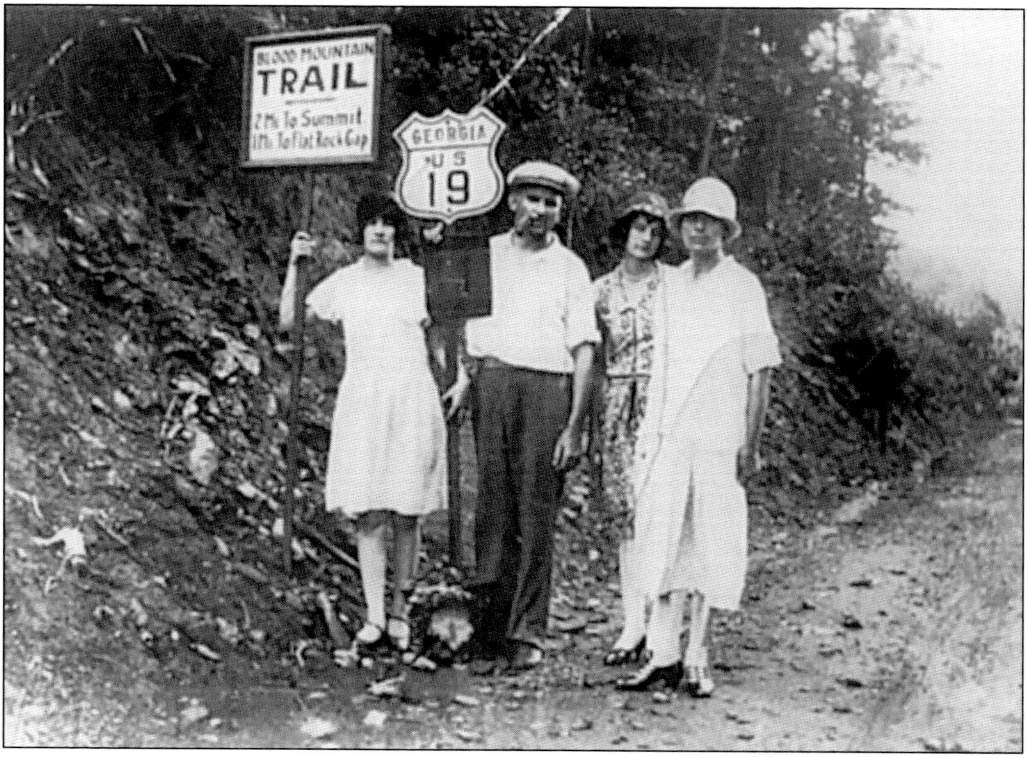

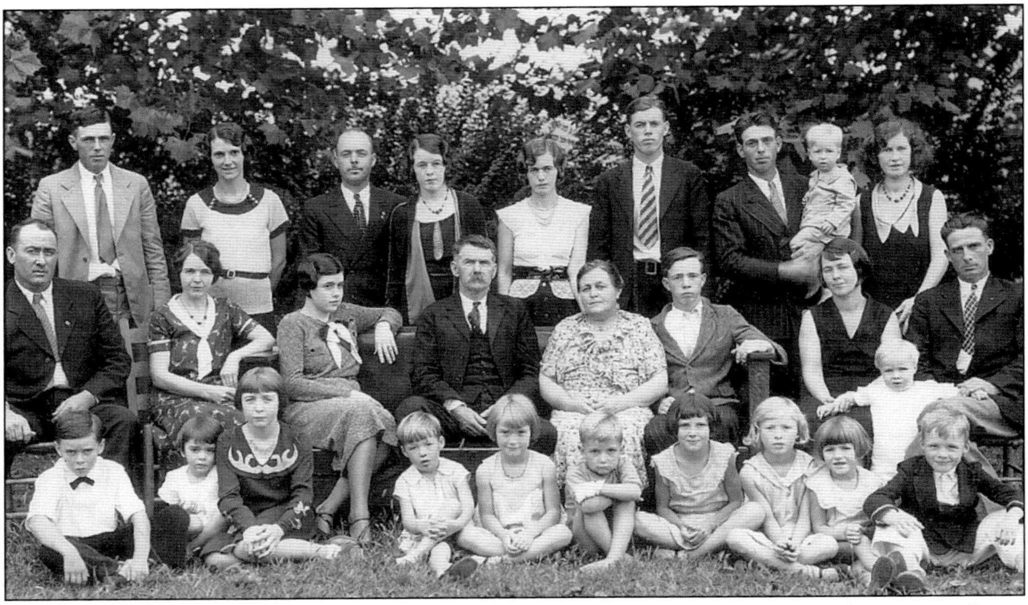

Pictured in this photograph *c.* 1934 (from left to right) are (first row) Jack Teague, Doris Teague, Hazel Teague, Mildred Jordon, Betty Mauney, and Tommy Mauney; (second row) Tom Teague, Minnie Mauney Teague, Johnny Mauney, Charles Stanhope Mauney, Theadosia Mauney, Charles Mauney, Williard Manny Jordon, and Joe Jordon; (third row) Clyde Mauney, Irene Mauney, Ed Mauney, Bess Mauney, Alice Mauney, Rush Mauney, Roy Mauney, Billy Mauney, and Willie Nicholson Mauney. (Courtesy of Liz Adkins.)

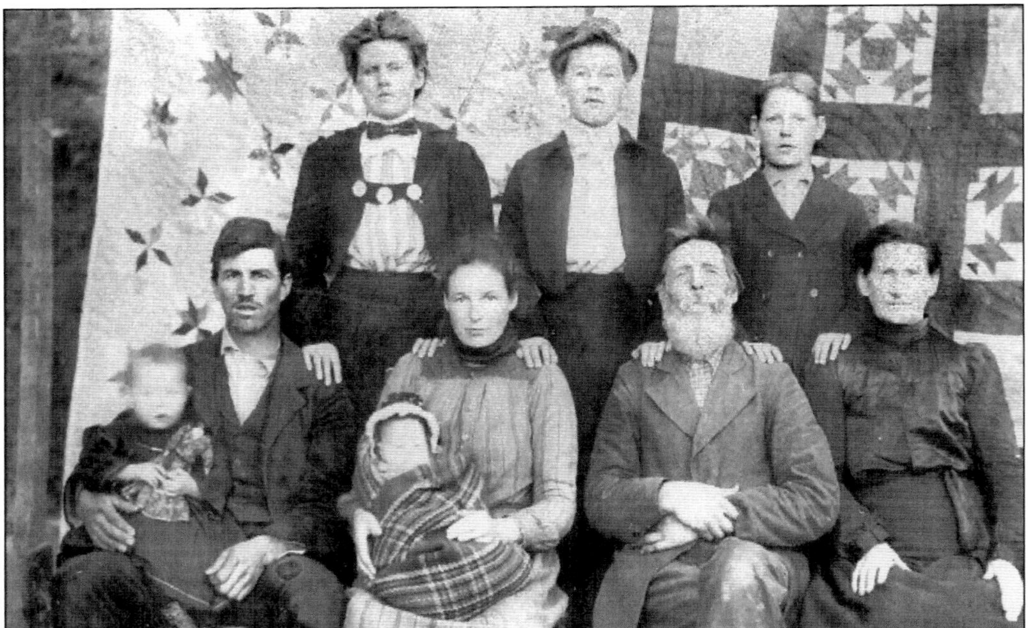

This Dills Family poses here in 1908 at an old house about one mile from Mt. Pleasant Church. Those pictured include (front row) James Martin Smith (holding daughter Bertha Smith), Theodosia Dills Smith (holding son Oral), George Washington, and Margaret E. Clement; (back row) Alice Dills, Elbie Dills, and Frank Dills. (Courtesy of Martha Clayton Clement.)

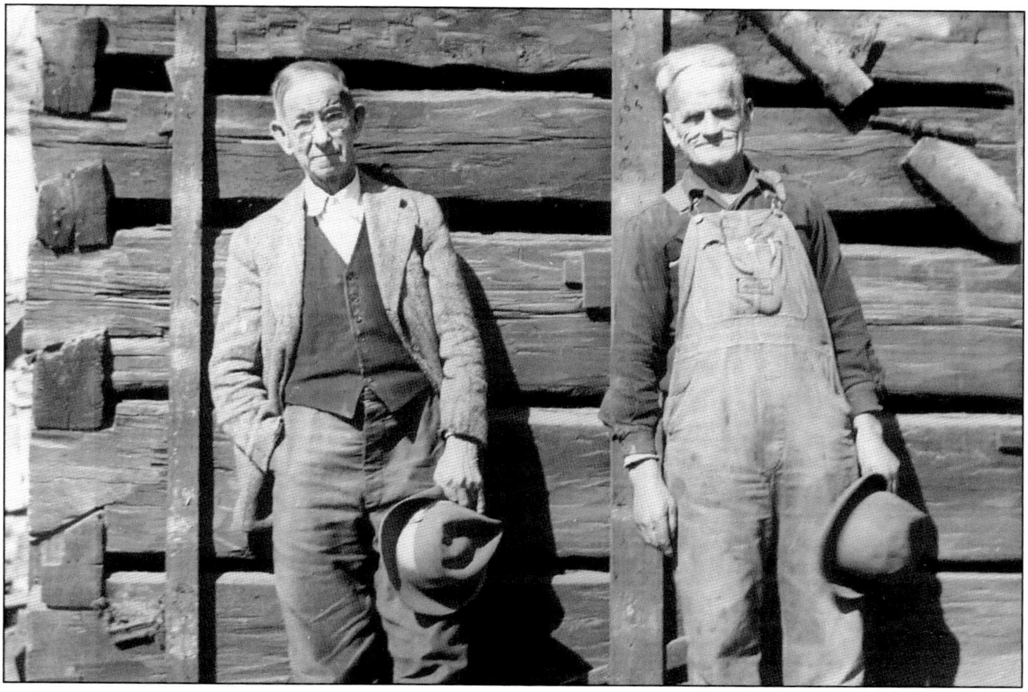

Billy May and Dock Thomas pose in this 1954 picture. (Courtesy of W. Lake Stroud.)

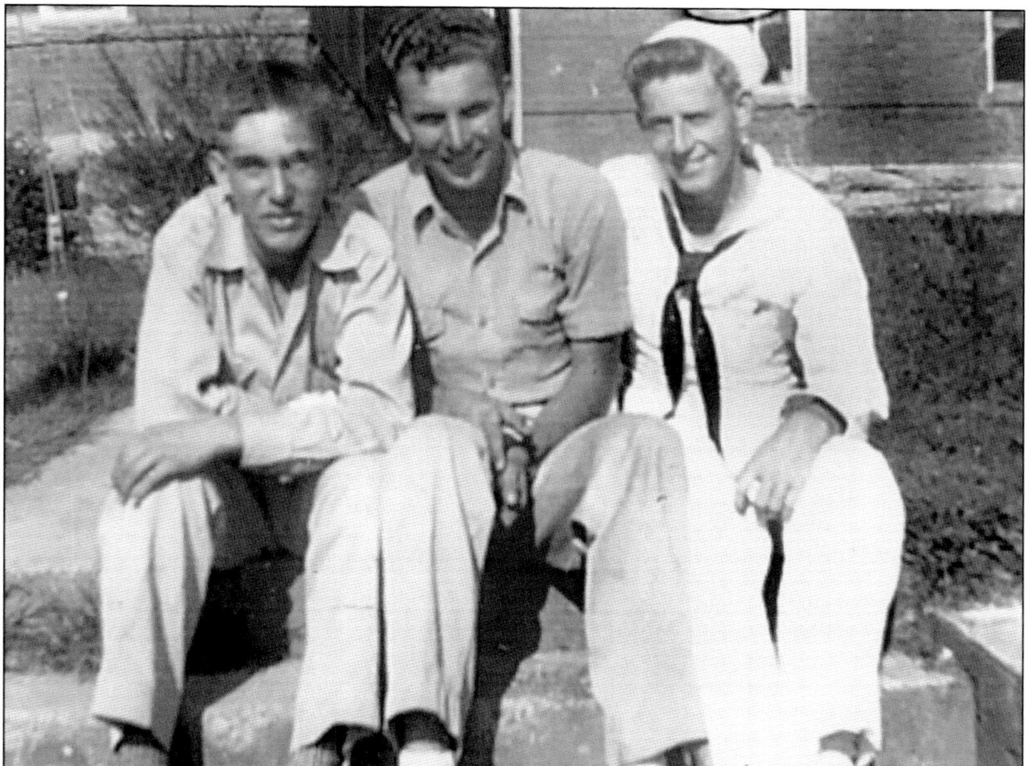

Raymond Akins, Carlton Colwell and Candler Jones are on the courthouse side steps in this August 1945 photograph. (Courtesy of Barbara Davenport.)

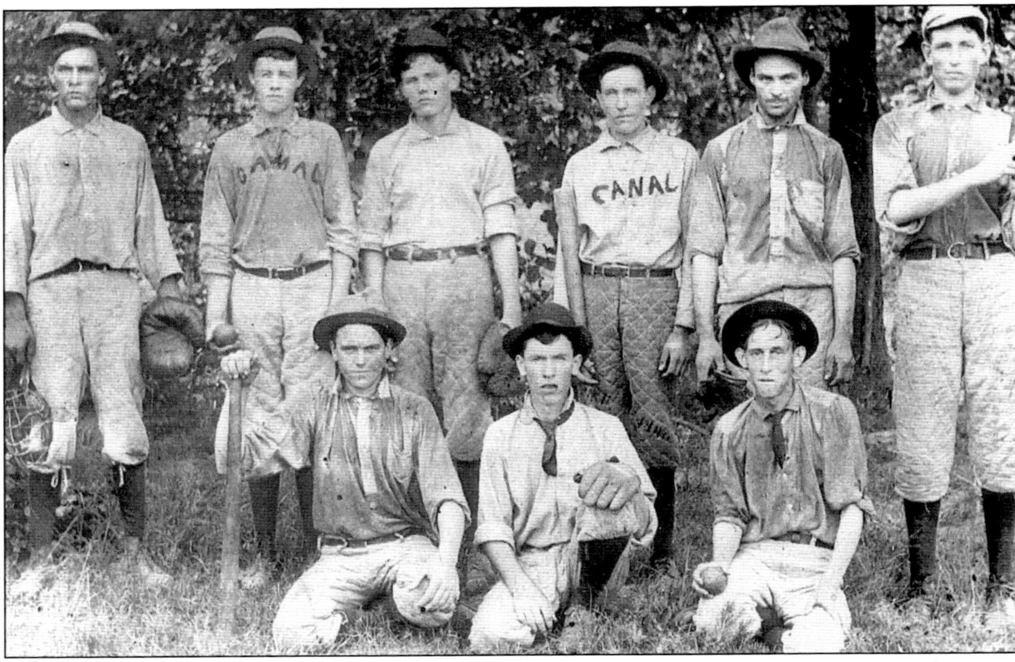

Members of the 1908 Canal Lake Baseball Team 1908, from left to right, are (front row) Homer Brackett (right field), Gus Brackett (second base), and Elisha Fair (second base); (back row) George Young (catcher), McAfee (pitcher), Garnett Brackett (first base), Thurman White (center field), Jim Brackett (third base), Asbury M. McGlamery (short stop). (Courtesy of Melva Lynn Drake.)

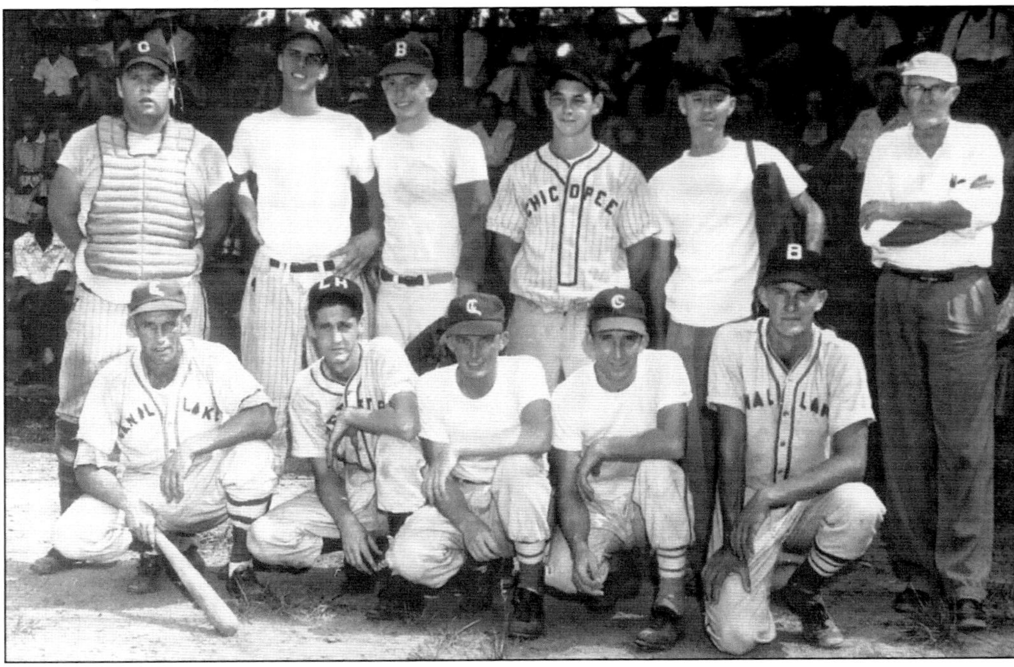

Members of the all star team in 1954 included Ford Bryant, Jake Winter, Bill Drake, J.W. Payne, Jack Lance, Doug Casper, Glen Whitmore, Bill Brannon, Jack Waters, and Arthur McAfee. (Courtesy of Melva Lynn Drake.).

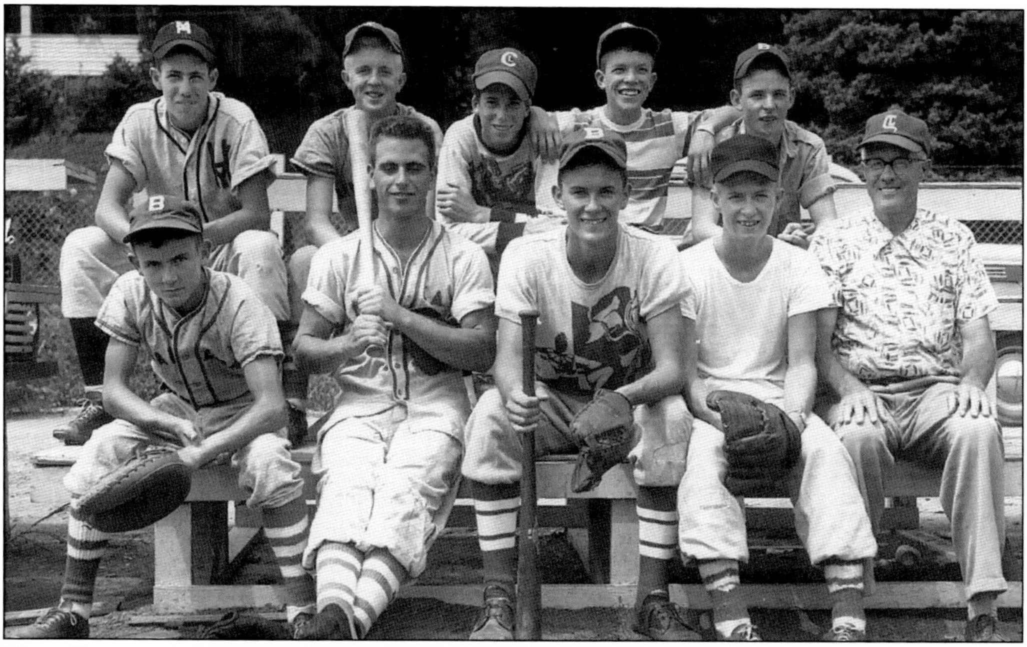

The all star team members (from about 1953), from left to right, are (front row) Bud Akins, James Kelley, Jack Lance, Freddie Register, and Arthur McAfee; (back row) Jerry Hood, Gene Rogers, J.M. Rich, James Butt, and Bill Stephens. In 1949, a baseball field was built on what was once a neighbor's corn field. The team MAC sponsored was named Canal Lake Baseball Team. After seeing the response of the many young people wanting to play ball, MAC decided to build a permanent field on his own property. With the help of several neighbors, a ball field with a covered grandstand was built in 1950–1951 at Canal Lake on the Murphy Hwy. Some of those who played at Canal Lake would later become a U.S. congressman, governor of Georgia, professional baseball player, major league manager, doctor, pharmacist, real estate employees, politicians, business owners, construction company owners, and other professionals. (Courtesy of Melva Lynn Drake.)

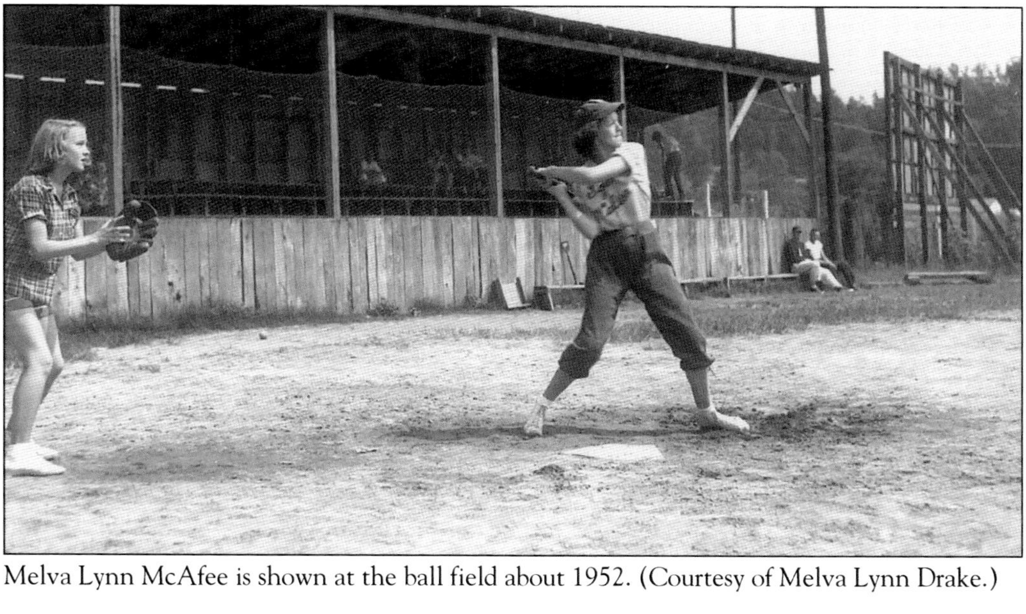

Melva Lynn McAfee is shown at the ball field about 1952. (Courtesy of Melva Lynn Drake.)

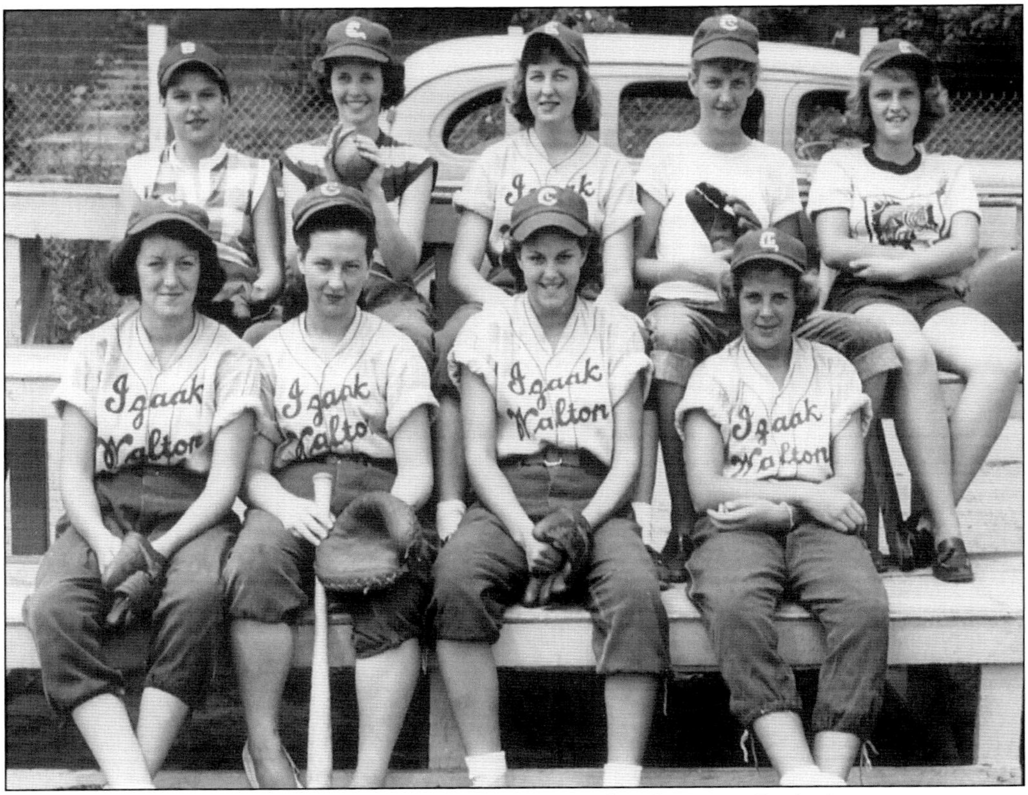

Shown here is a girls softball team, *c.* 1950. (Courtesy of Melva Lynn Drake.)

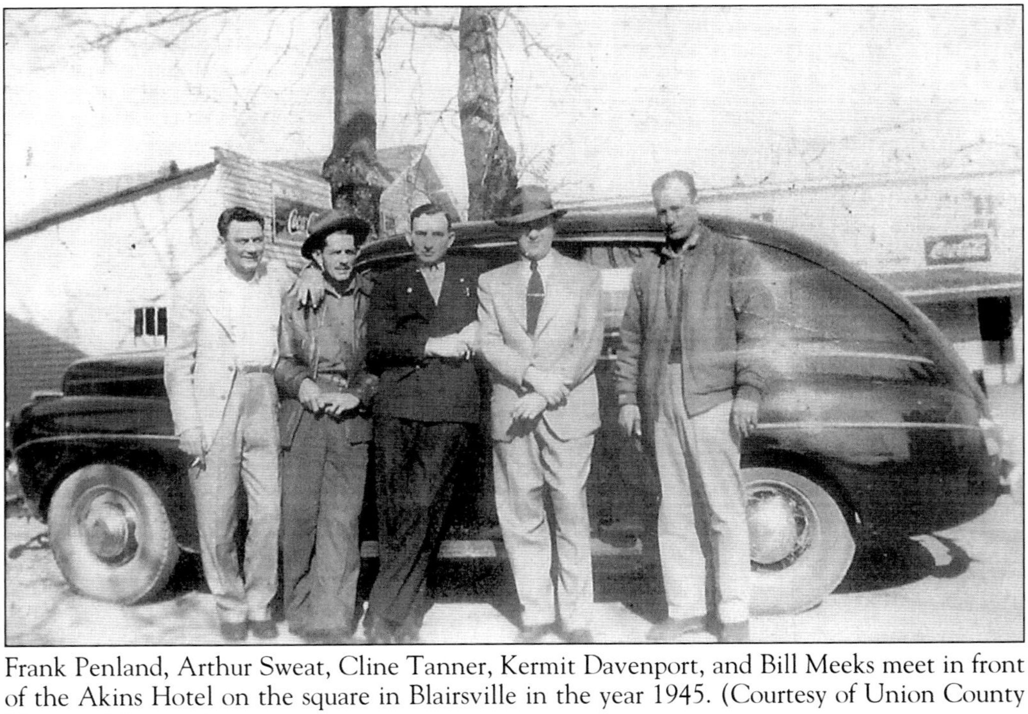

Frank Penland, Arthur Sweat, Cline Tanner, Kermit Davenport, and Bill Meeks meet in front of the Akins Hotel on the square in Blairsville in the year 1945. (Courtesy of Union County Historical Society.)

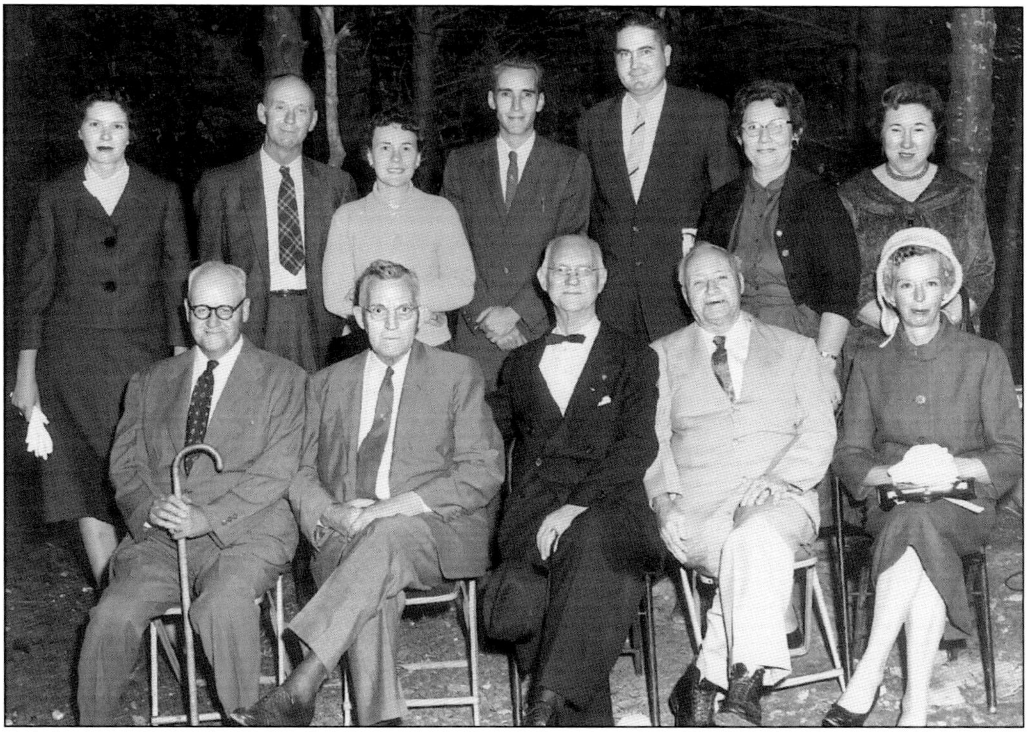

Byron Herbert Reece Memorial Society members included, from left to right, (front row) Wade Murrah, Judge T.S. Candler, M.D. Collins, Dr. J.M. Nicholson, and Eva Mae Reece; (standing) Jean Reece Rispoli, T.J. Reece, Lorena Turner, Preston Turner, Harold West, Louise Butt, and Austine Carr. (Courtesy of Union County Historical Society.)

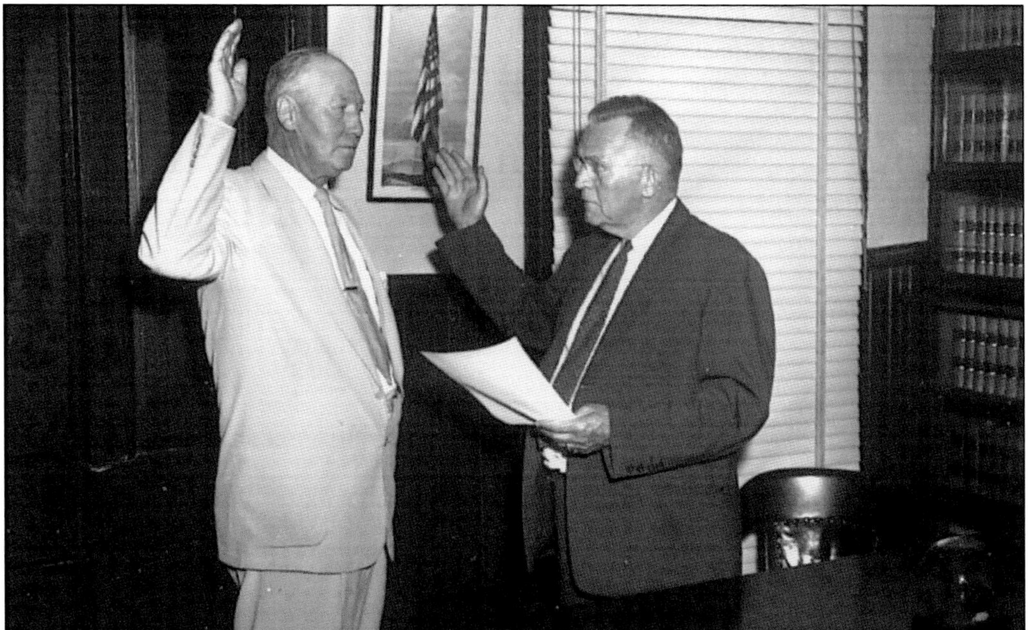

Obediah Pruitt, Mayor of Blairsville and Federal Marshall, is sworn in by Judge T.S. Candler c. 1950. (Courtesy of Union County Historical Society.)

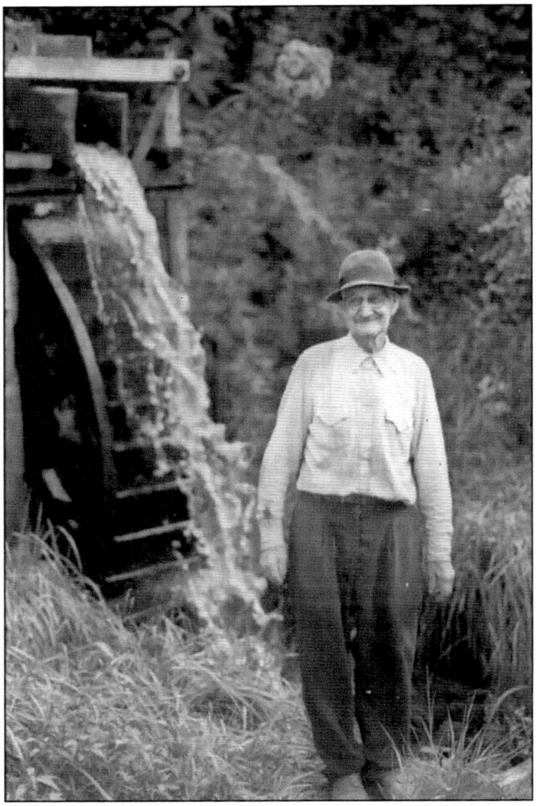

Elisha Payne, born 1899, was noted as one of the last "True Mountain Men." He was born in a log cabin not far from where he lived all his life. He was an inventor, carpenter, blacksmith, farmer, father of six, and husband, to wife Doll, for over 70 years. (Photograph by Ted Oliver.)

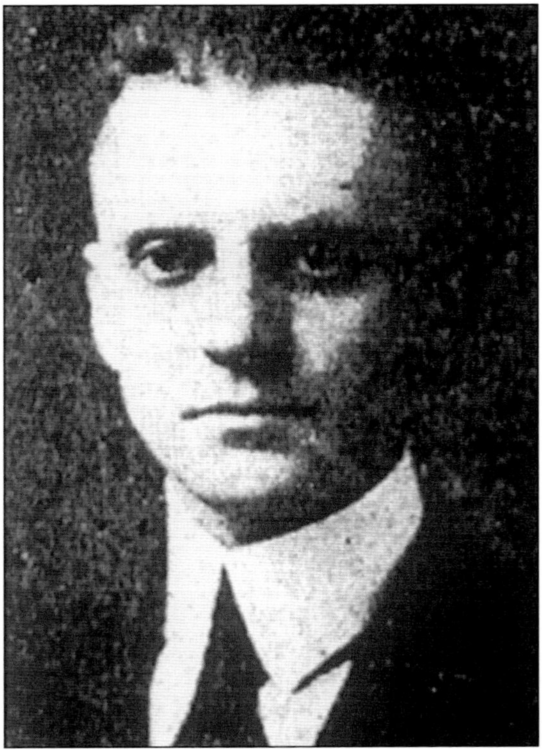

Grady Miller was born in Union County. He was a professor of history from 1922–1925 and dean of Young Harris College from 1925 to 1932. He served as a state senator in the late 1920s. Grady lived in Choestoe and walked through Trackrock to Young Harris to attend school. Grady was father to Zell Miller, who became governor of Georgia and a United States Senator.

Byron Herbert Reece is shown with his father and mother in front of fireplace at old homestead on route 129 south of Blairsville. Byron Herbert Reece produced an enduring body of poetry and fiction from the sounds and spirits of his North Georgia homeland. His five volumes of verse draw deeply from the lyrical wellsprings of nature and the Bible. Reece was a bright and solitary schoolboy, a graduate of Blairsville High School who grew up in such rural isolation. He won *American Poet Magazine*'s annual poetry award in 1943. Reece's first volume of poetry, *Ballad of the Bones*, was published in 1945. By 1952, Reece had been nominated for a Pulitzer Prize in poetry (for *Bow Down in Jericho*, 1950). He received the Georgia Writers Association's literary achievement award five times.

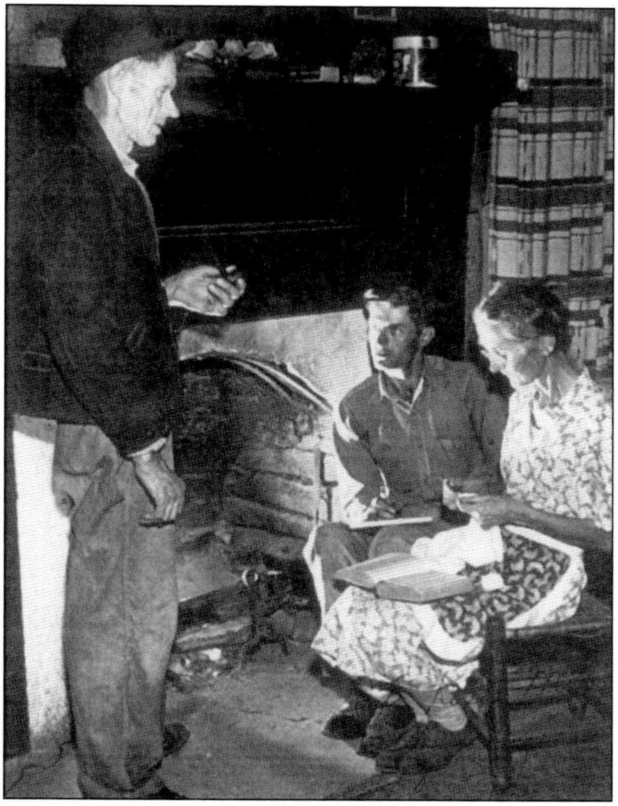

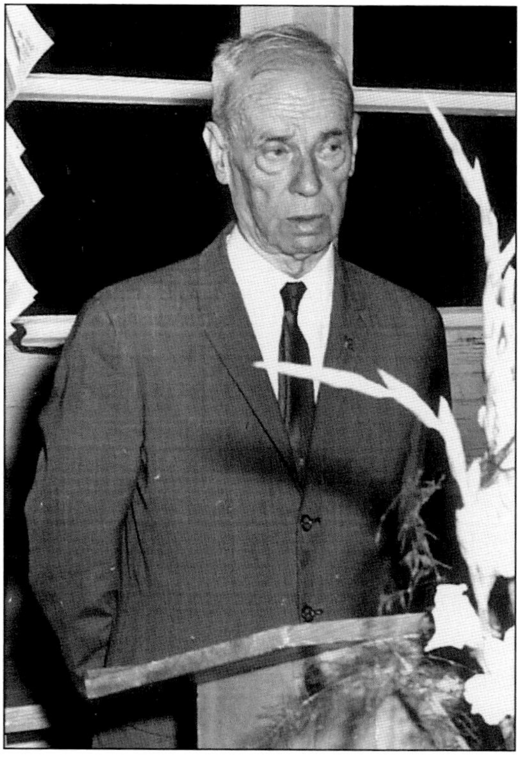

Dr. Jack Lance, born in Union County, was President of Young Harris College (1930–1942) and later worked for the State Board of Education.

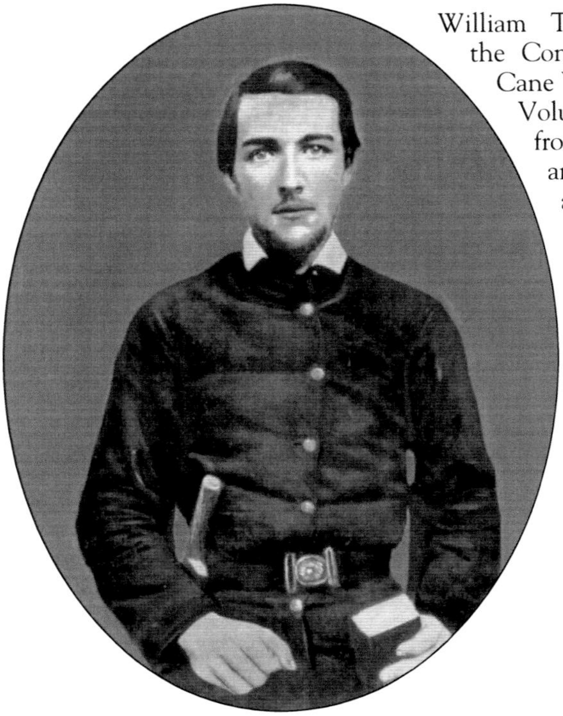

William T. Addington (1840–1862) served in the Confederate Army in Company K "Young Cane Volunteers" of the 23rd Regiment Georgia Volunteer Infantry. The 23rd Regiment served from Virginia, to South Carolina, to Florida, and back to Virginia. He took ill with fever and died in Virginia shortly after this photo was taken in 1862. (Courtesy of Union County Historical Society.)

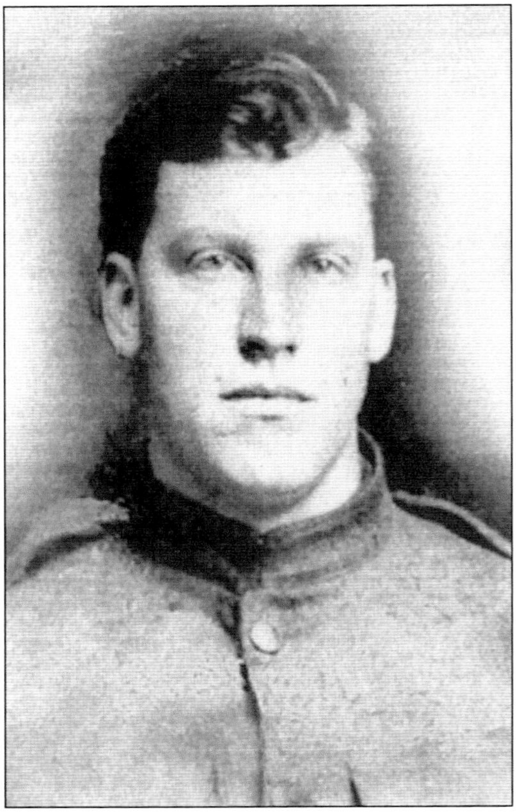

Private Ira Cornelius Spiva, U.S. Army Company "A" 9th Infantry, was killed in action in World War I. He died on September 12, 1918 and was the first Union County soldier killed in the war.

Leon Davenport (c. 1952) had an impressive military career in the Army. Davenport retired as a major after serving 23 years in infantry and armor. He served during a portion of WORLD WAR II, the Korean War, and the Vietnam War. He was cited for heroism on five occasions. Davenport was decorated with three awards of the Silver Star, Purple Heart, and many others—including a Bronze Star with "V" for Valor. It is believed that Davenport is the most decorated military man ever to have lived in Union County.

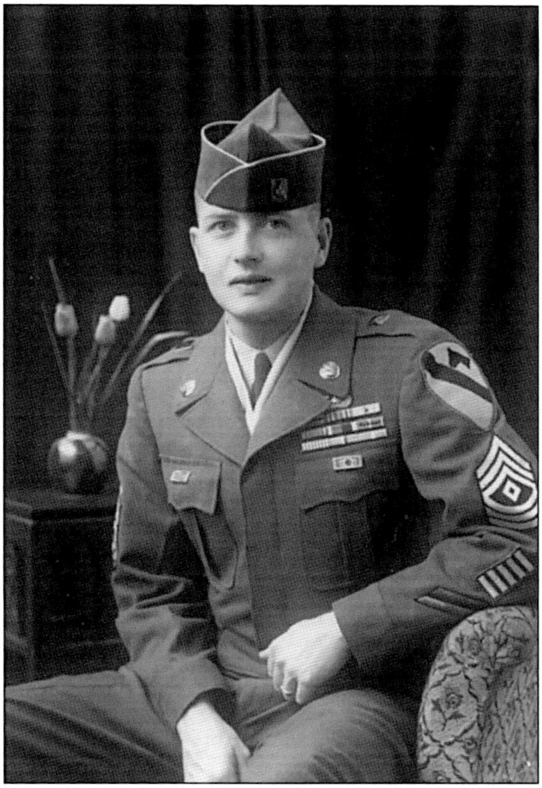

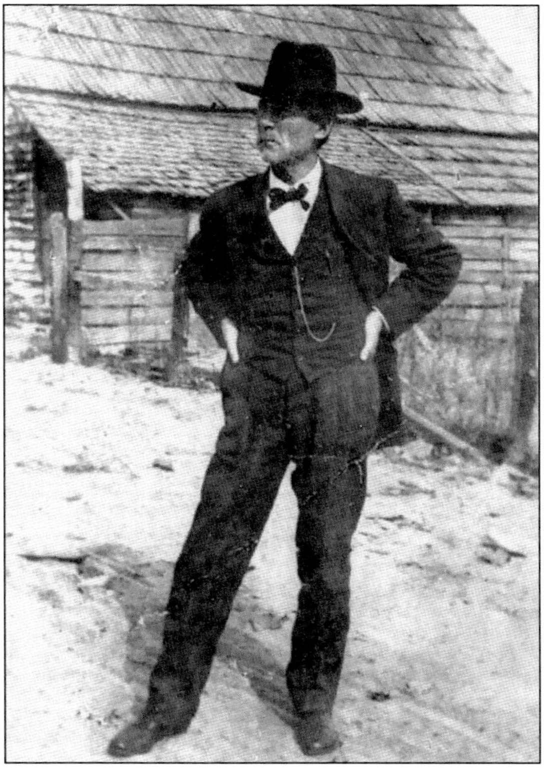

Early pioneer Buck Candler was the father of T. S. Candler and Zeke Candler.

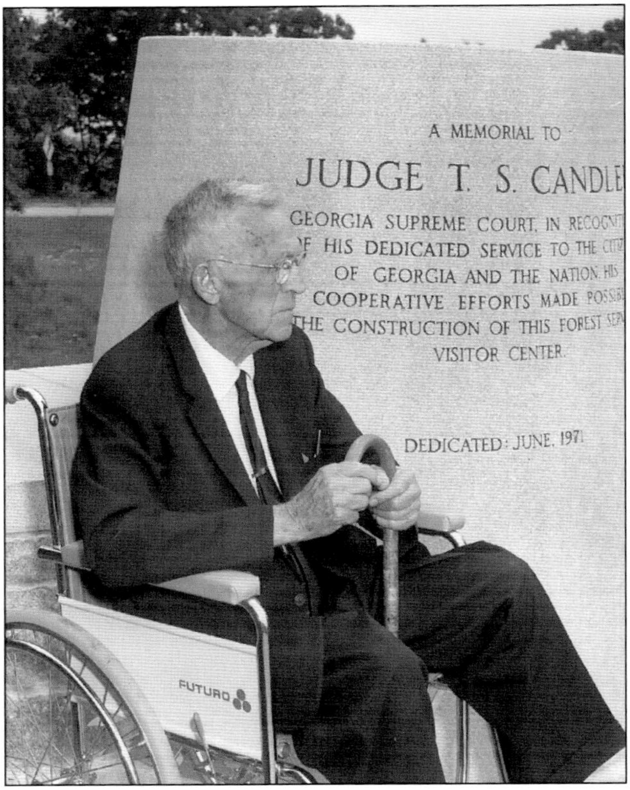

Judge T.S. Candler was a justice of the Georgia State Supreme Court. He began education with blue back speller in a one-room schoolhouse in Blairsville. From 1915 to 1939, Tom served as mayor of Blairsville and as Union County attorney. He served on the school board and was United States Commissioner in the Northern District of Georgia for 12 years. In 1939, Candler was appointed trial judge. In 1943, he served on the commission, which drafted the 1945 Georgia Constitution. As a result of that Constitution, an additional judge was added to the Supreme Court. Governor Arnall appointed Judge Candler to that position. In his 22 years on the Georgia Supreme Court, 8,527 cases were docketed. Judge Candler received many awards and recognitions in his distinguished career.

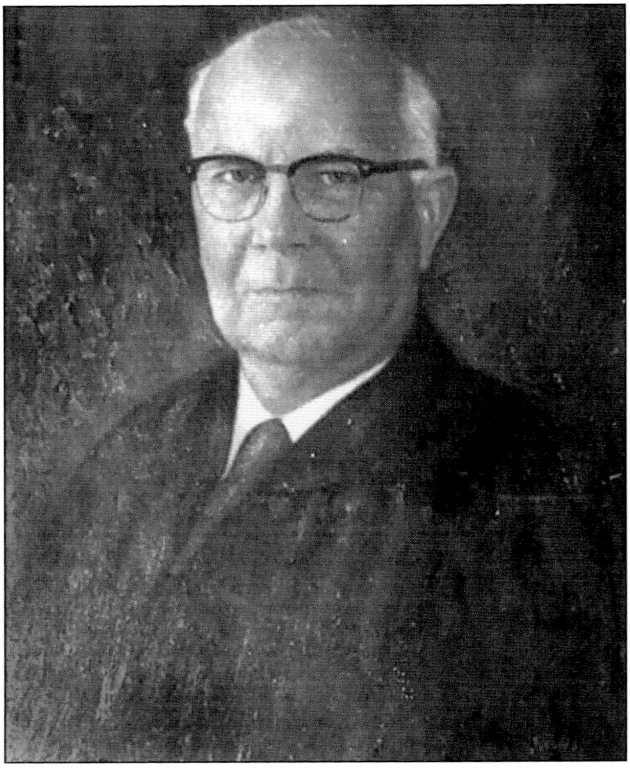

Chief Justice W.H. Duckworth, born in 1894 in Choestoe, served on the Georgia Supreme Court for 32 years, the last 20 as Chief Justice. He served as assistant attorney general for the state. After being told by the governor he was too young to be appointed to the Supreme Court, Duckworth ran for office in 1937. He was elected in a three-candidate race. Justice Duckworth wrote the decision in the famous three governors case. At age 74, after being elected since 1937 without opposition, he ran for office against two opponents—and won. Eight months following the overwhelming victory, he died.

Joseph E. Brown moved to Union County as a boy. The old Brown home was on the present site of the Woody Gap School. He left Union County for school in South Carolina driving a yoke of oxen to be sold for his board and tuition. In 1849, he became a state senator. He was elected governor 1857, reelected 1859, 1861, and 1863—the only man to have four times been elected governor of Georgia, including two terms while Georgia was in the Confederate States of America. During the Civil War, Brown's views on state's rights conflicted with President Davis' efforts to centralize the Confederate government. Brown was appointed to Chief Justice of the Georgia Supreme Court in 1868. Brown was appointed to the U. S. Senate in 1880 and served until 1891.

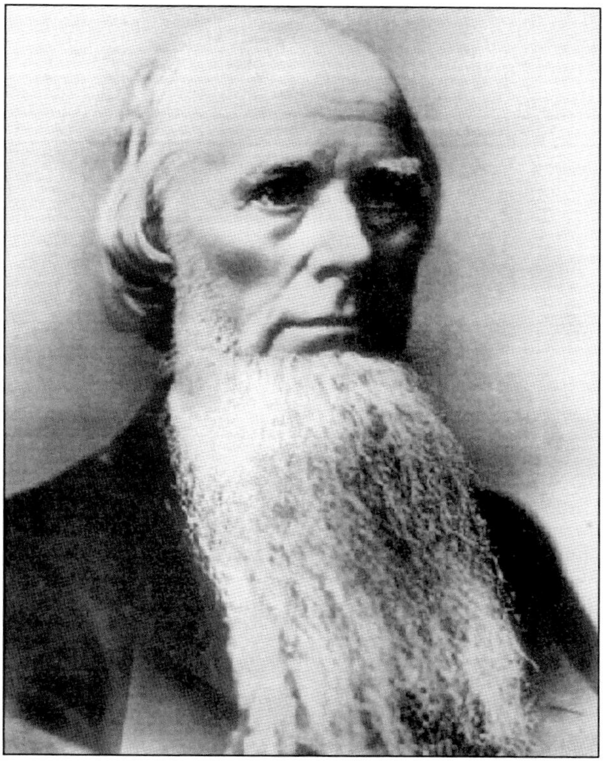

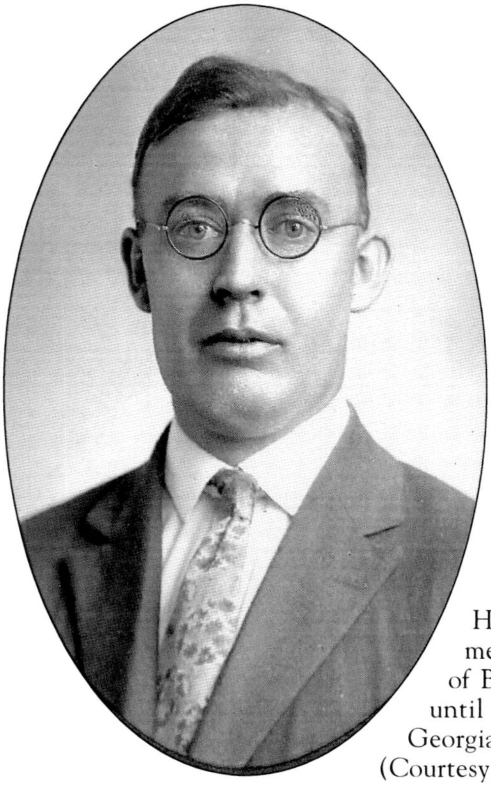

Herbert Monroe Edge, born in 1892, was a medical doctor serving the North Georgia town of Blairsville and the surrounding area from 1936 until his death in 1974. He also served in the Georgia State Senate, representing the Ninth District. (Courtesy of Dale Elliott.)

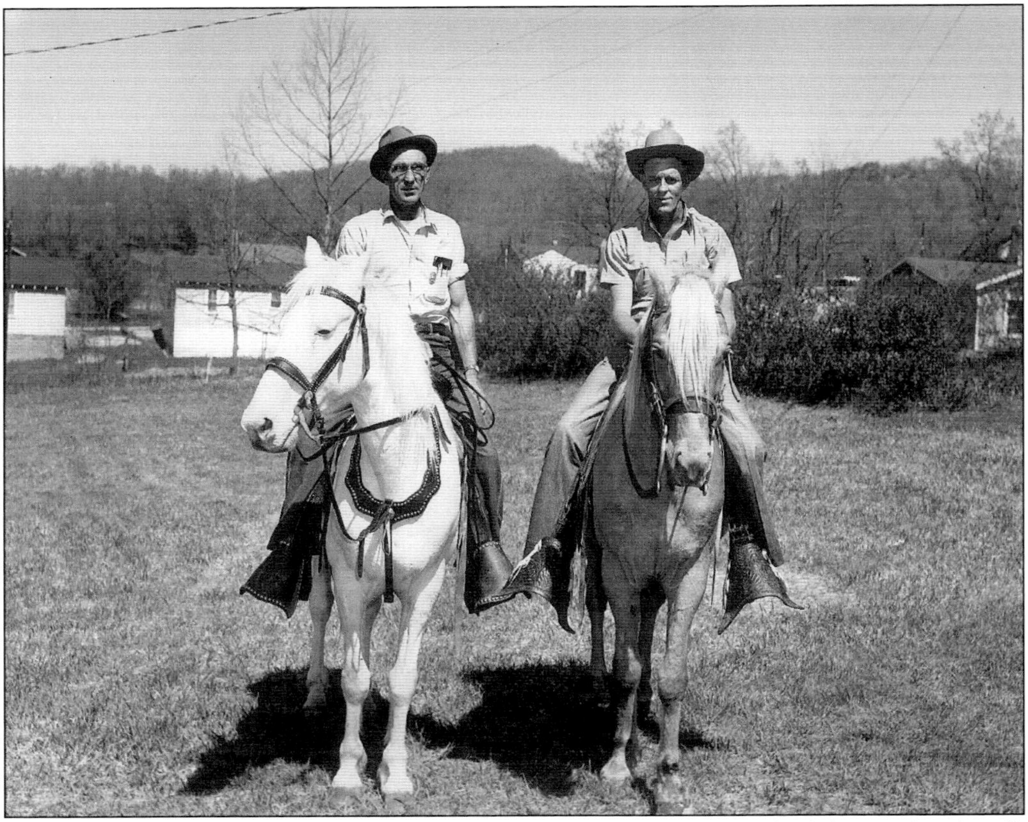

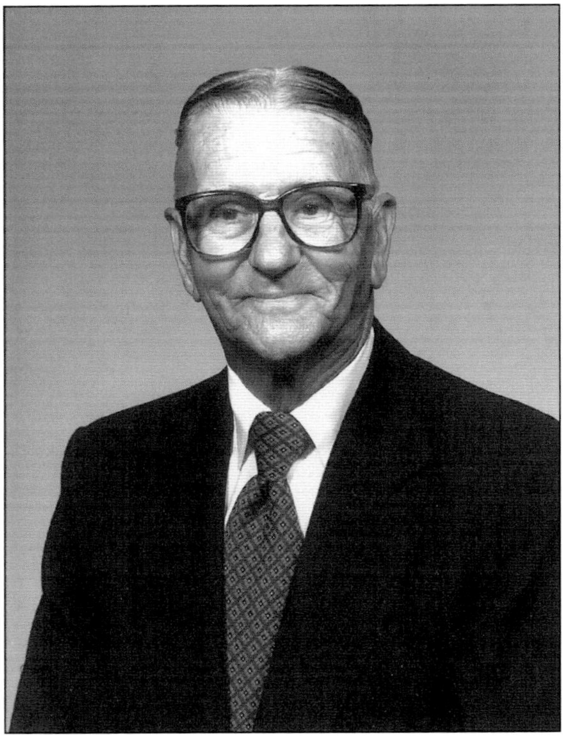

Harlan Duncan (right) served as sheriff of Union County for 21 years and as a Georgia state patrol officer for 18 years. His law career lasted more than 40 years. Duncan began law enforcement with the police department of Blairsville then as a deputy of Union County. He once chased bank robbers and confiscated a drug airplane. He served in the U.S. Army during WORLD WAR II. Seen with Harlan is Wayne Collins (left), who served as sheriff of Union County from 1957 to 1964. (Courtesy of Tommy Duncan.)

Virge Kelley, lifelong resident, served as sheriff of Union County from 1953 to 1956. Kelley served during a time of moonshine runners, catching his share of bootleggers. (Courtesy of Betty Williams.)

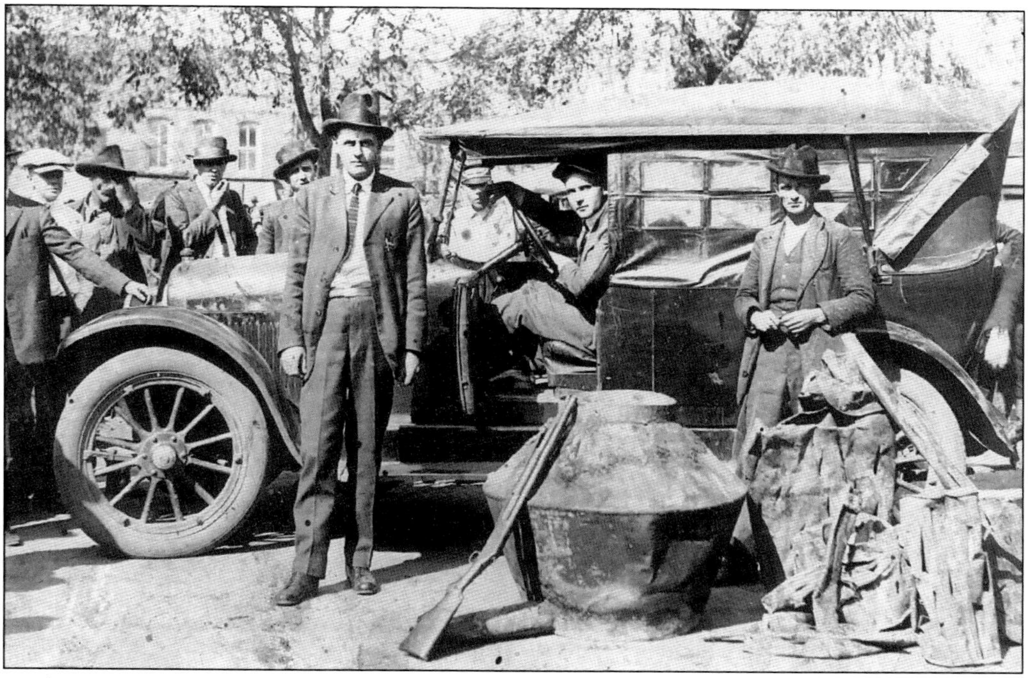

With "still" evidence for a court case are Frank Laransey Souther, standing with top hat; Grayson Souther, in car; and Jake Burton Kelly, standing right. (Courtesy of David Friedly.)

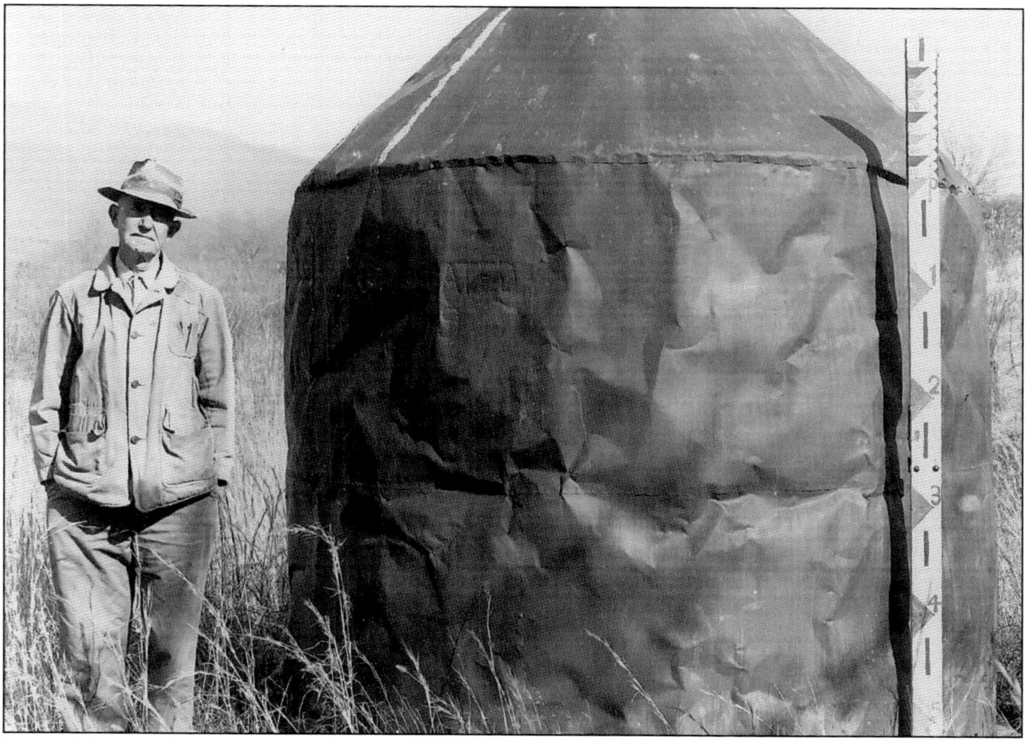

James Monroe Gray was sheriff when this very large still was captured. He served as sheriff from 1949 to 1952. (Courtesy of W. Lake Stroud.)

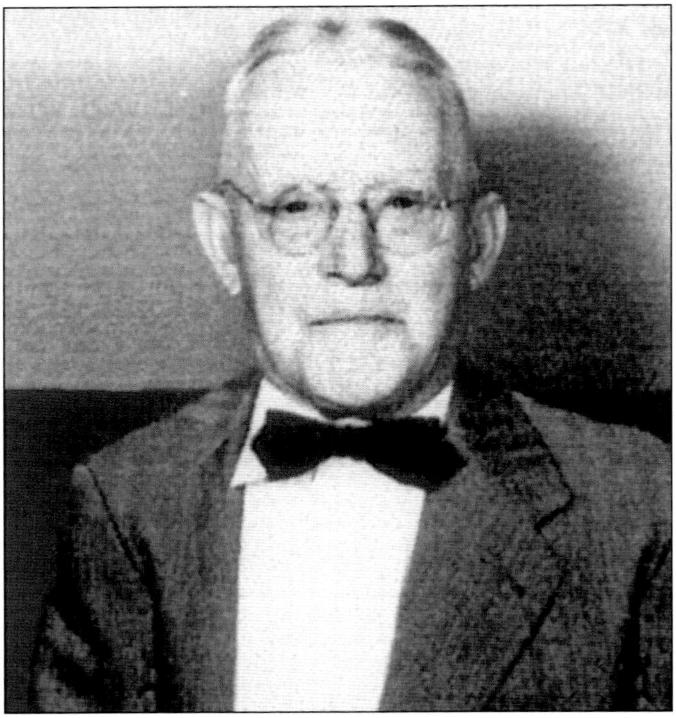

Following in his father's footsteps, Ed Jones became a U.S. Marshall prior to returning to Union County to serve as sheriff. He served as sheriff of Union County for 28 years. Several of Ed's deputies, including Virge Kelley and Harlon Duncan, later became sheriff in Union County. (Courtesy of Union County Historical Society.)

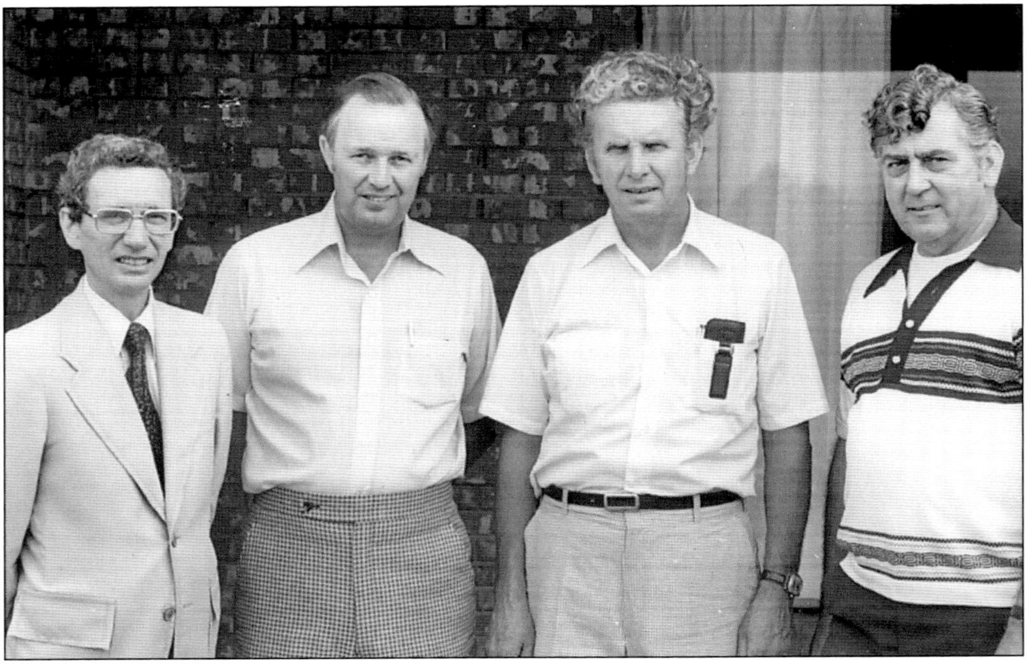

Union Countian Carlton H.Colwell, third from left, was born 1926. He enlisted in the United States Army in 1944, and was elected to the Georgia House of Representatives in 1964. He served for 30 years in this position. Carlton's contributions to the community have been numerous. He is seen here with Congressman Ed Jenkins, State Senator John Foster, and State Representative Ralph Twiggs. Both Foster and Jenkins were born in Union County and Twiggs grew up in the area. (Courtesy of Union County Historical Society.)

Six

Around the County

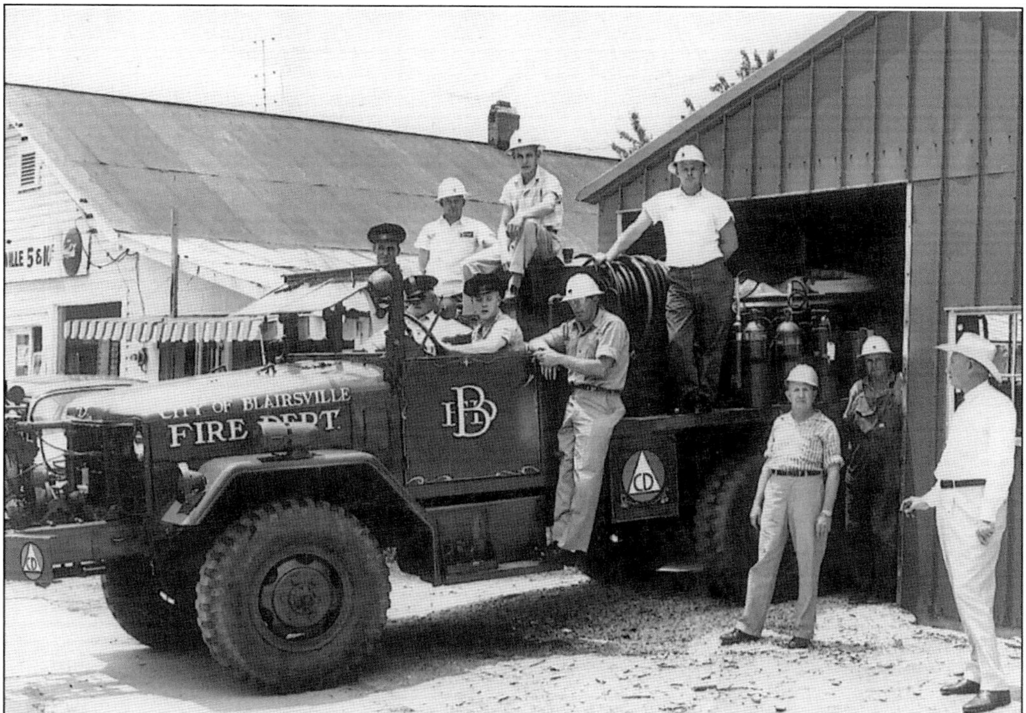

Union County Volunteer Fire Department is pictured in May 1960. In the photo, left to right, are Paul Kelly, J.B. Barfield, Sam King, Charles Rogers, Bobby Jackson, Neal Collins, Ron Davenport, Terrell Jones, Truman Jarrett, and Obe Pruitt. Notice the building beside the fire department is the original 5 & 10 store. (Courtesy of James Jones.)

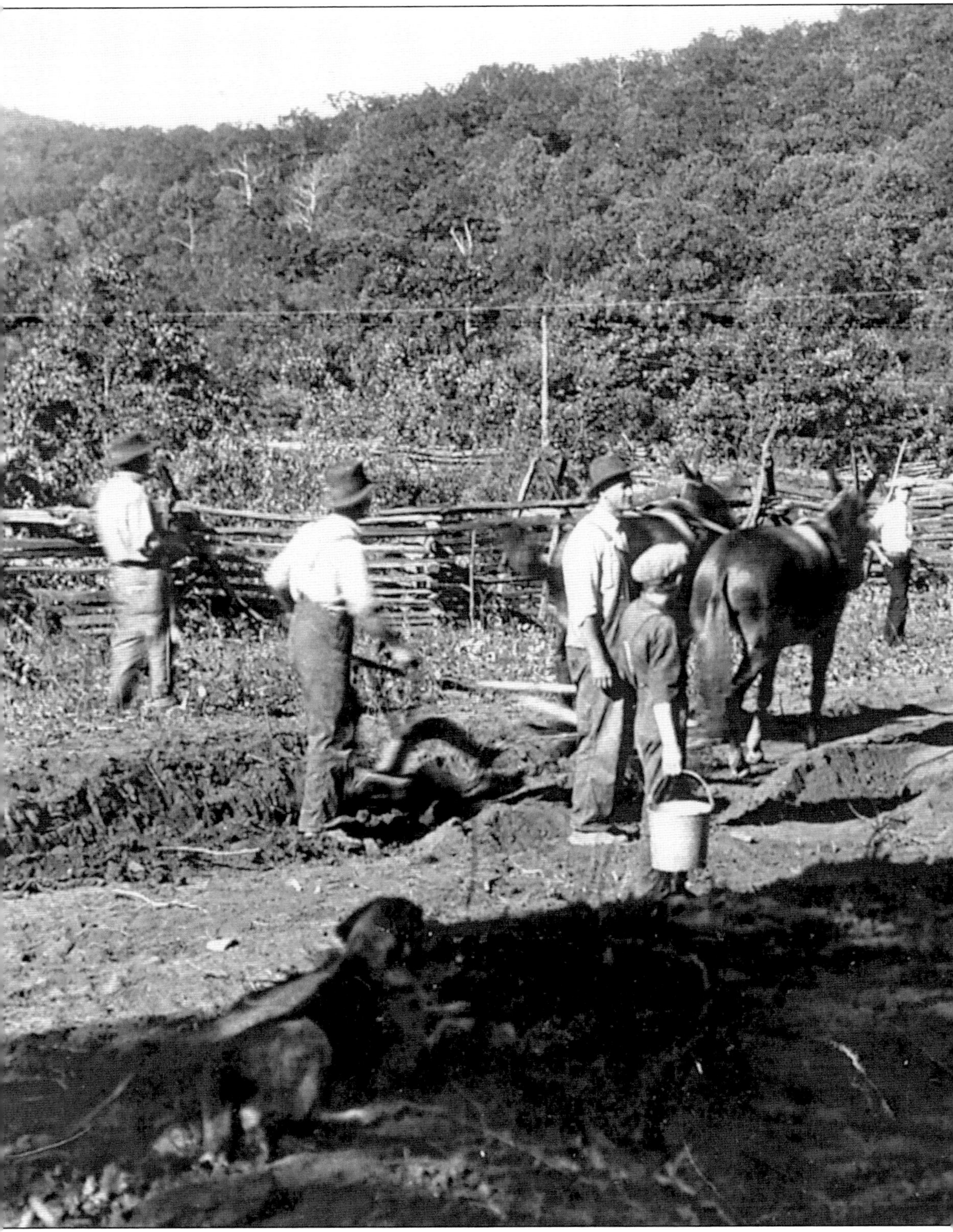

Building a road in Union County required a lot of hard work by many people and many animals.

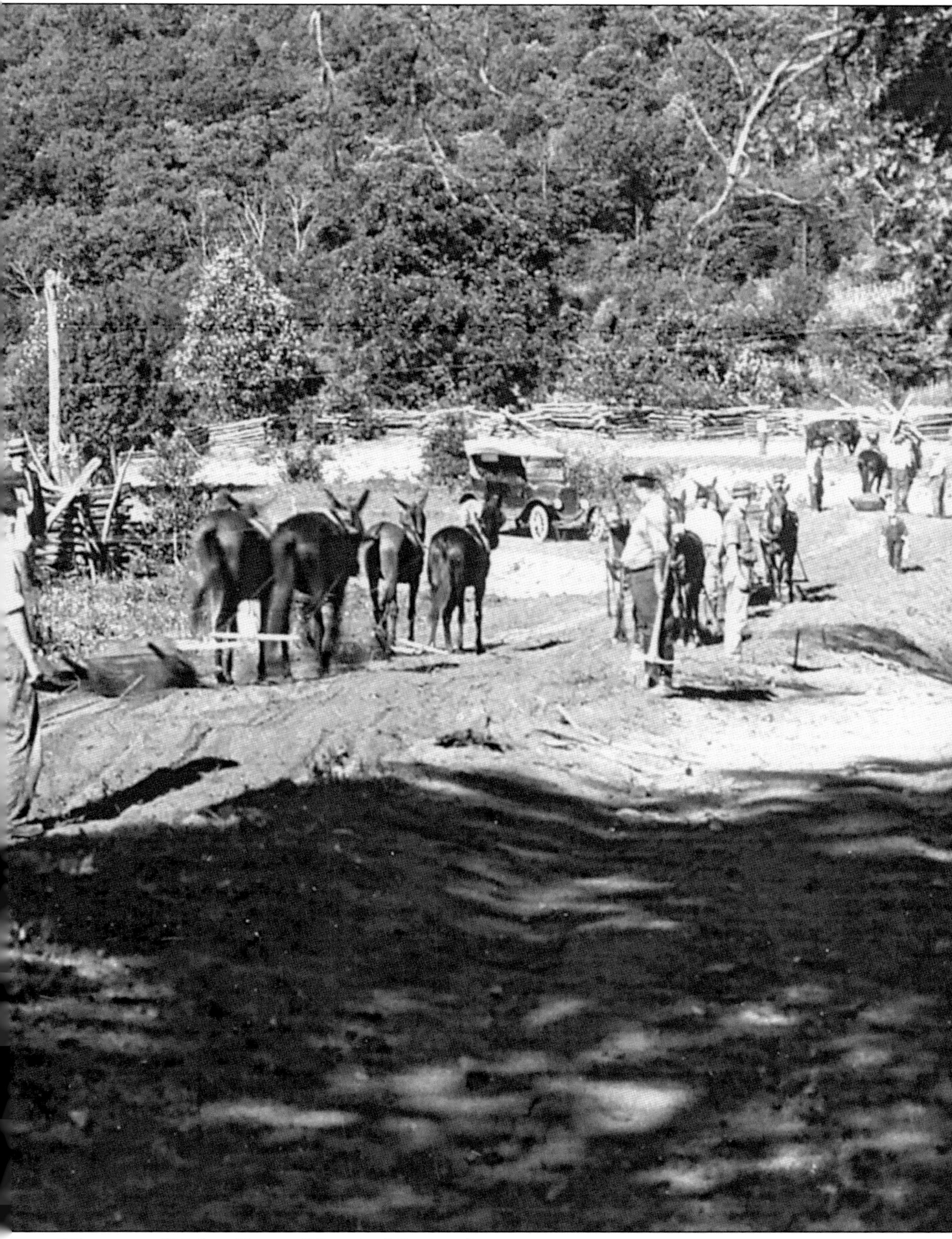

(Courtesy of Union County Historical Society.)

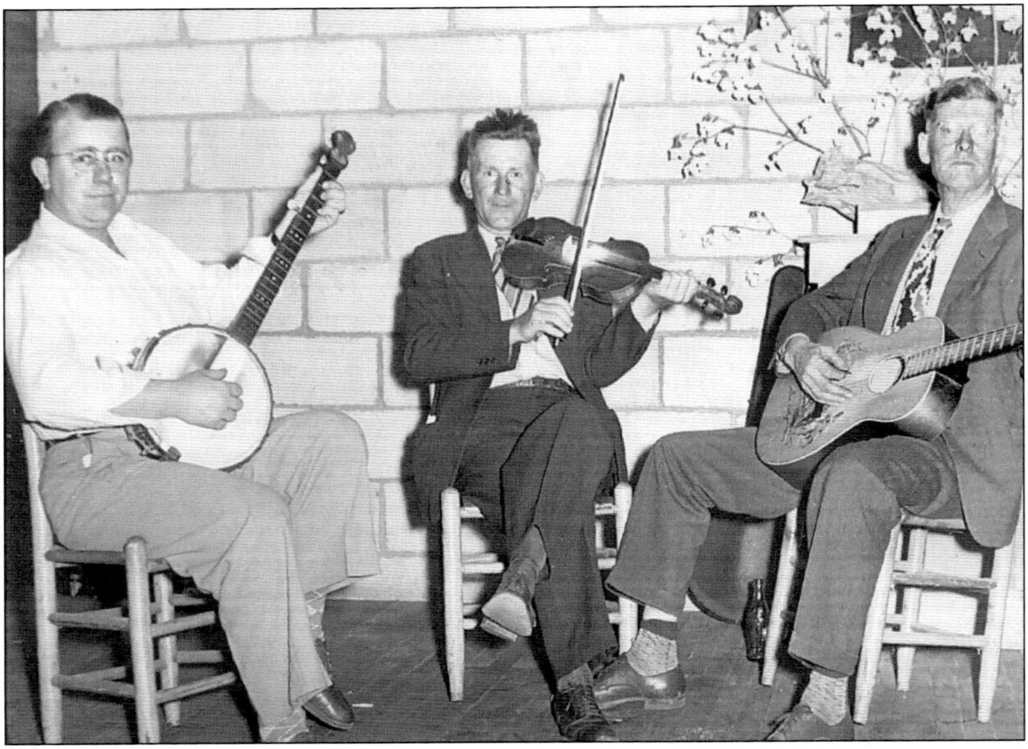

Musicians in the 1940s and 1950s played for most any occasion. Local musicians included Claude Partin, Walter Rogers, and Red Henderson. (Courtesy of Frances Fair Partin.)

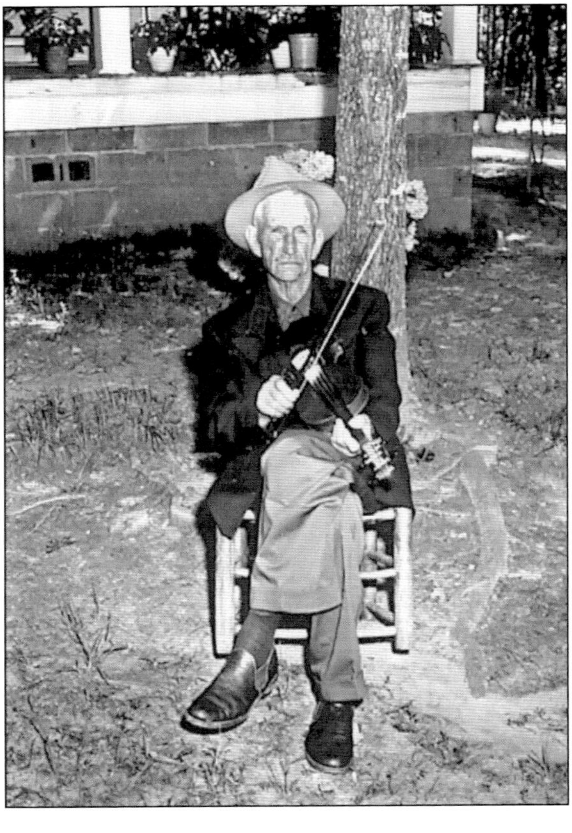

William Bracket (1872–1965) ran a corn mill, kept bees, raised boxwoods, and loved to play the fiddle. (Courtesy of Union County Historical Society.)

Mary Jo Miller was born October 6, 1896 in Union County, Georgia. She died September 16, 1966. She is buried in Arlington National Cemetery in Arlington, Virginia. She served in the United States Army from 1927 until 1956 retiring as a lieutenant colonel. Her occupation was a nurse. She returned to Blairsville after retiring from the Army. She built a home on the Young Harris Highway where her father and mother had a home and a farm. Her father was Isaac Newton Miller (1854–1933) and her mother was Josephine Butt Miller (1857–1948). Her home was moved to Weaver Road after her death. (Courtesy of Union County Historical Society.)

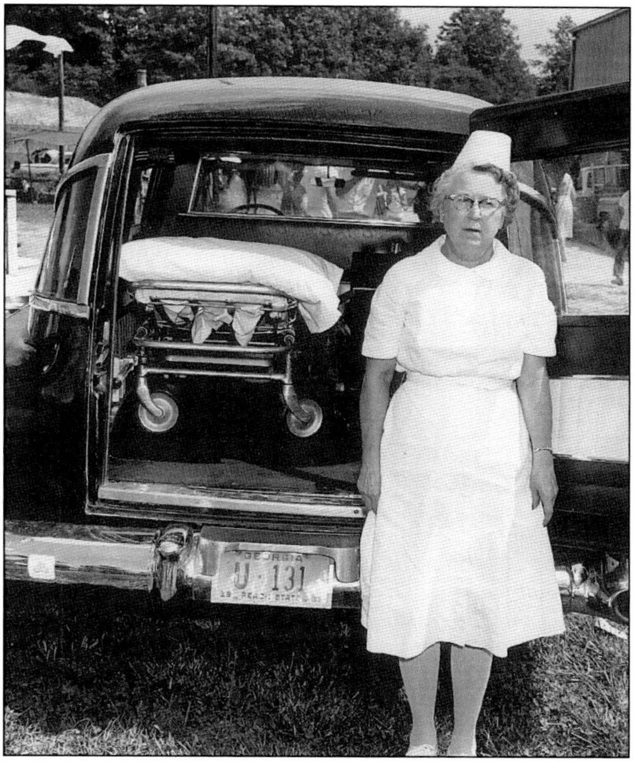

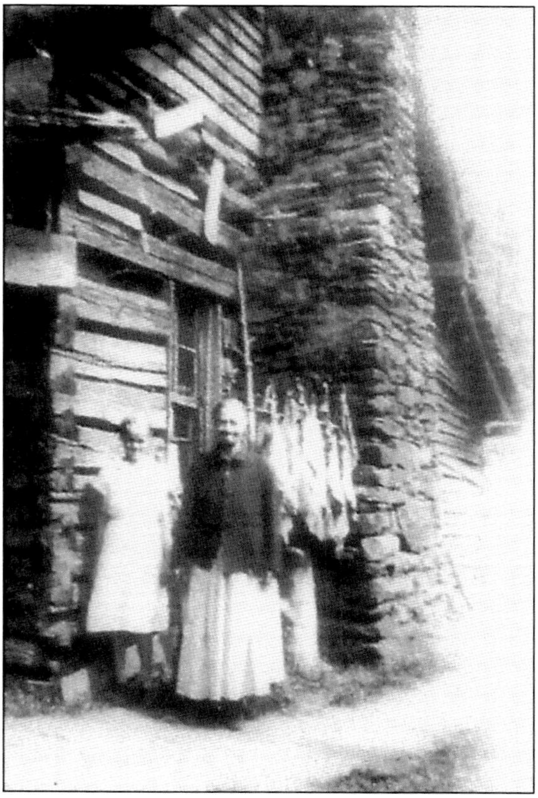

Aunt Mary Wheeler, also known as Granny Wheeler, was one of the midwives for the Suches area. She had a saying about natural child birth. "Of course it's natural, just a natural thing God made and put on women. When apples are ripe they will fall, and when it's time for a baby to be born, it's a coming." Granny Wheeler delivered hundreds of babies within the Suches area and many outside the area. Most times there was no reward. Sometimes she was paid 50 cents and later on as much a dollar. Fathers and mothers often had no cash, so they paid with fruits or vegetables. This photo was taken at Granny Wheeler's cabin in the early 1950s when she was approximately 92 years old, and still "catchin' babies. Tobacco hangs behind Granny Wheeler in the photograph.

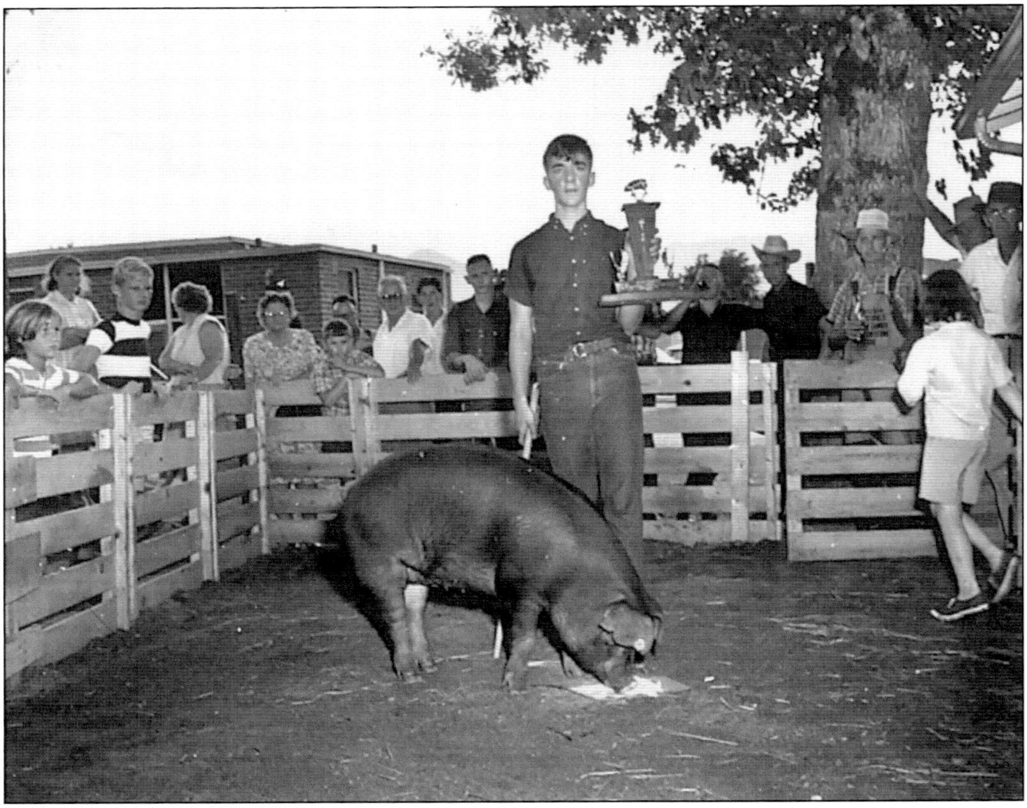

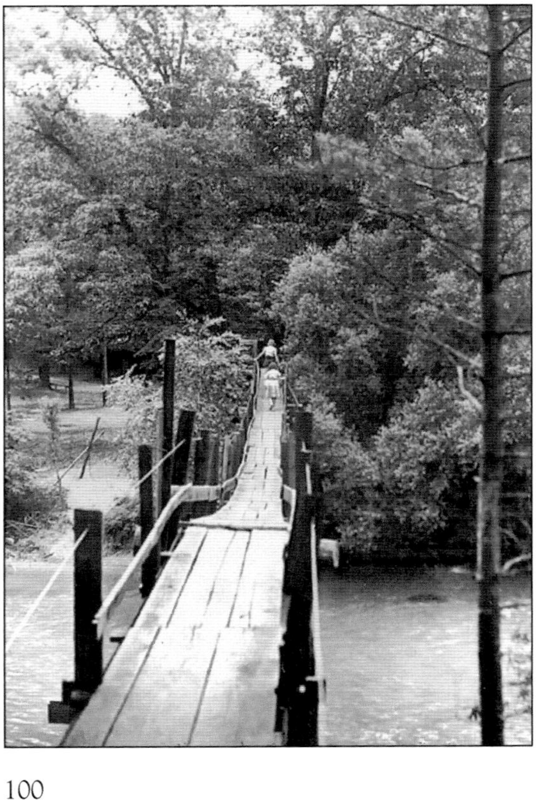

This picture was taken in 1966 at the University of Georgia Experiment Station with either 4H or FFA judging. (Courtesy of Union County Historical Society.)

Shown here is a foot bridge over water at Canal Lake, c. 1940. (Courtesy of Melva Lynn Drake.)

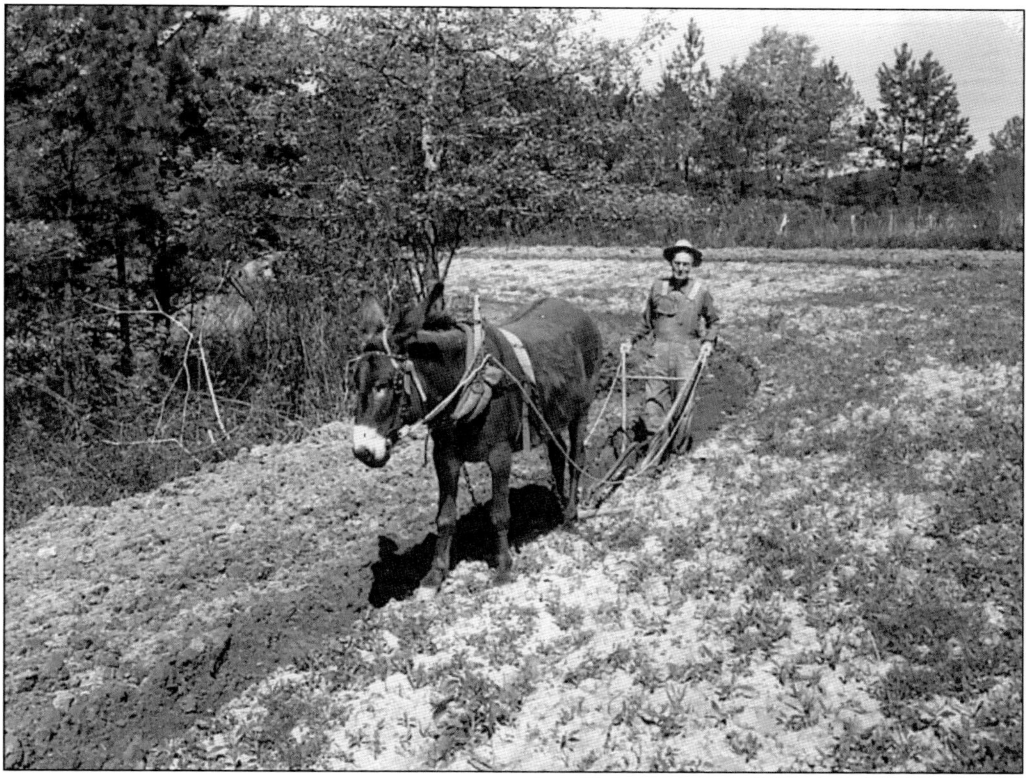

Ned Chastain is planting his garden in 1965 with mule Jennie. This was a typical spring chore around the county for decades. (Courtesy of Union County Historical Society.)

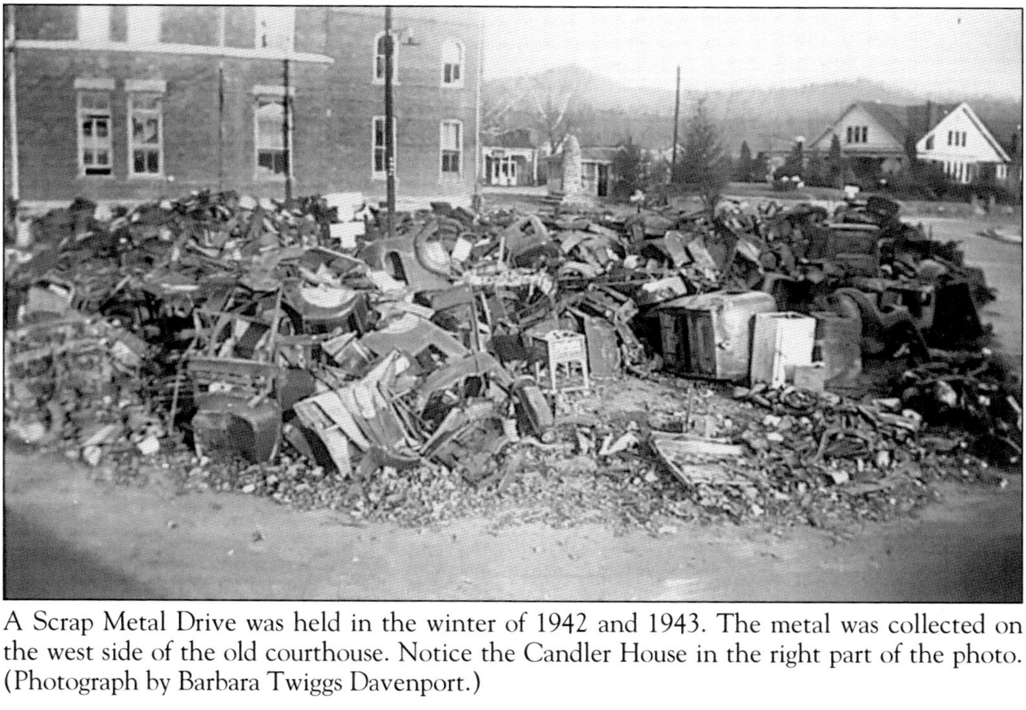

A Scrap Metal Drive was held in the winter of 1942 and 1943. The metal was collected on the west side of the old courthouse. Notice the Candler House in the right part of the photo. (Photograph by Barbara Twiggs Davenport.)

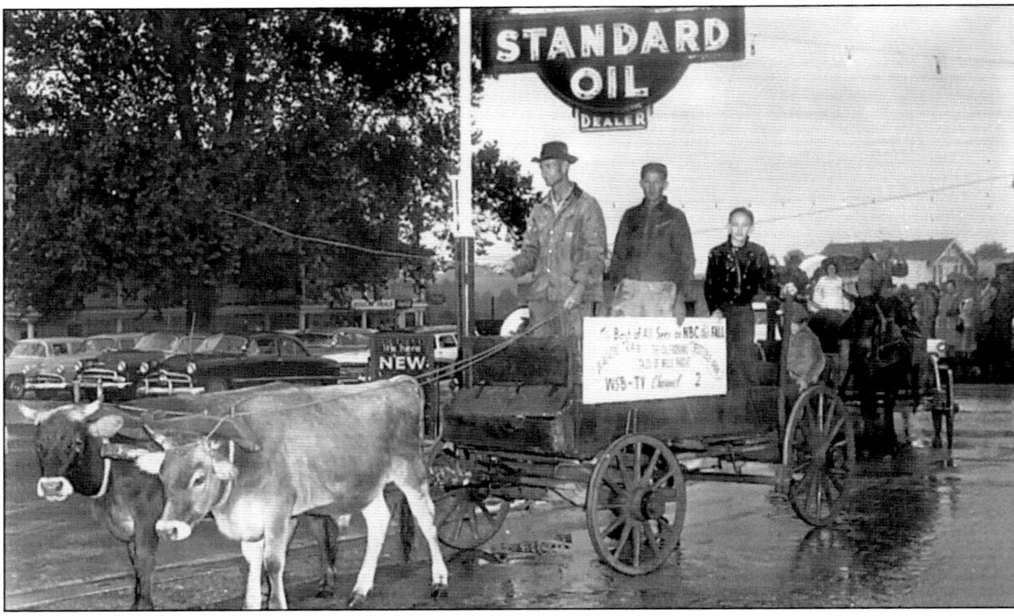

A parade in 1957 features oxen pulling a wagon. The sign on the wagon advertises "The Best of All Seen on NBC this Fall." WSB TV Channel 2 advertised *Wagon Train*, *Restless Gun*, *The Californians*, and *Tales of Wells Fargo*.

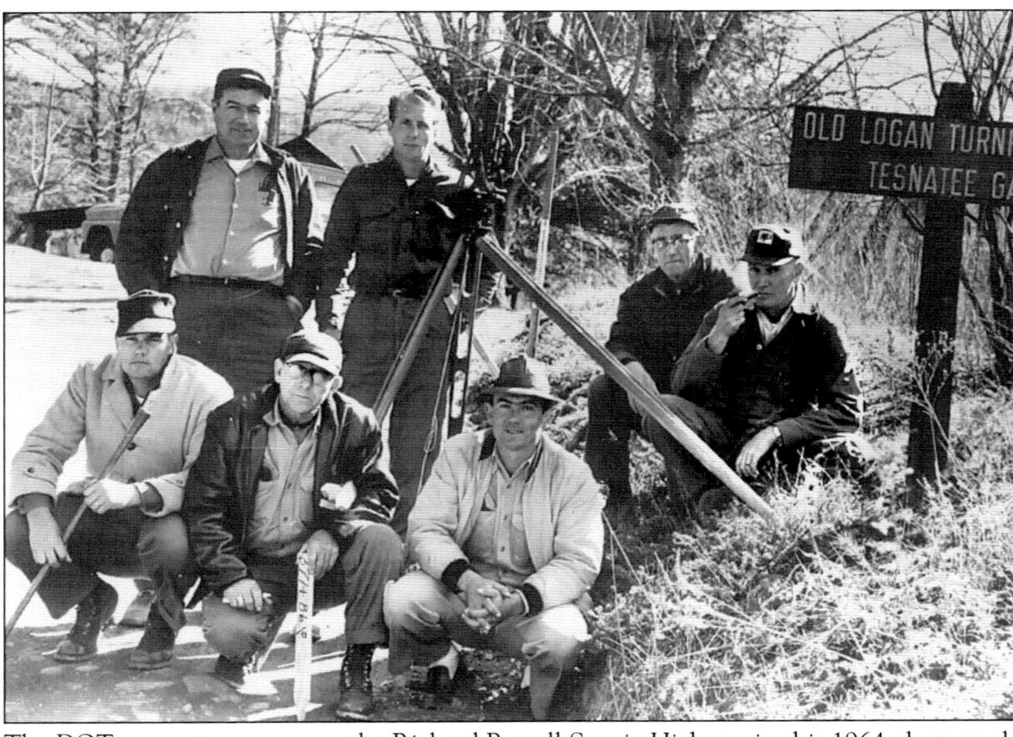

The DOT survey team pose on the Richard Russell Scenic Highway in this 1964 photograph. The sign shows they are on the Old Logan Turnpike near Tesnatee Gap. From left to right are (front row) Max Hawsley, Charlie Hicks, Bud Akins; (back row) Glenn Roberts, Glenn Hamby, Winferd Berrong, and Robert Rogers. (Courtesy of Union County Historical Society.)

George Lanning holds his muzzleloader rifle in this 1953 picture. (Courtesy of W. Lake Stroud.)

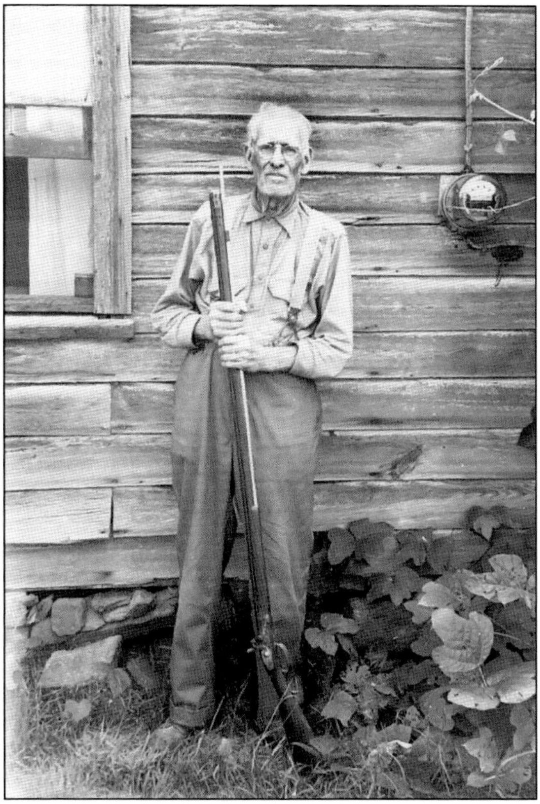

Hoyt Hamby cooks sorghum syrup at the Sorghum Festival in Union County. (Courtesy of Union County Historical Society.)

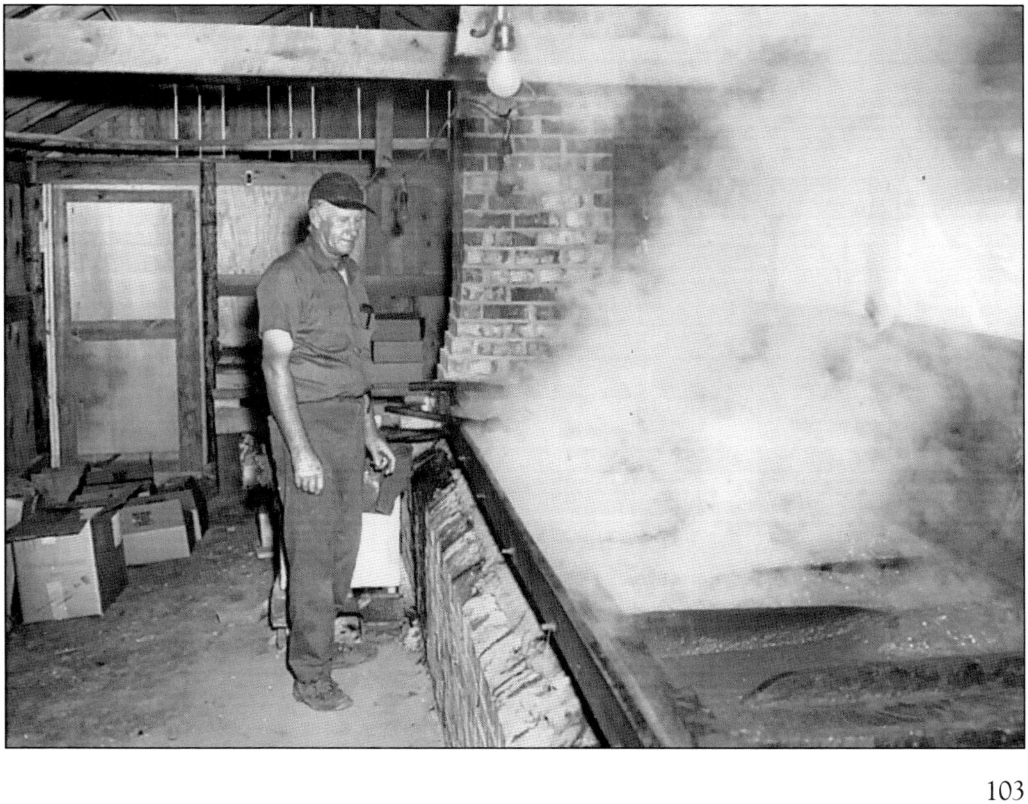

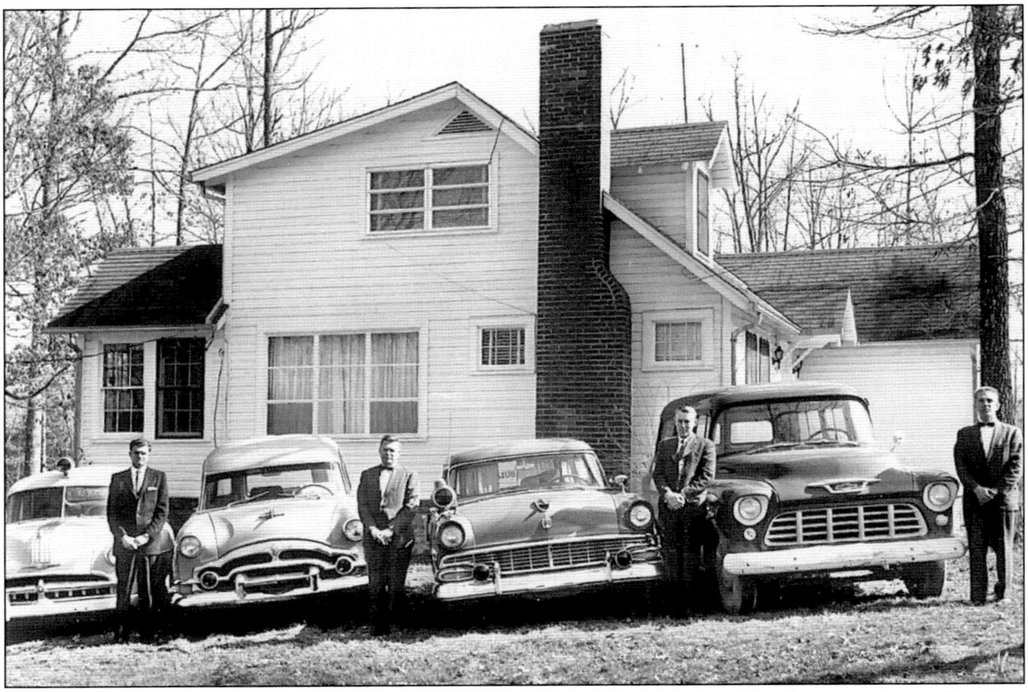

Akins Funeral Home, *c.* 1950s, provided ambulance service. Seen in this photograph are Hughes Colwell, Pat Akins, C.A. Rogers, and Raymond Akins.

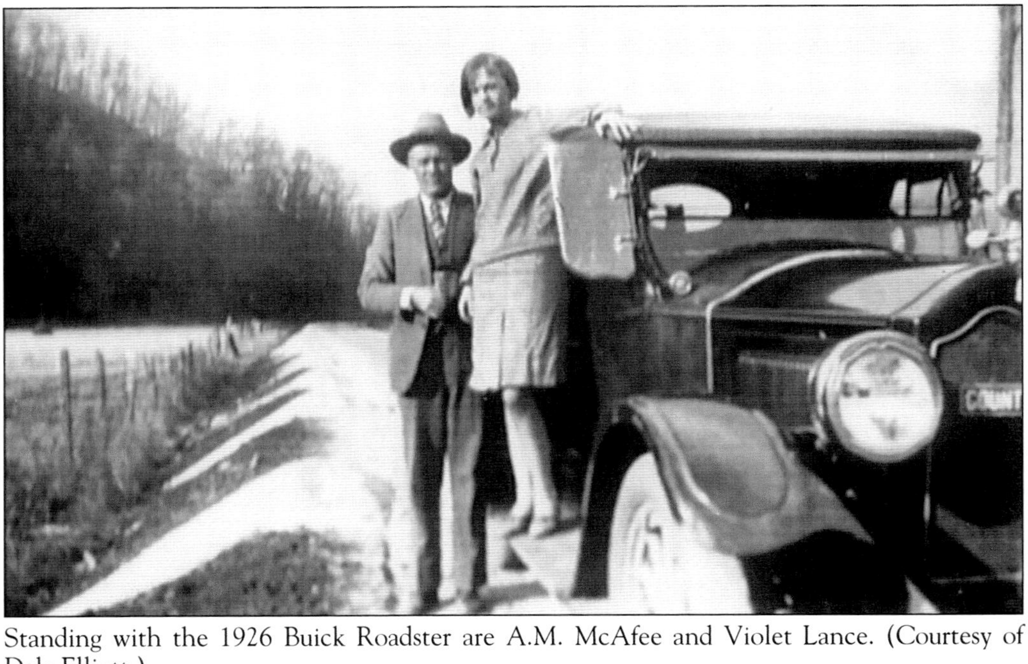

Standing with the 1926 Buick Roadster are A.M. McAfee and Violet Lance. (Courtesy of Dale Elliott.)

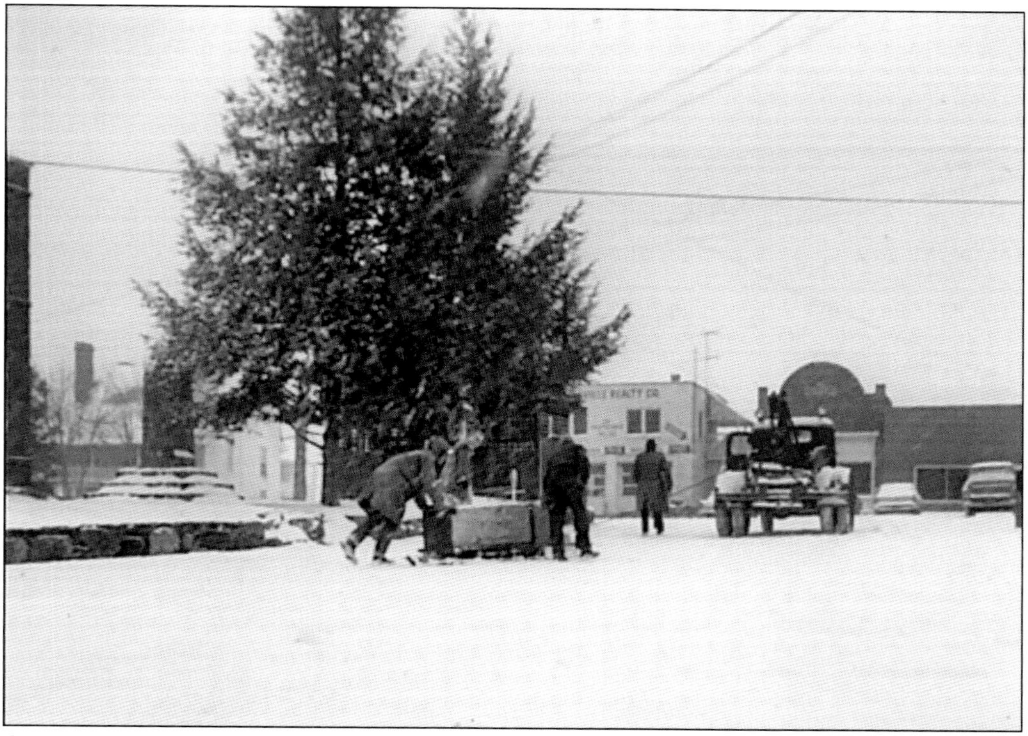

On a snowy day in Union County, relocating the bank from one place to another is underway for Union County Bank. In this 1960 scene, a wrecker is being used to pull a bank safe across the snow to the new location. (Courtesy of Charles Rogers.)

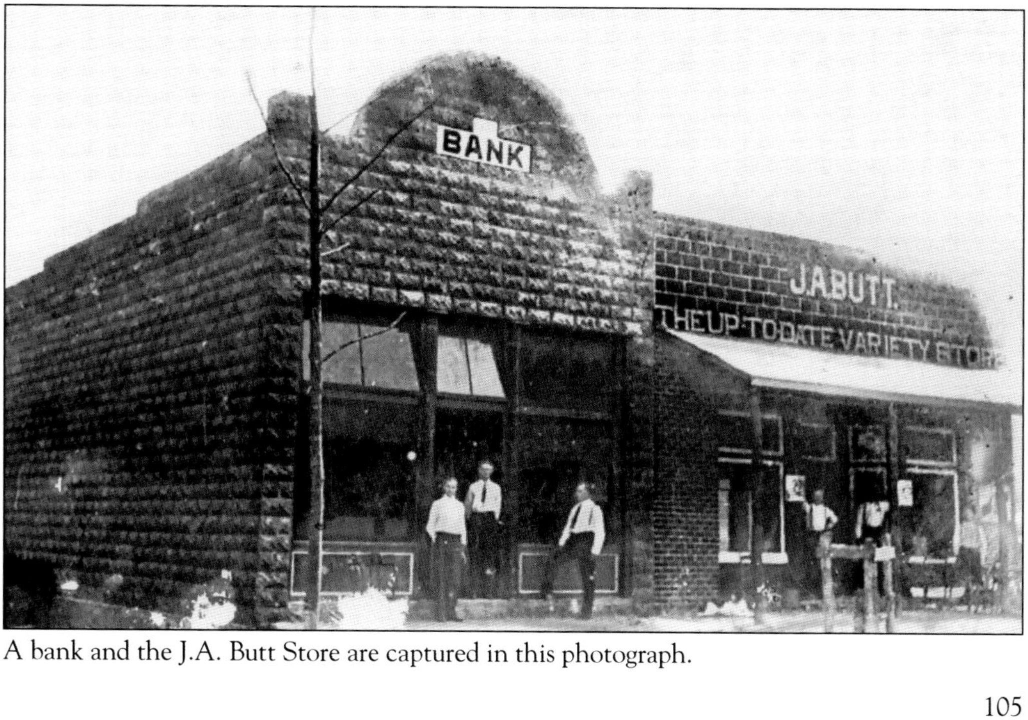

A bank and the J.A. Butt Store are captured in this photograph.

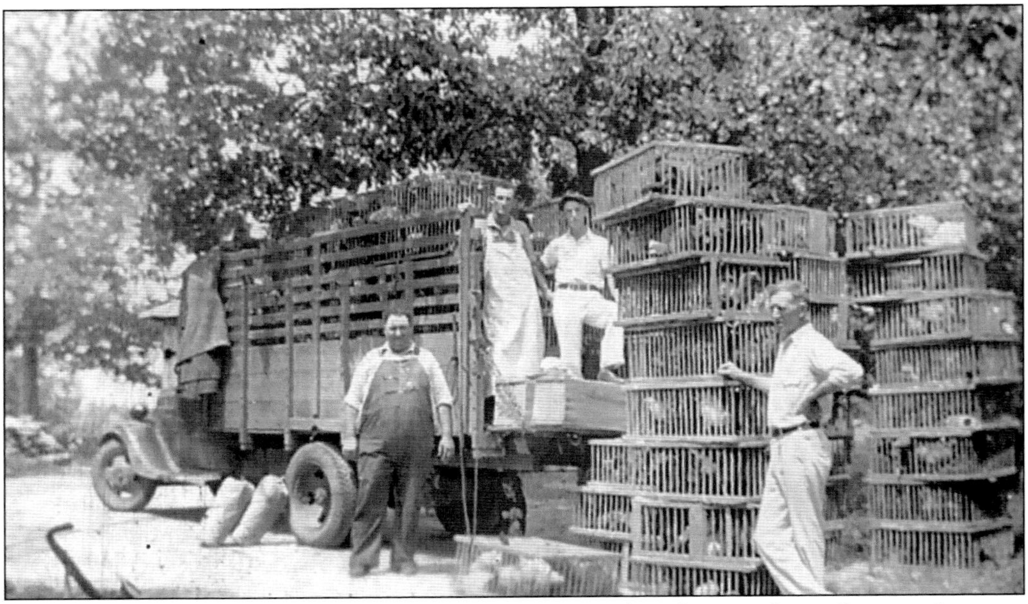

Here are the Chicken and Egg Men—also known as Traveling Grocery Store. Seen in photo are Henry Deaver, Jimmy Young, Virge Burnett, and Earnest Hill. (Courtesy of Jimmy Deaver.)

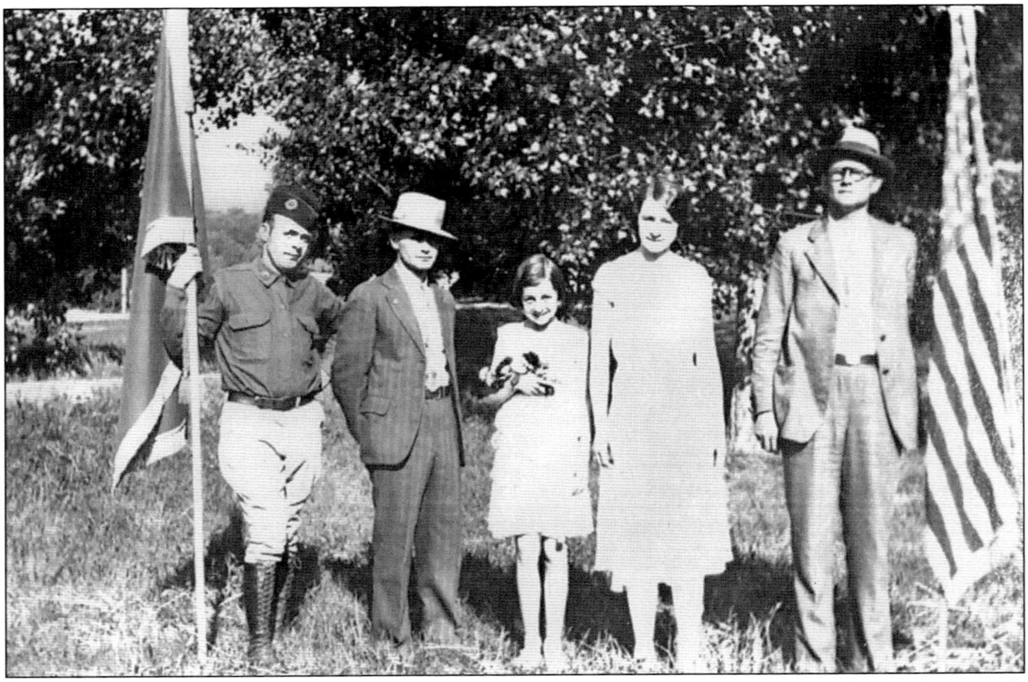

Ed Mauney, Press Davenport, Betty Laura Candler, Stella Hemphill, and Claude Hughes watch as the American Legion presented a medal to Betty in 1930s. (Courtesy of Dale Elliott.)

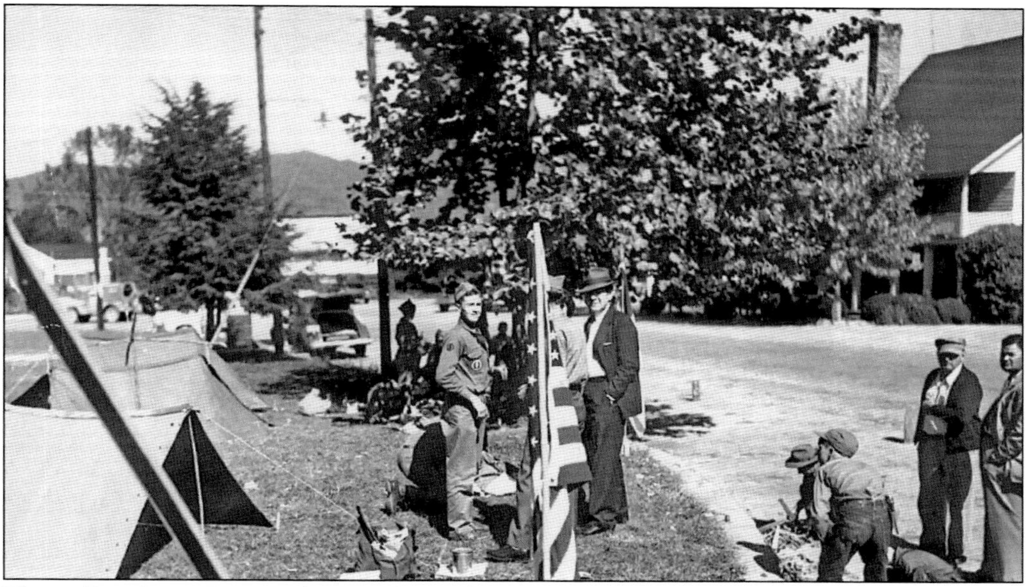

This is Boy Scout Day on the courthouse lawn c. 1950. Included in the photo are Scout Bob Hill, Scoutmaster Rev. Claud Boynton, and Superintendent of Schools Pat Helton. This is the view looking north toward Dr. Wellborn's house. (Courtesy of Bud Hill.)

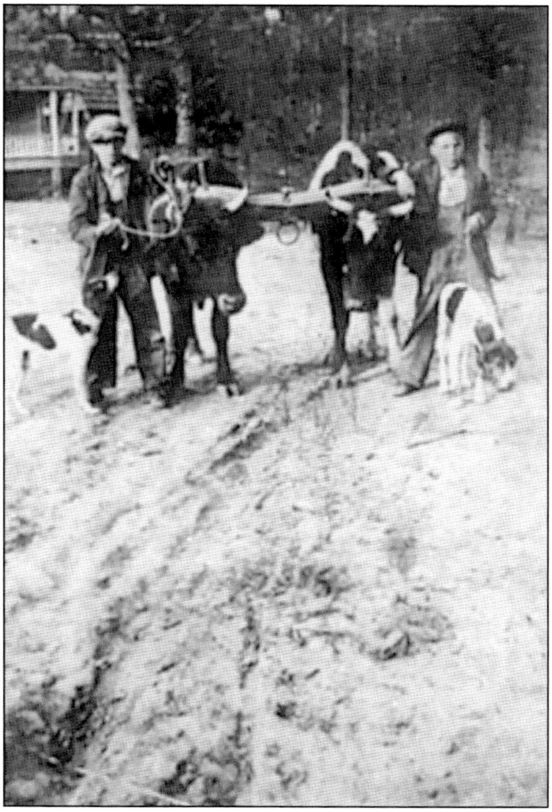

Wayne Collins (who became sheriff of Union County) and Neal Collins (who became ordinary of Union County) are pictured with their steers and dogs c. 1920s.

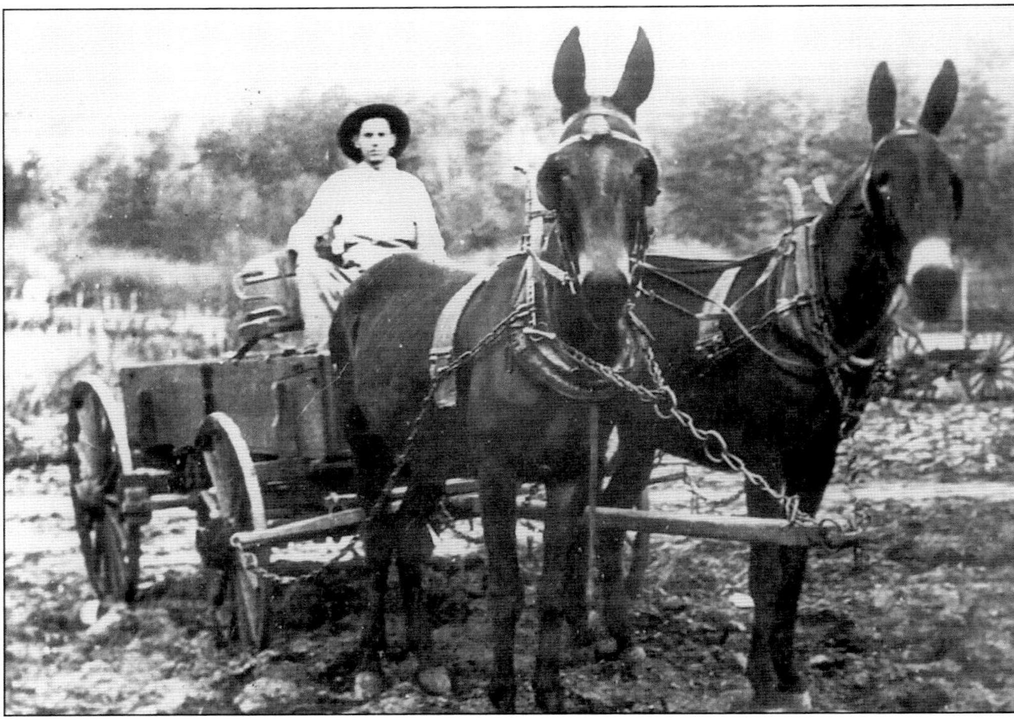

Oscar Cannon hauled from Cleveland to Blairsville in the mid-1920s. (Courtesy of Dale Elliott.)

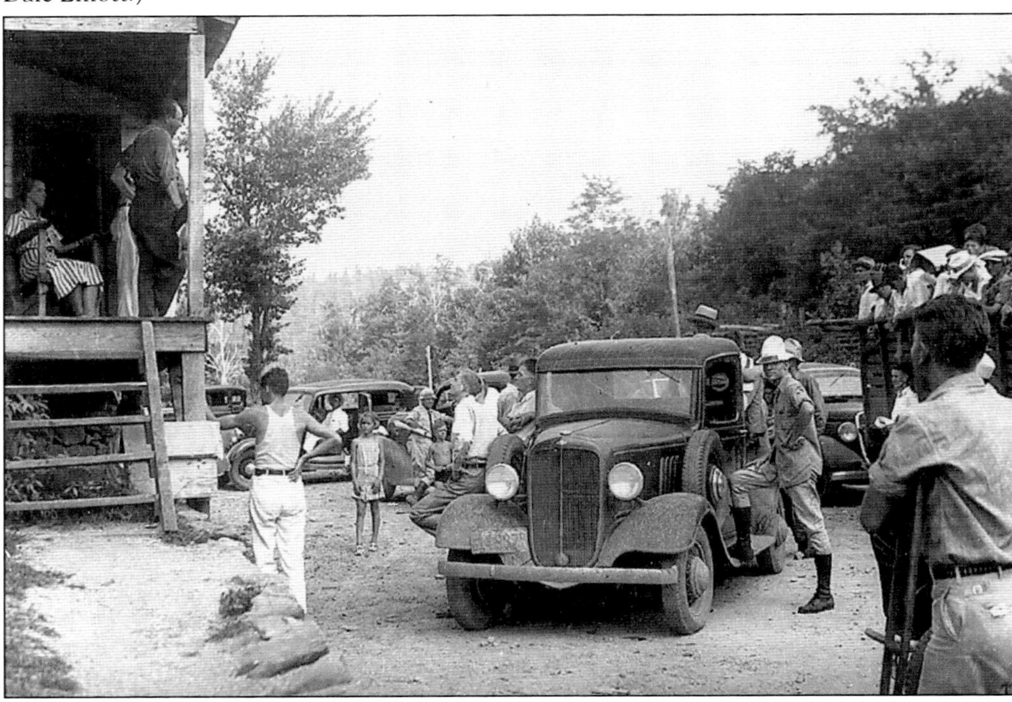

The person in this photo, believed taken in the Suches area, is identified as Ranger Arthur Woody (leaning against the post) of the Chattahoochee National Forest talking to the crowd in 1945.

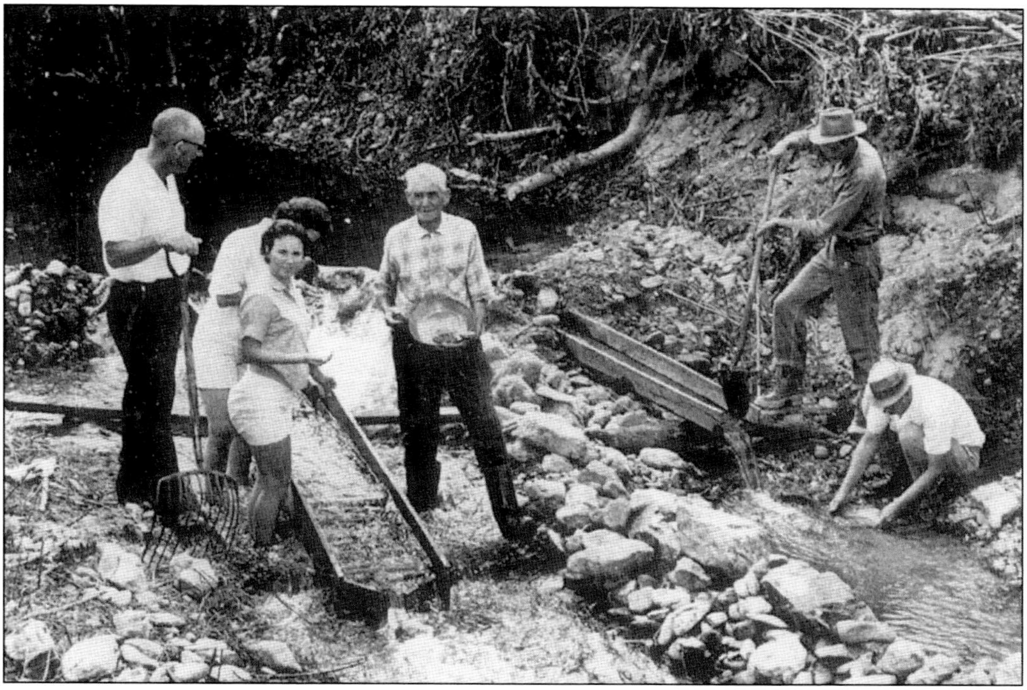

Mr. Bill Fortenberry demonstrates how to pan for gold in Coosa Creek. A reported $2,000,000 was taken from streams and mountainsides in the early days of the county.

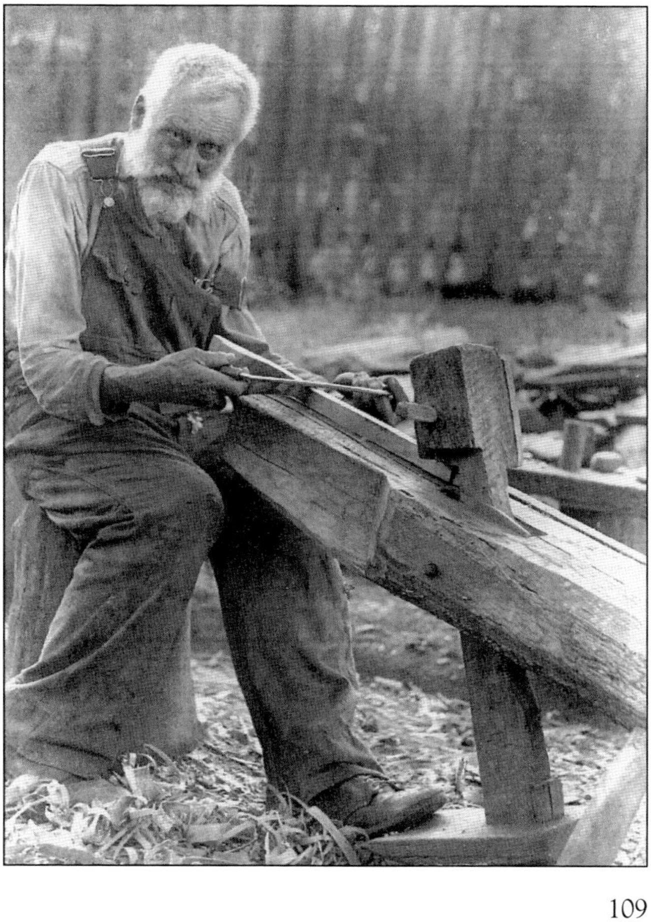

Jason Reid, chair maker, sits at the shaving horse *c.* 1930. (Photograph by Doris Ullman.)

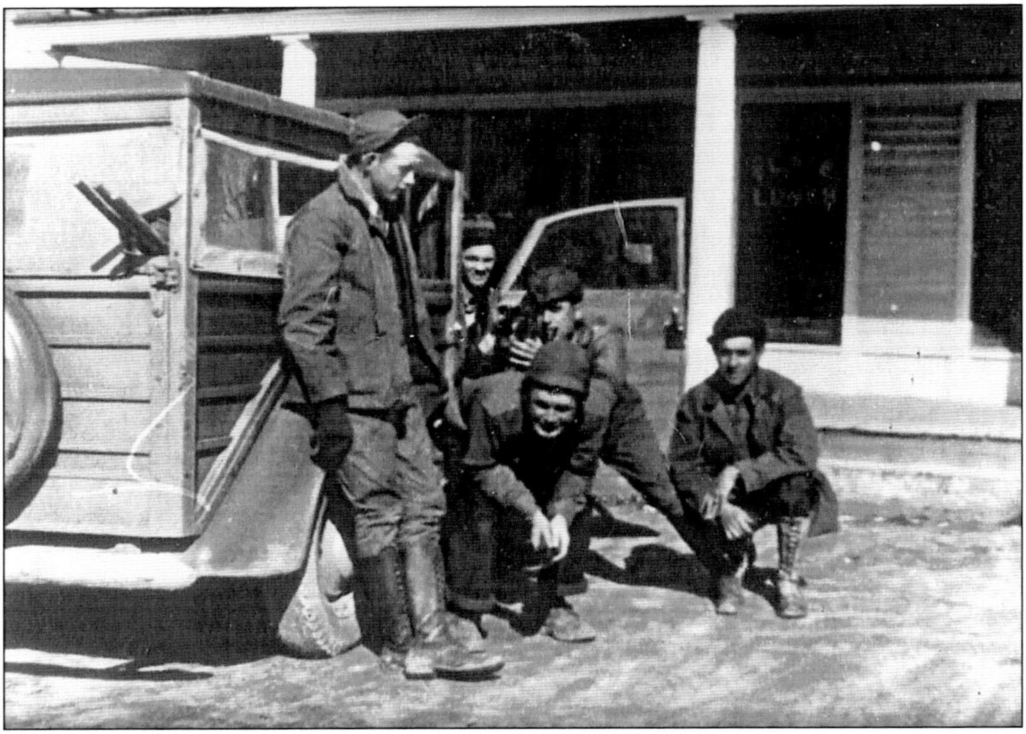

This TVA crew brought electricity to the county in the 1940s. (Courtesy of Katherine Litton.)

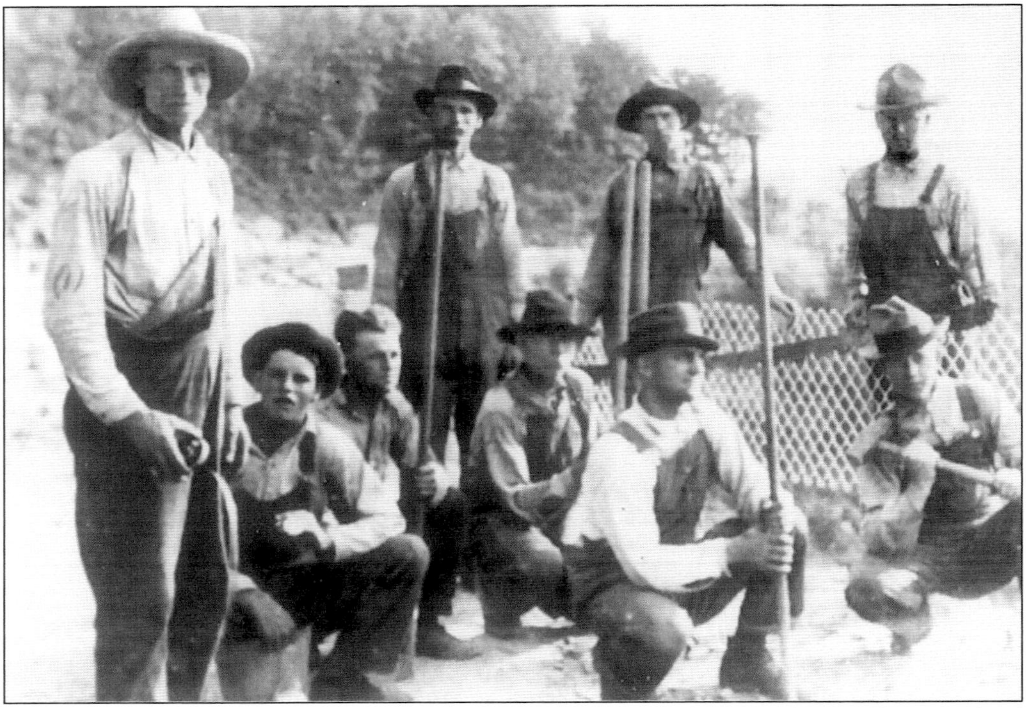

These men are building the road across Neel Gap 1926. From left to right are (front row) Ed Townsend, Tom Wilson, Steve Spiva, Ben Wilson, and Hub Collins; (back row) J.F. (Jep) Souther (contractor), Uley Collins, Jess Souther, and Ivan Collins. (Courtesy of Ray Rogers.)

Seven

Structures and Scenic Places

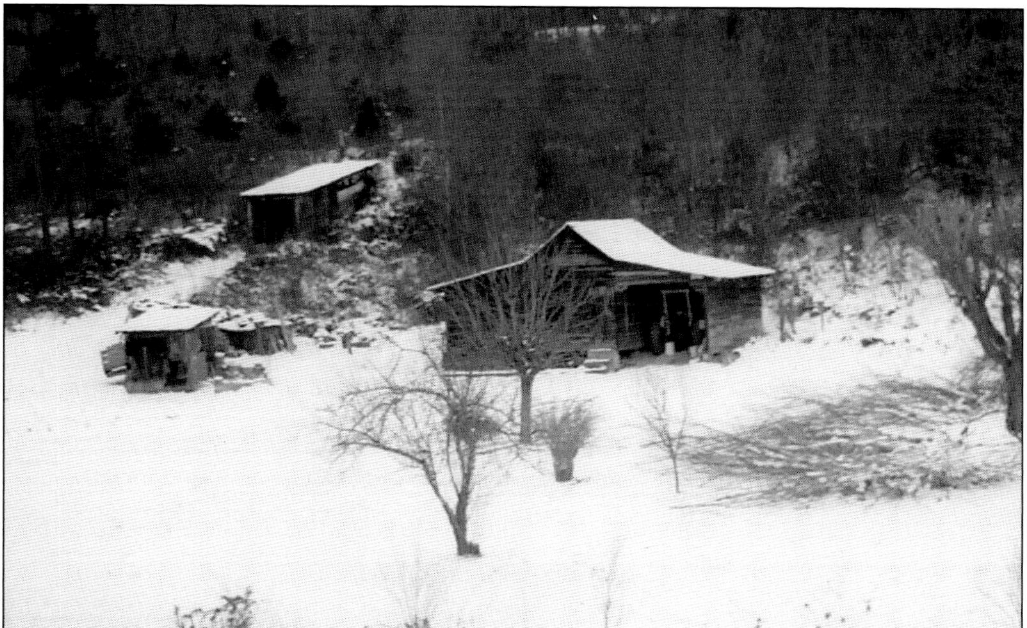

Rustic structures such as these have been typical in Union County throughout the decades. This is a winter scene with a lot of snow. (Photograph by Norman Cooper.)

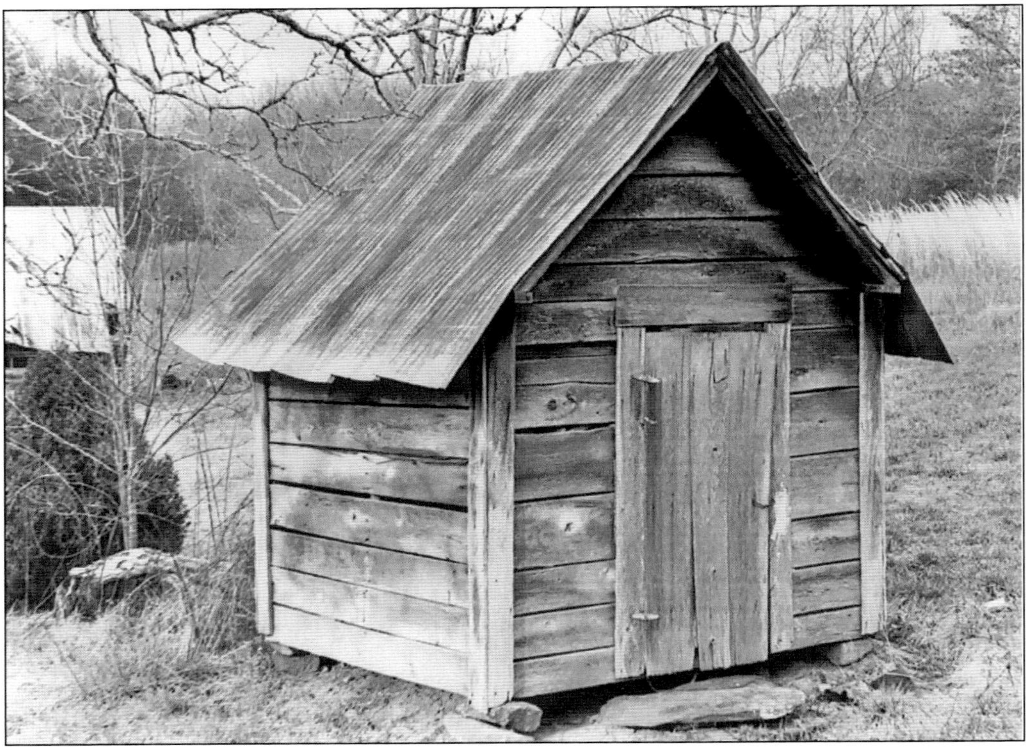

A smokehouse is seen near Choestoe. (Courtesy of Union County Historical Society.)

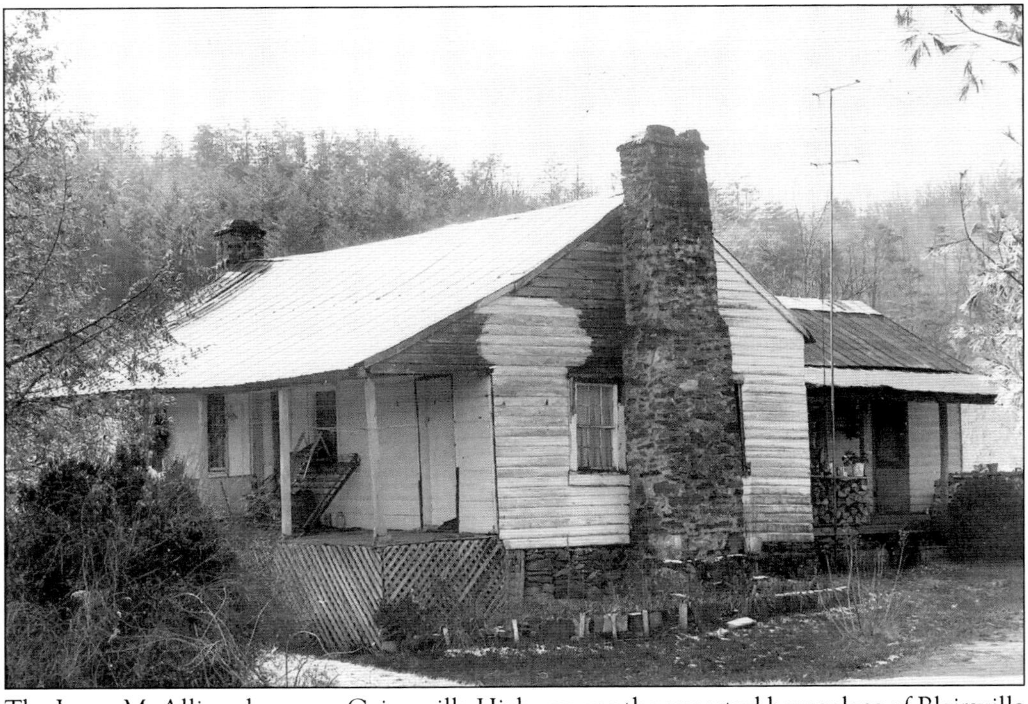

The James M. Allison home on Gainesville Highway was the ancestral homeplace of Blairsville Mayor Charles Allison and Union County Ordinary Frank Allison. (Courtesy of Union County Historical Society.)

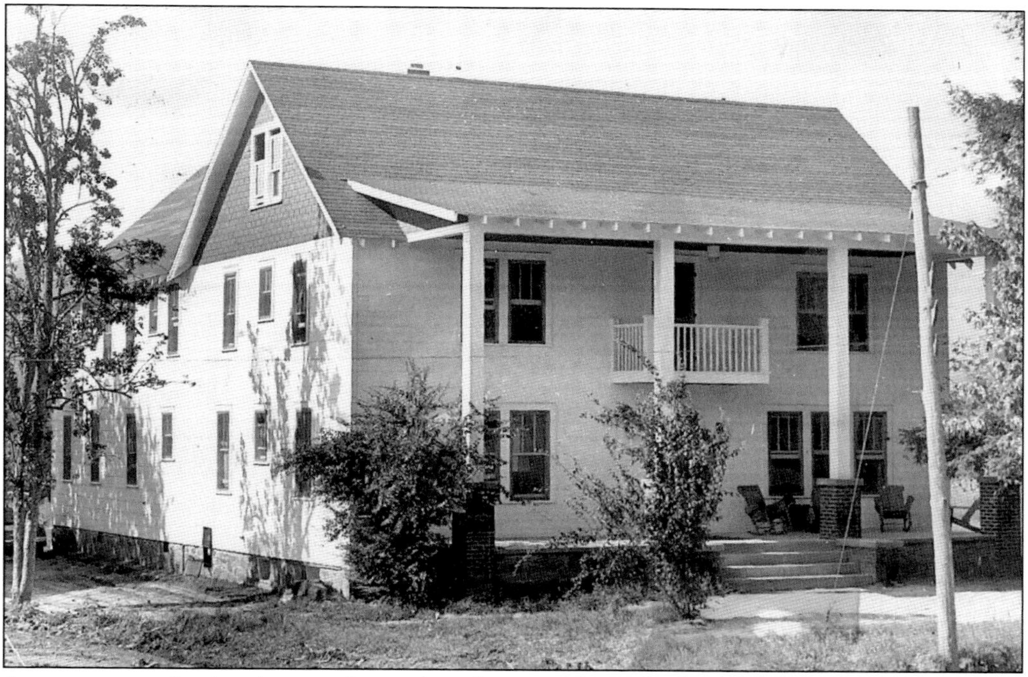

A newspaper clipping (year unknown) is shown and on the back of this photo reads, "Sale of the recently remodeled Jones Hotel to Erwin B. Akins, WWII veteran. One of the most modern hotels in North Georgia, the Jones Hotel was completed by J.T. Jones in 1939 and has been operated by him since its construction." Thurman and Edith Jones were owners and operators of this facility until 1950. Meals were prepared and served on the lower level. (Courtesy of James Jones.)

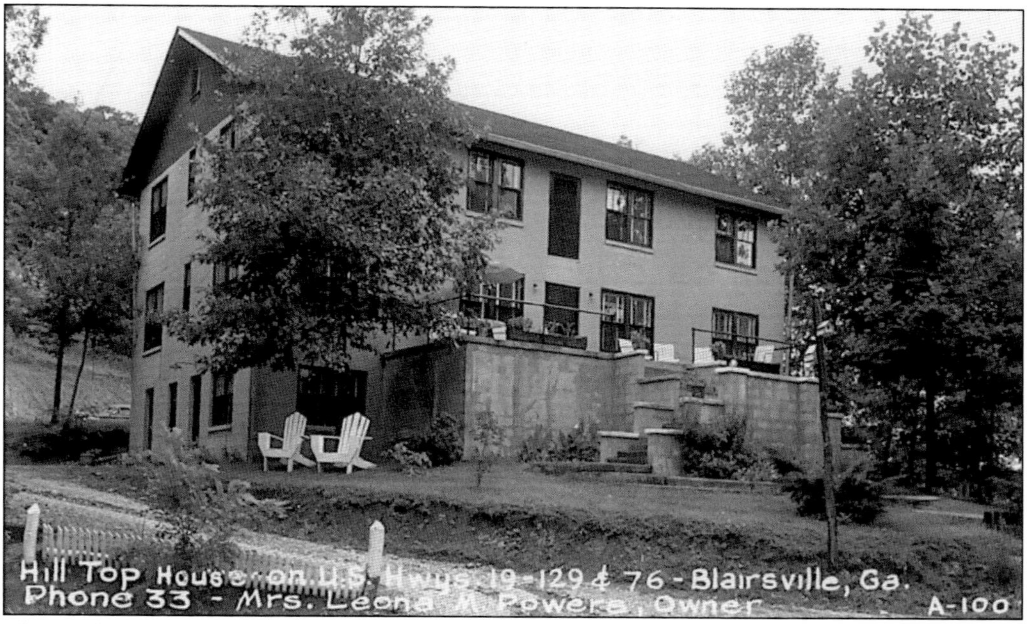

This undated photo postcard shows the Hill Top House on U.S. Hwy 19-129 & 76 in Blairsville. Note the phone number—c. 1950—reads "Phone 33, Mrs. Leona M. Powers, Owner." (Courtesy of James Jones.)

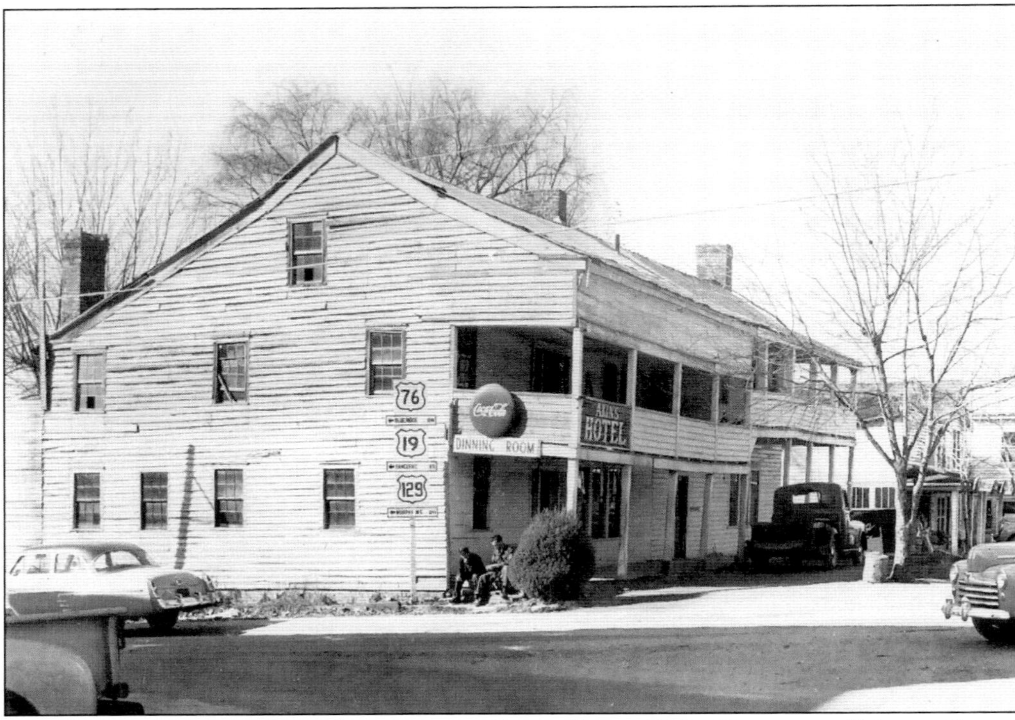

This is the Akins Hotel on the square in Blairsville, *c.* 1950. (Courtesy of Union County Historical Society.)

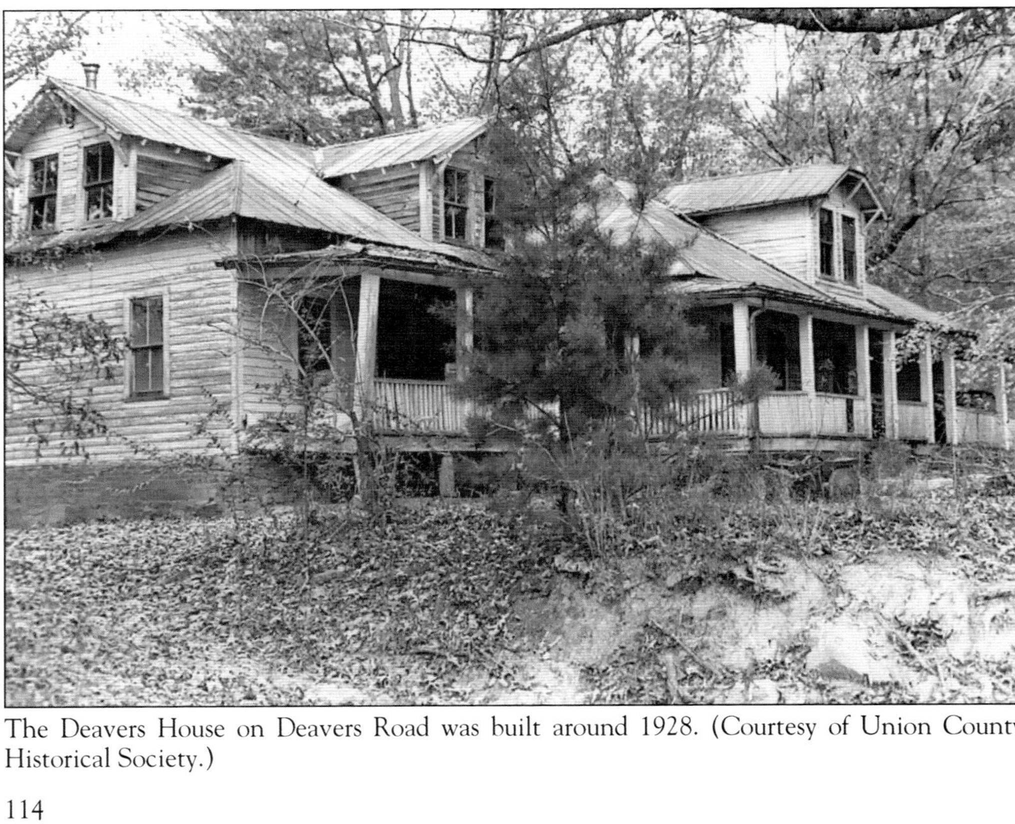

The Deavers House on Deavers Road was built around 1928. (Courtesy of Union County Historical Society.)

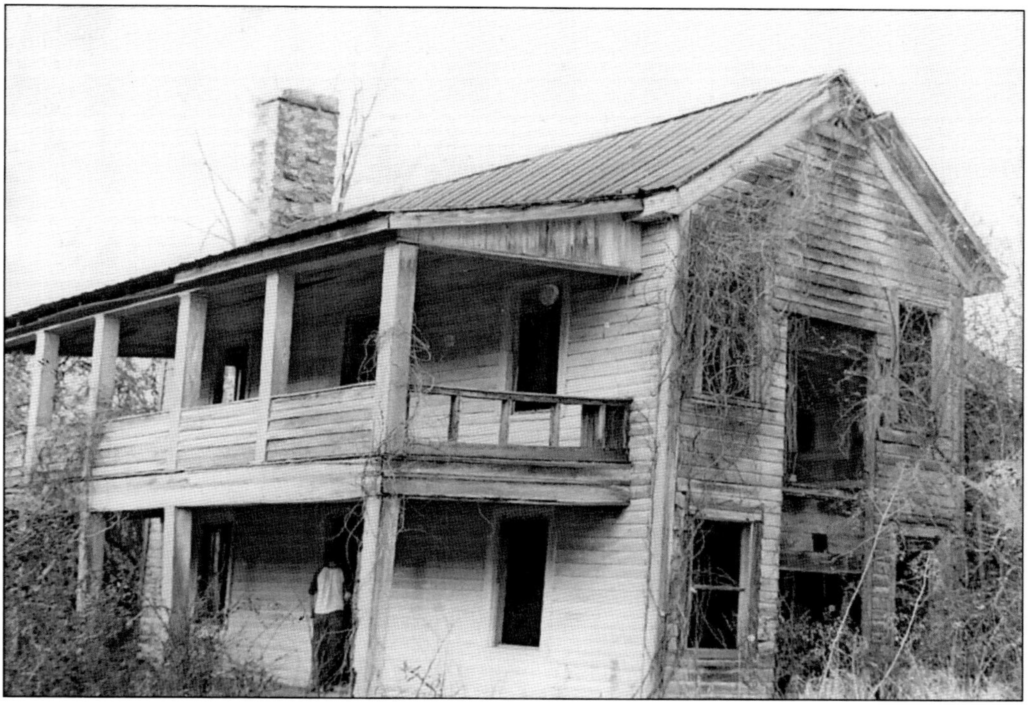

Here is the Bob "Red" Lance House. Lance bought the property near the Georgia and North Carolina border in 1917. Lance was Ordinary of Union County and a representative. He was also remembered as a contractor. To reach the rooms on the back wing, a person had to go outside to the porch from the main house. It was noted as one of the finest homes in Union County.

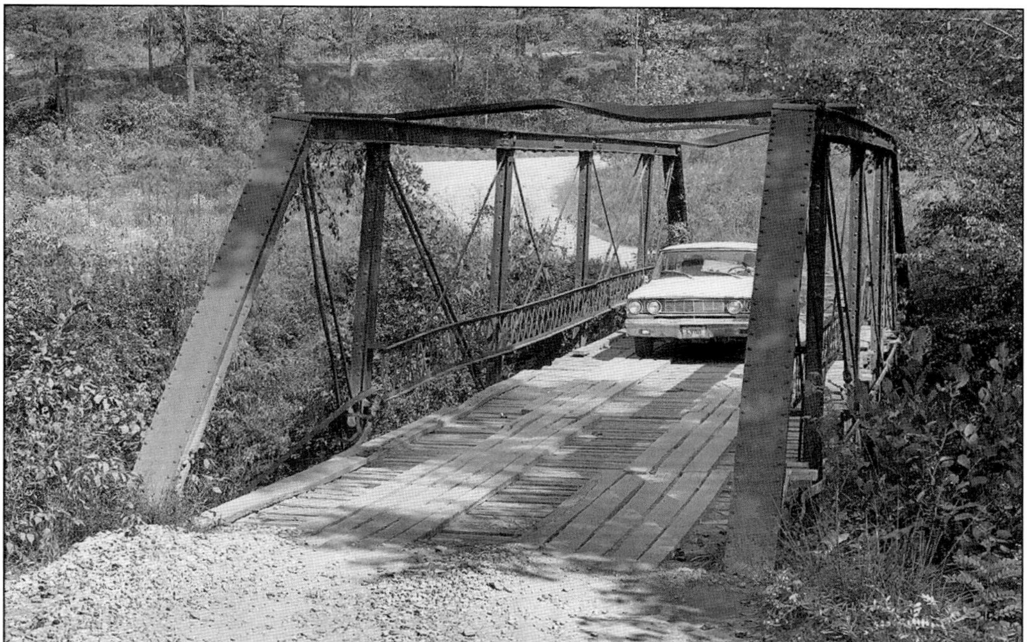

This is the Nicholson Bridge, a one-lane bridge near the Gainesville Highway.

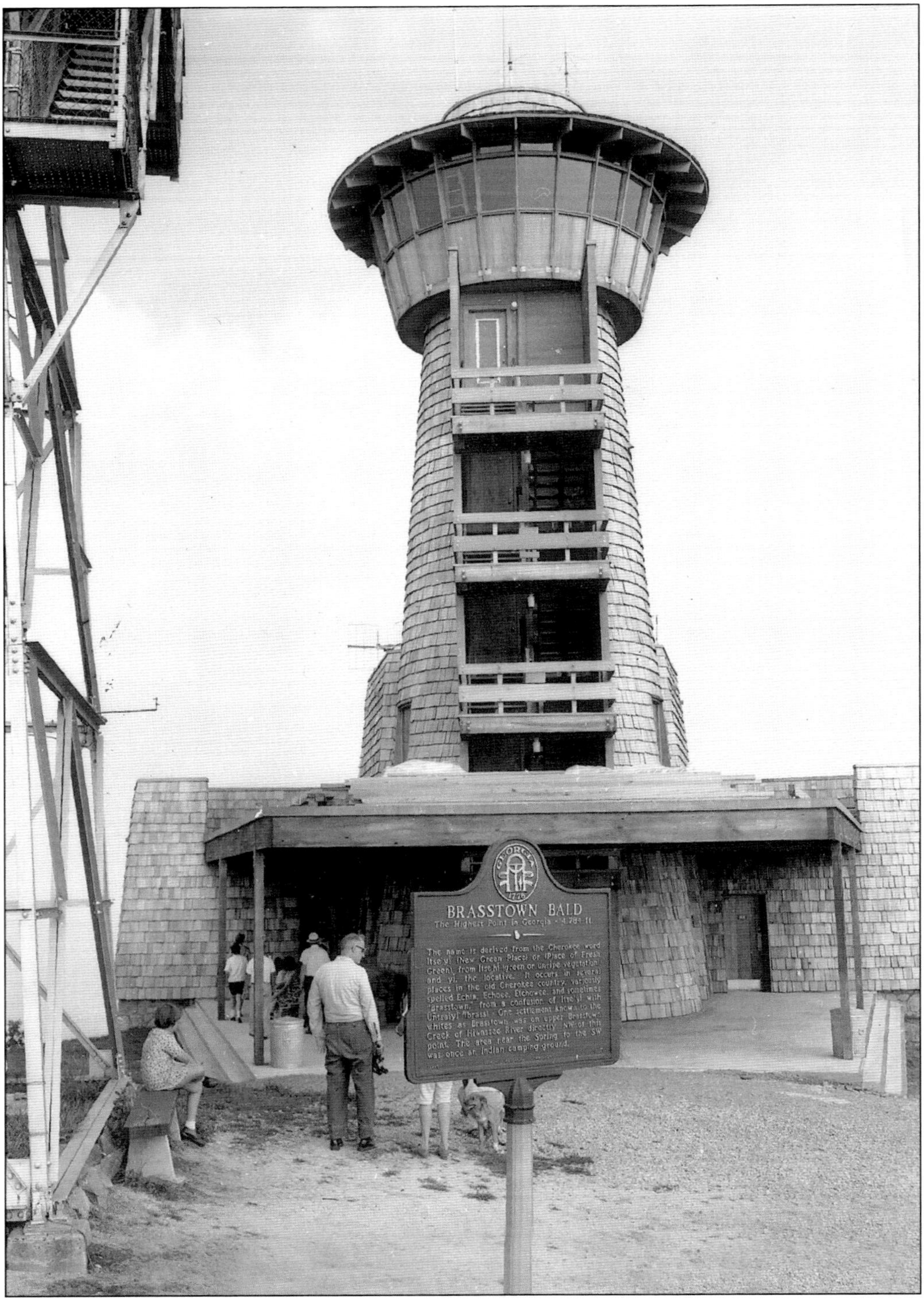

Brasstown Bald is the highest point in Georgia at 4,784 feet. The name is derived from the corruption of the Cherokee word meaning "new green place" or "place of fresh green." (Courtesy of Union County Historical Society.)

In 1935, the State of Georgia had the CCC construct a 33-foot high lookout house out of stone and wood to replace the wooden tower on Brasstown Bald. The tower was manned by Forest Service personnel. In 1947, the Forest Service removed the Georgia owned tower and put up the steel tower seen at right. This was used until it was replaced by another structure (shown opposite page). In 1965, the steel tower was given to the Georgia Forestry Commission. (Courtesy of Union County Historical Society.)

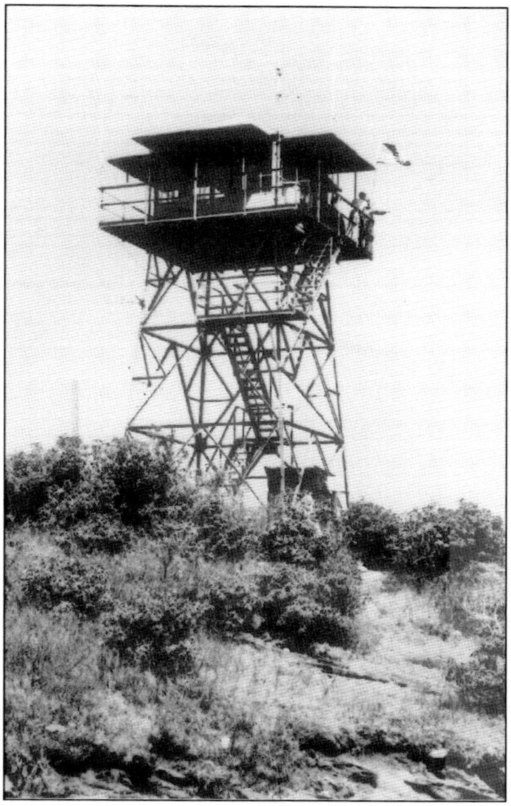

A typical combination of scenic beauty and older structures was common to the area for centuries in Union County. This is known as the Uncle Bill Souther house in the Town Creek Area. (Courtesy of Union County Board of Education.)

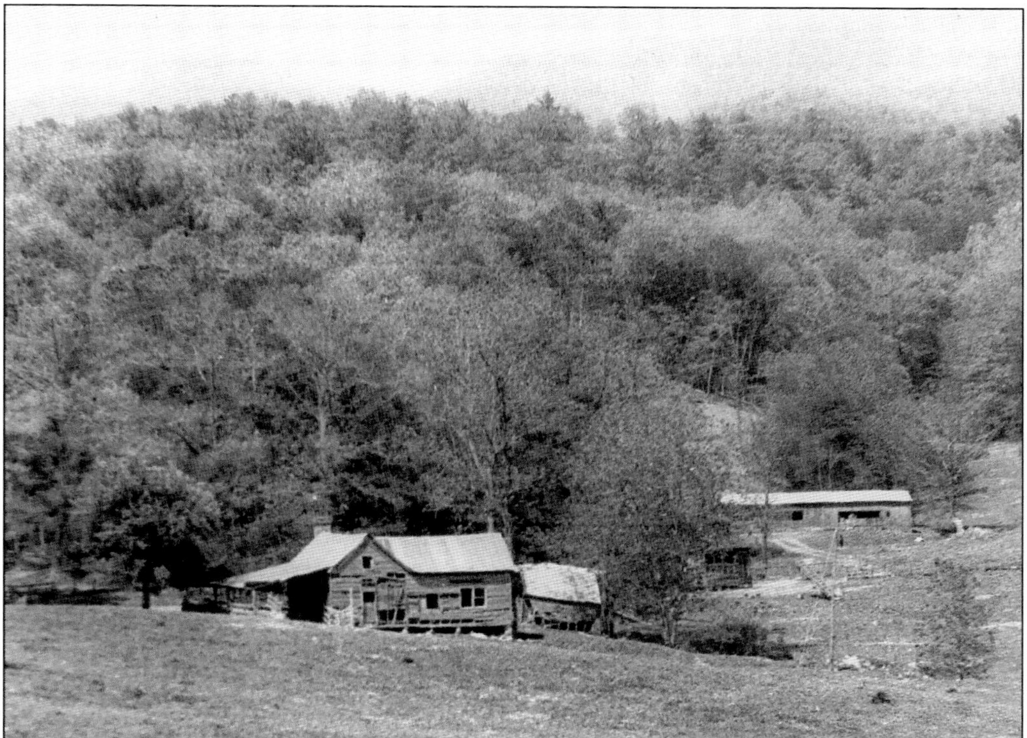

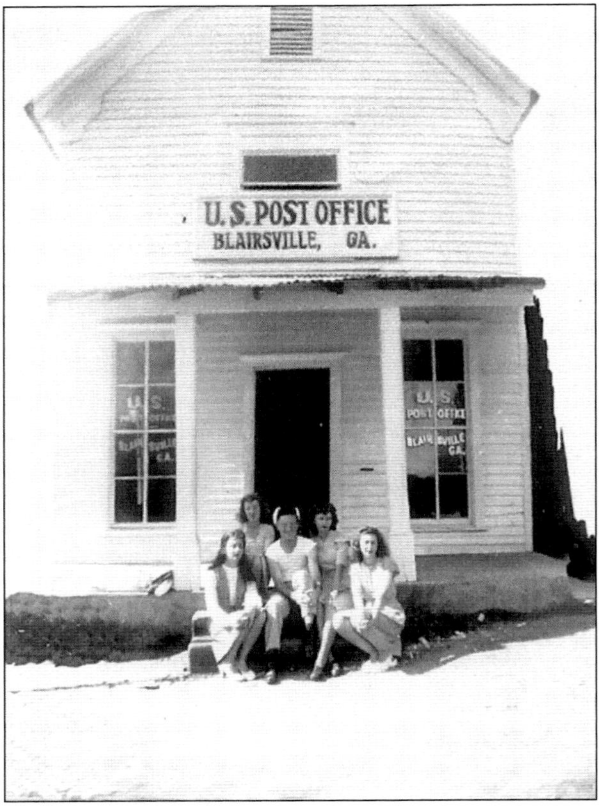

The United States Post Office sits on the square on the northeast side of the courthouse in Blairsville, 1945. Seen in the photo (from left to right) are Barbara Twiggs, Francis Colwell, unidentified, Eleanor Akins, and Antoinette Annette Akins. (Courtesy of David Friedly.)

Hunter-England House, sometimes called the Twiggs Place, was built around 1834. Legend has it that construction of the house had to be stopped to help round up Indians. Harriet England raised 11 children here. Some consider this the oldest house in the county. (Courtesy of Union County Historical Society.)

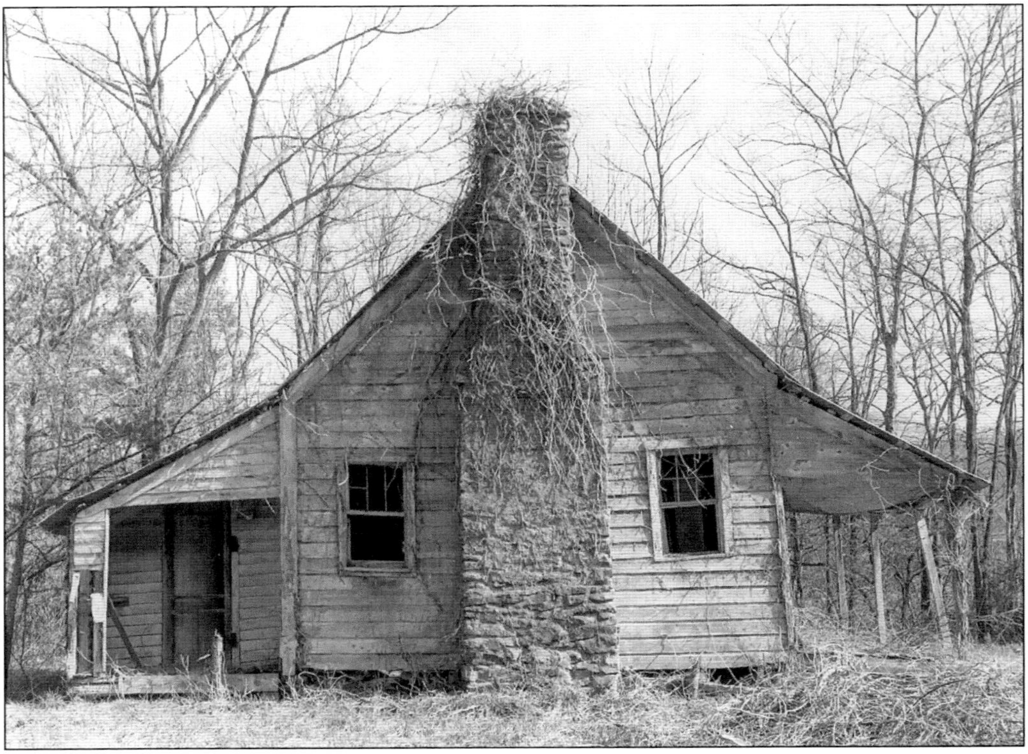

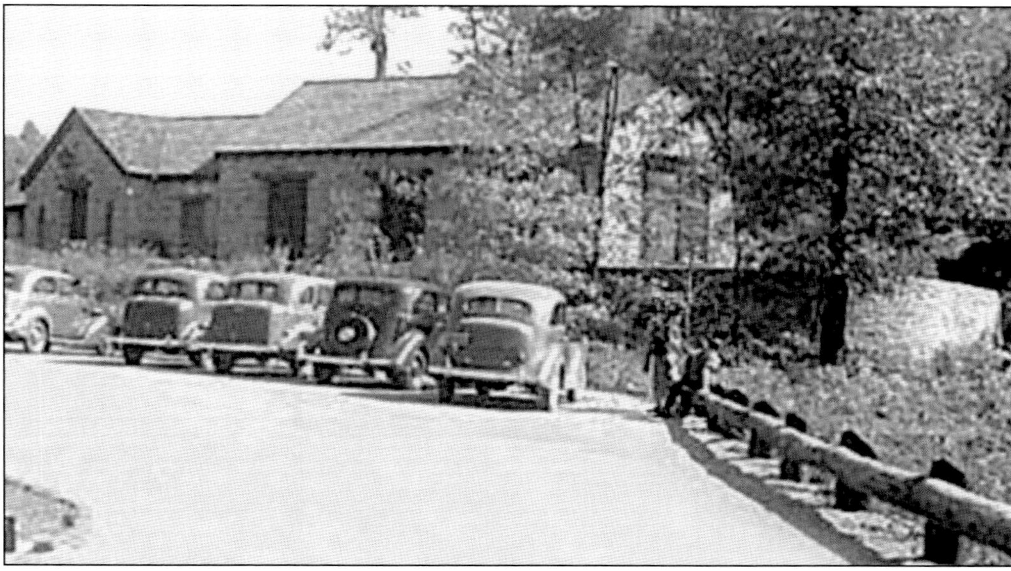

This photograph of the Vogel Lodge (now Walasi-Yi), *c.* 1939, was taken two years after completion of the lodge. It shows the building looking from the south end.

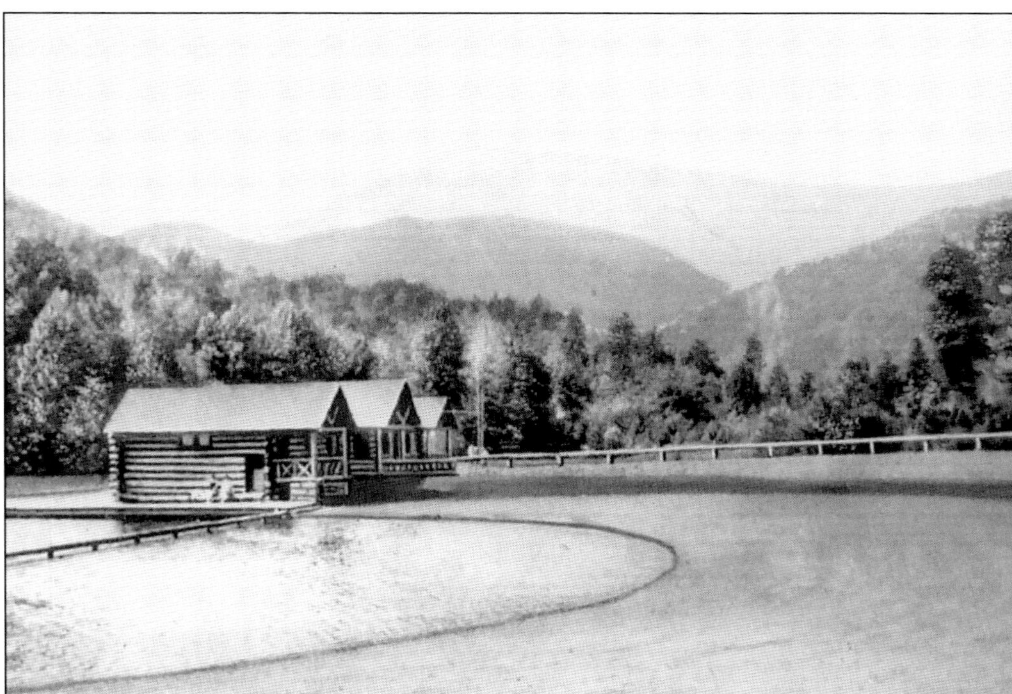

Lake Trahlyta at Vogel State Park is seen as it appeared on a postcard in the 1930s.

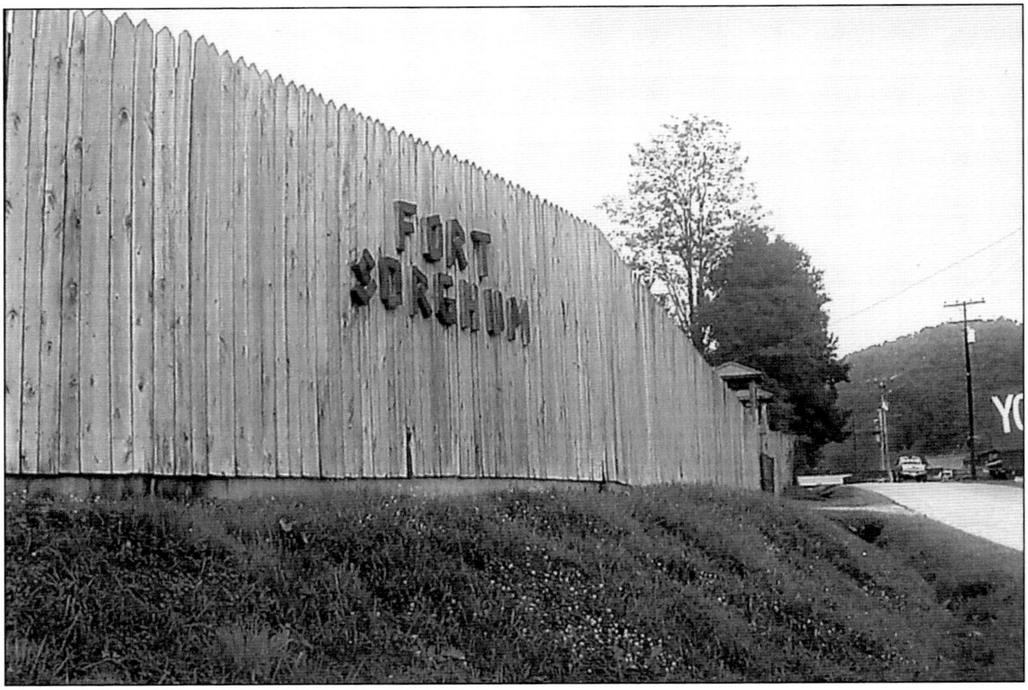

For decades, the event drawing the greatest number of visitors to the area has been the annual Sorghum Festival, held at Fort Sorghum in Blairsville. (Photograph by Norman Cooper.)

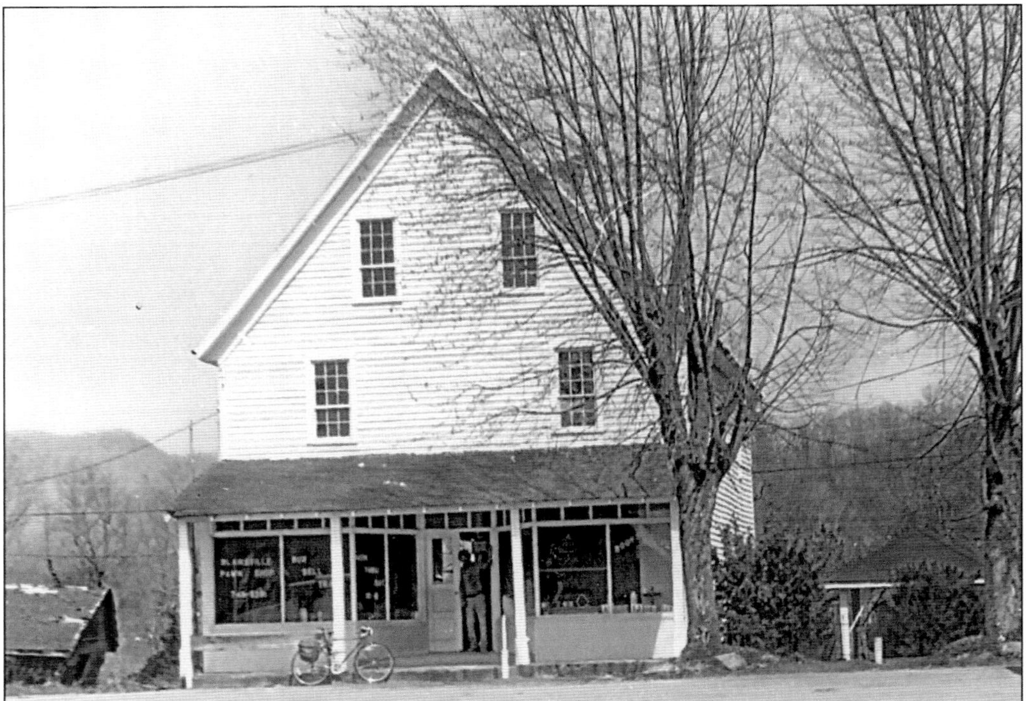

This picture captures a store that once stood on the square in Blairsville.

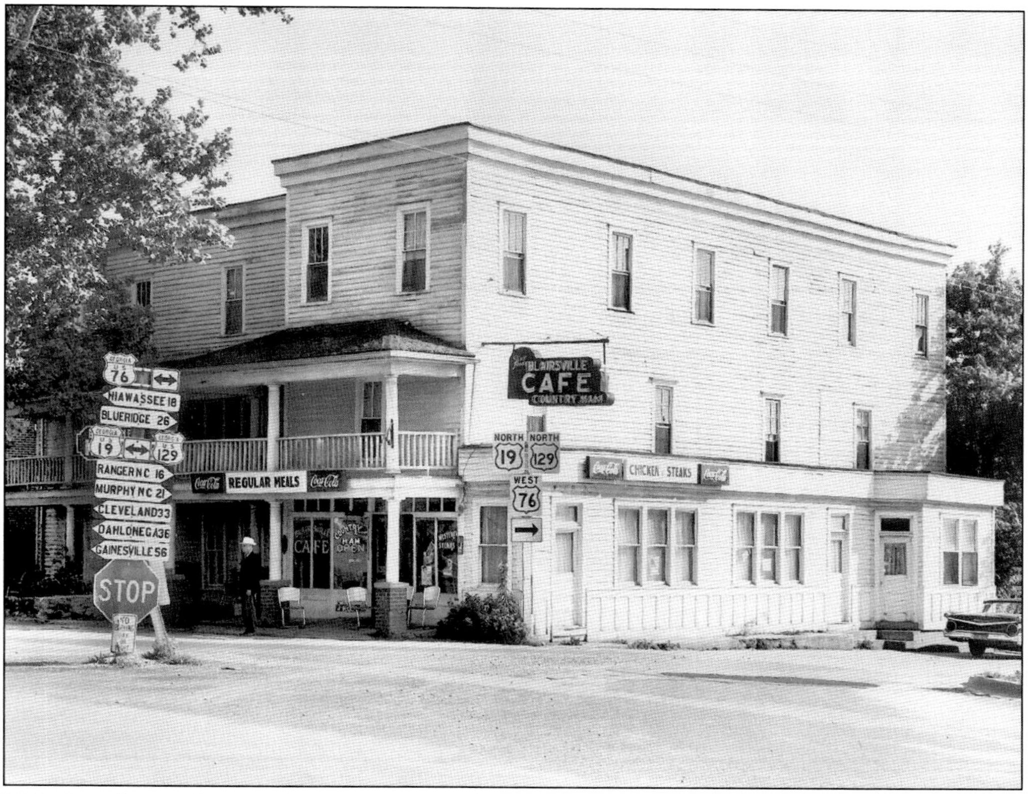

This hotel was known by two names during its existence—Blairsville Hotel and the Christopher Hotel. This is a photo after a third story was added. (Courtesy of Union County Historical Society.)

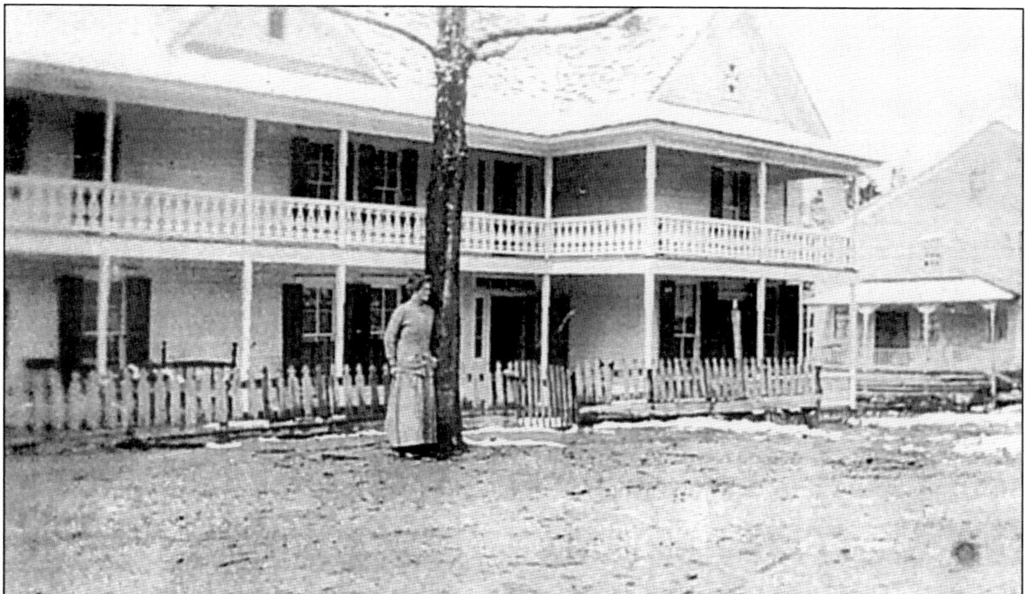

The Christopher Hotel is seen in the early 20th century. (Courtesy of Marjorie Christopher.)

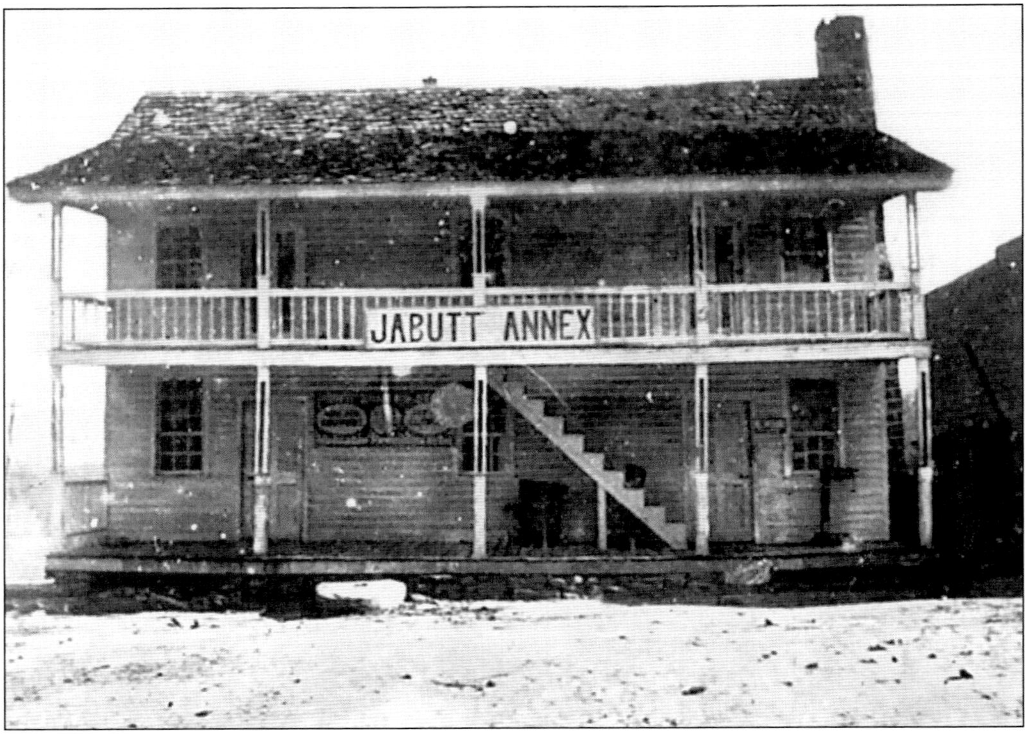

This early 1930s photo of the J.A. Butt annex was located on the corner of the square, next to the J.A. Butt store. This was a popular attraction during court week.

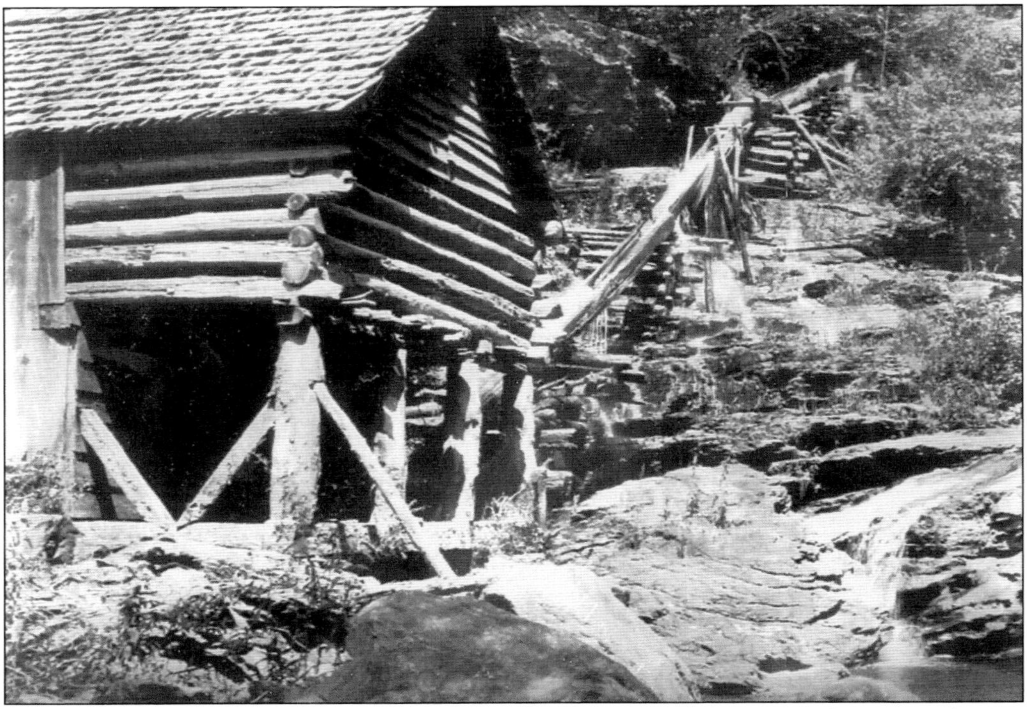

The Canada Creek Falls mill was located in the Canada District, near where Woody Gap School was built. (Courtesy of United Community Bank.)

Waterfalls have been around for centuries. They have been favorite recreational spots for decades with the early settlers. Getting to and observing Helton Creek Falls, a natural water fall, was a challenge prior to the time when roads were cut close to the falls. In this time elapsed photo, which shows the flow of water, snow can be seen on branches and the rocks in the foreground. Helton Creek Falls is a beautiful double waterfall set in deep hardwood forest. The total vertical drop is more than 100 feet. (Photograph by Norman Cooper.)

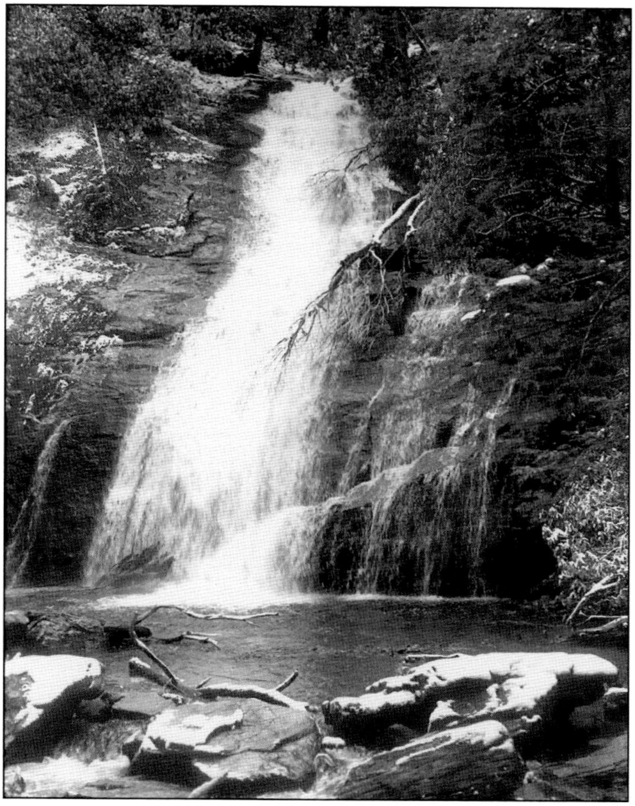

With the creation of the lake at the state park, Vogel State Park has a manmade waterfall. The lake was built by the CCC. This spectacular water fall has been a favorite site since the creation of the lake. (Photograph by Norman Cooper.)

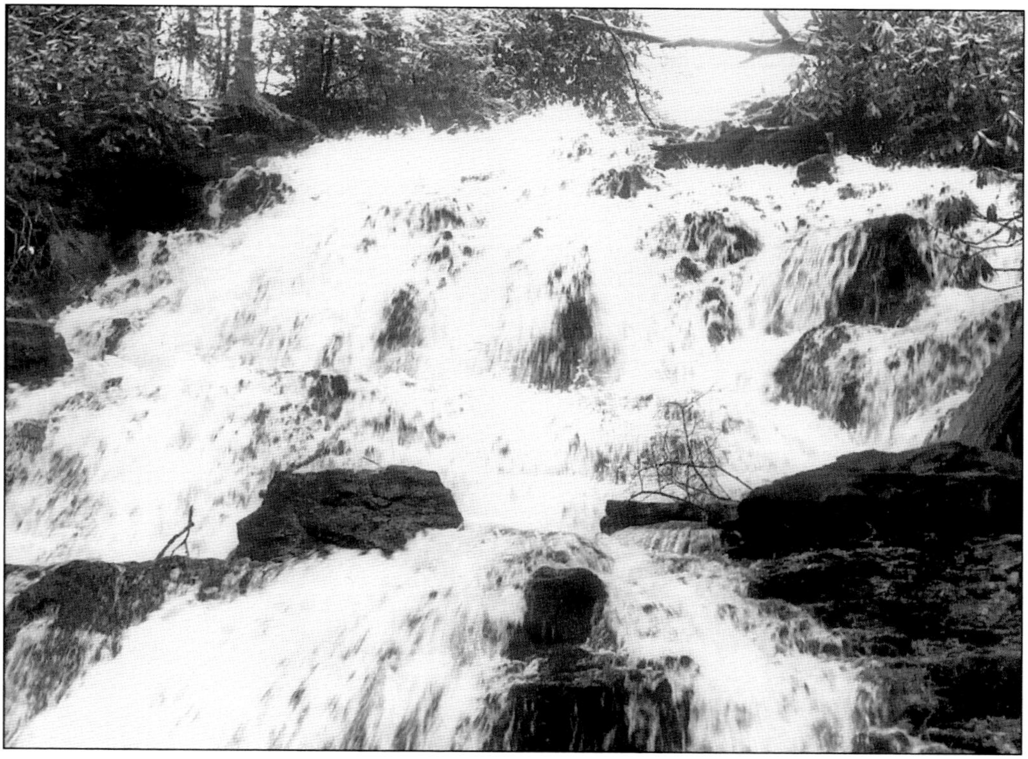

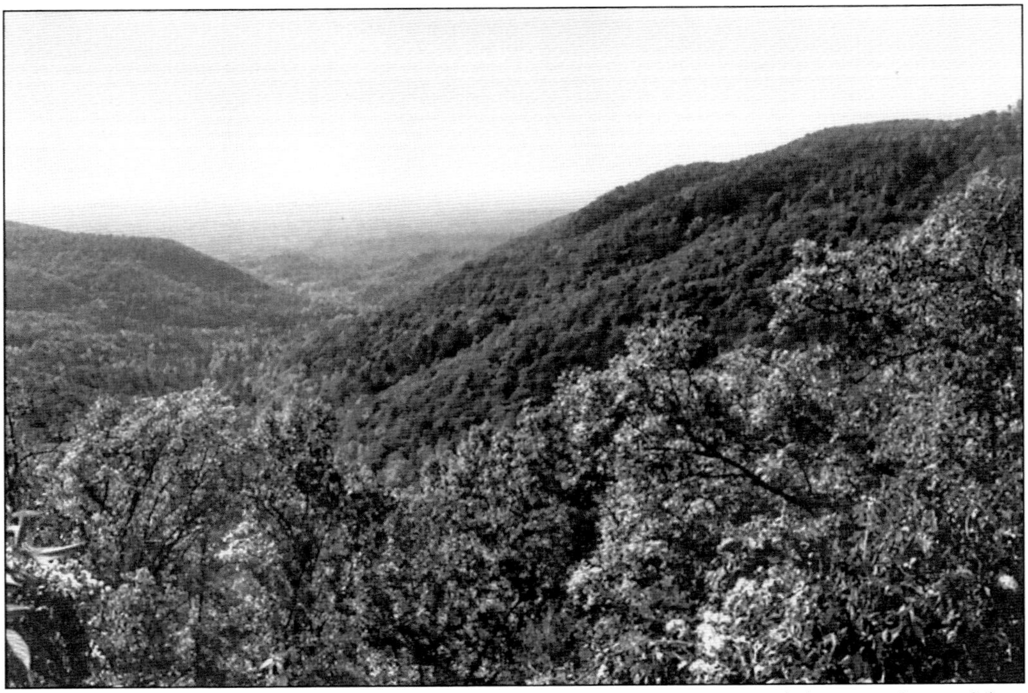

The Union County area of the Northeast Georgia Mountains is one of the most beautiful in the Appalachians. For many decades in the late 1800s and early 1900s, this beautiful yet rugged terrain separated those living in Union County from their neighbors farther south. (Photograph by Norman Cooper.)

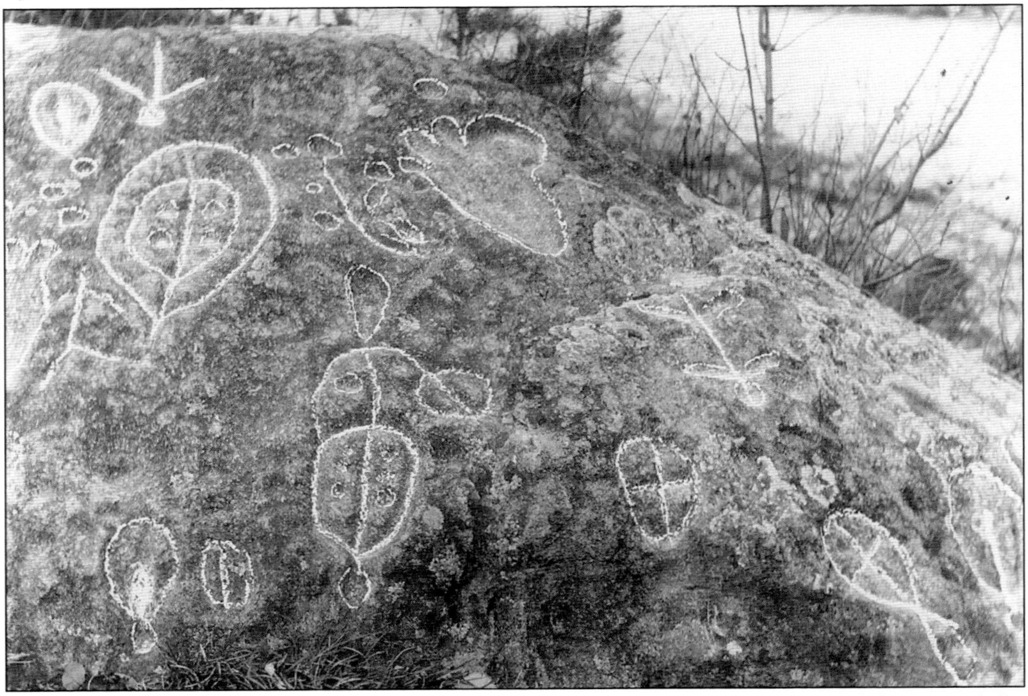

Trackrock Archeological Area has this stone many call the "mystery rock." (Photograph by Ed Mauney.)

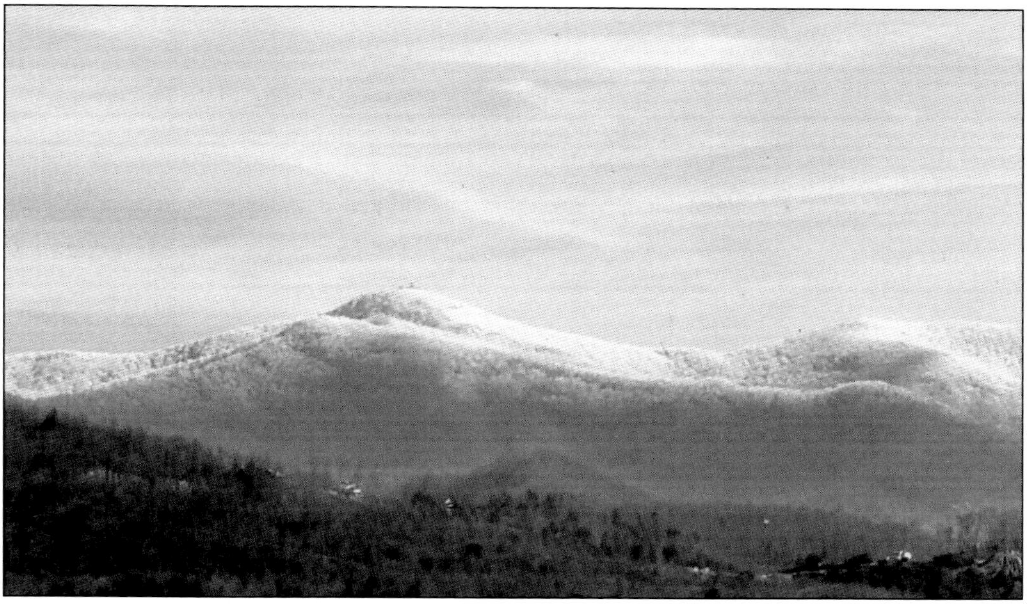

Go back one winter, go back 50 winters, go back 100 winters—it all looks the same to residents who gaze upon the snow covered mountains. The peak just left of center is Brasstown Bald, Georgia's highest elevation of 4,784 feet. Flora and fauna native to the region make the ranges unique. Scenes similar to this were common to many of the early pioneers and settlers. (Photograph by Norman Cooper.)

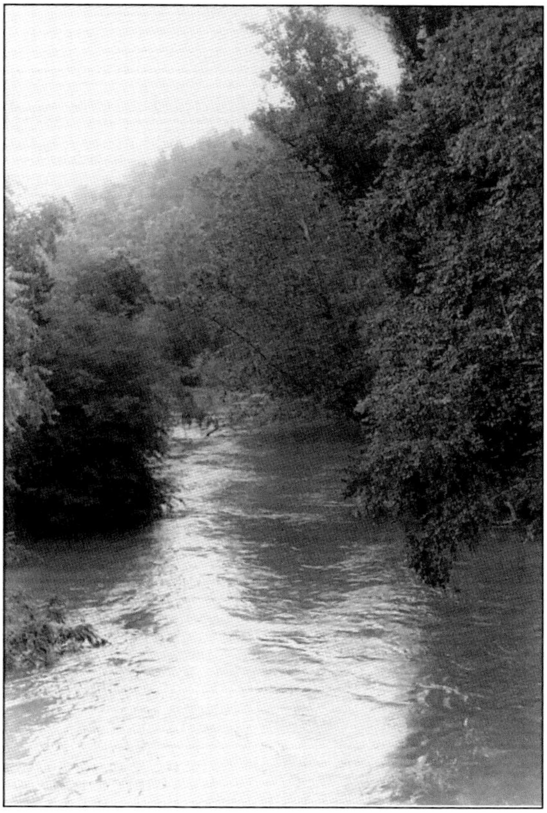

Nottely River is one of very few bodies of water in the country that runs south to north. This river, along with the creeks and streams connected to it, was a source of water for early settlers. Residents used the streams for drinking, bathing, washing, and for watering cattle and many other animals. (Photograph by Norman Cooper.)

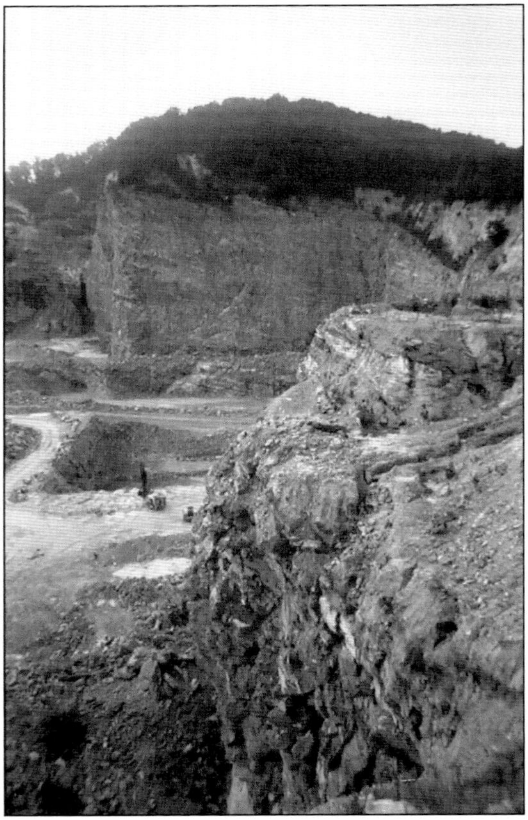

The rock quarry on Welborn Mountain has been described recently as "Union County's Grand Canyon." (Photograph by Norman Cooper.)

This photograph shows Lake Winfield Scott as it appeared on a postcard in the 1940s. (Courtesy of Union County Historical Society.)

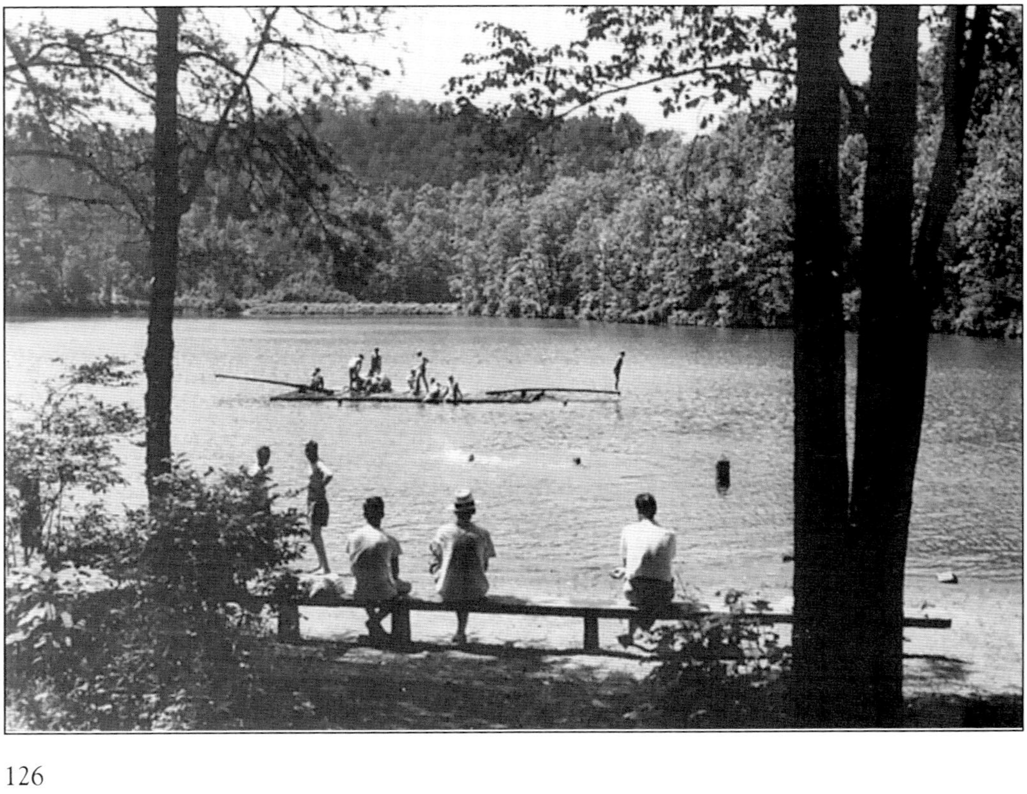

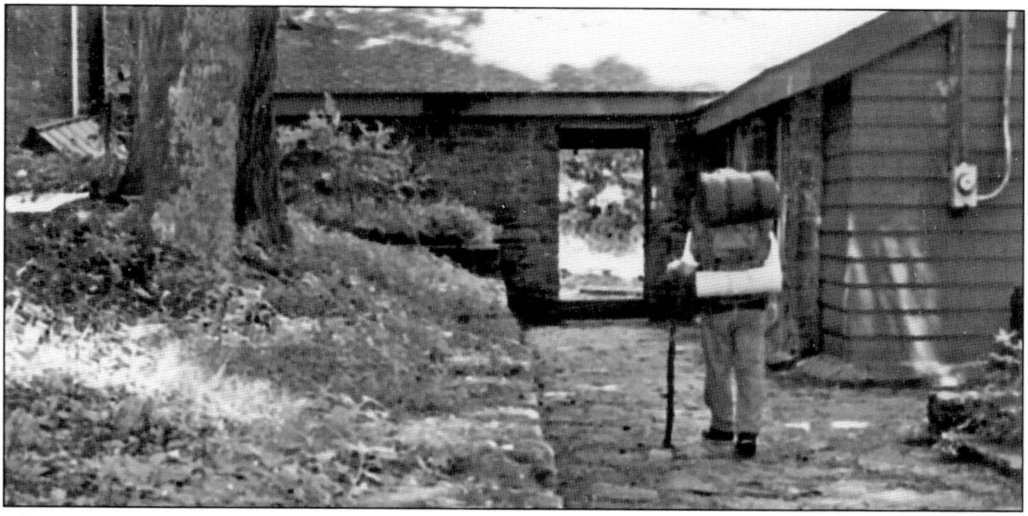

The Appalachian Trail is a wilderness footpath that winds over 2,100 miles along the crest of the Appalachian Mountains and runs through 14 states, from Georgia to Maine. The Appalachian Trail, which runs numerous miles through Union County, extends some 80 miles through the primitive areas of the Chattahoochee National Forest. Although rising, at times, to elevations of over 4,400 feet, the trail is mostly along ridges at elevations around 3,000 feet. It offers unlimited hiking adventure of exceptional challenge and variety. Ascents and descents are sometimes steep, but are often rewarded by scenic vistas from rocky outcrops and open summits. Pictured above is the only place where the trail goes through a structure or under a roof. The location is Neel Gap at the Walasi-Yi Center. Pictured below is a marker at the Walasi-Yi Center. (Photograph by Norman Cooper.)

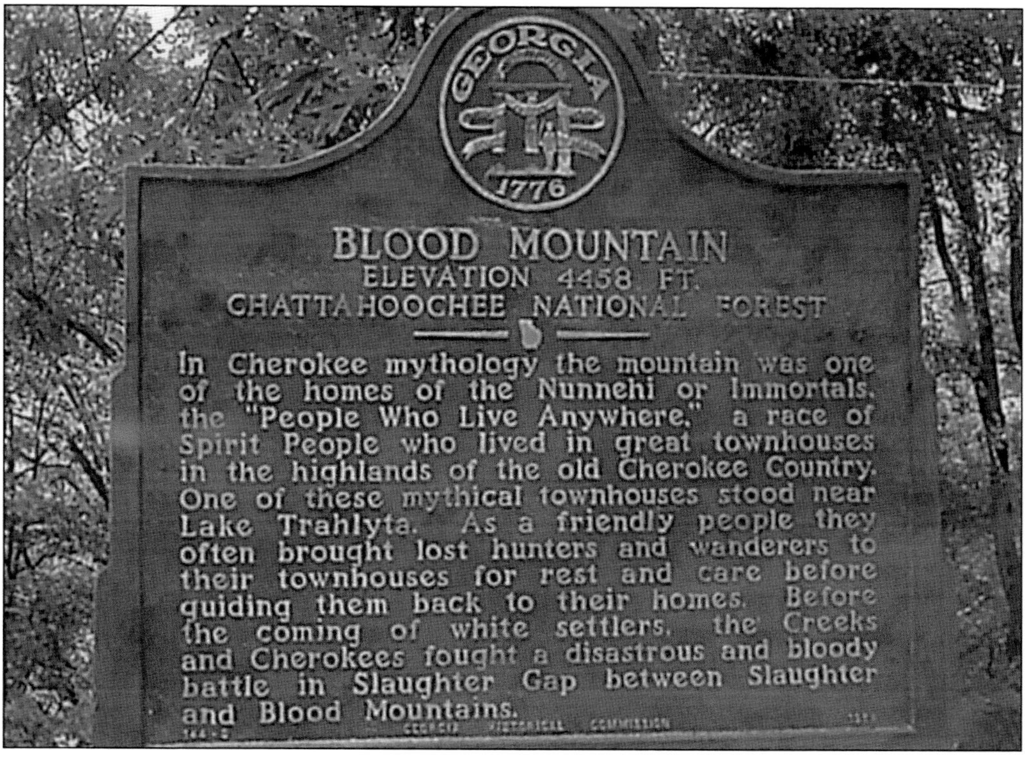

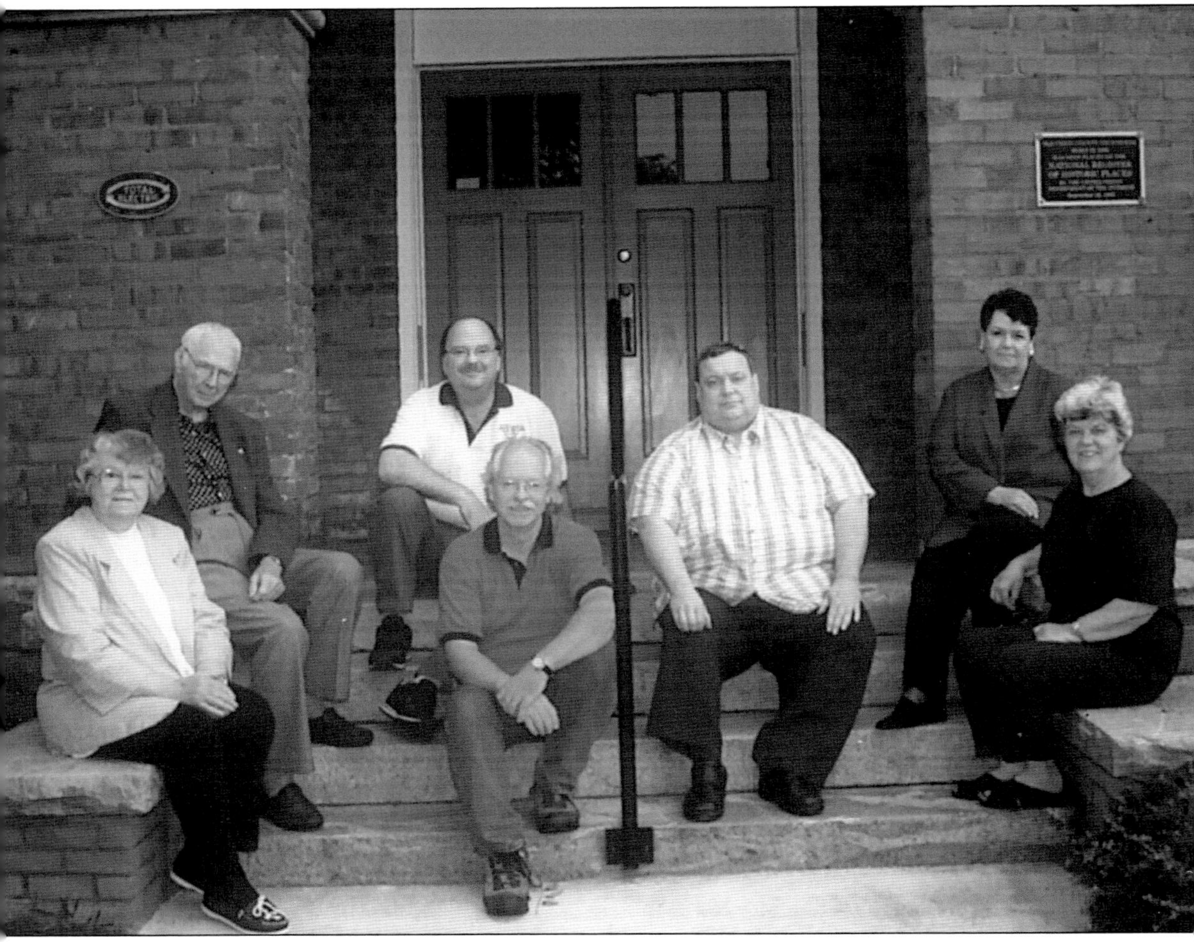

The Union County, Georgia Pictorial History Book Committee included Martyne Jokela, Dale Elliott, Norman Cooper, Steve Oakley, David Friedly, Jane Thompson, and Betty Jane Shuler.

Presenting this rich history—which spans numerous decades and is shown in thousands of photographs—in one pictorial book was no easy task. The goal of the committee was to include as much variety and uniqueness as possible to the work. The focus of this volume is Union County, Georgia pre-1970. The photographs of the restoration of the old courthouse in chapter one are an "added bonus." It is our sincere desire that you have enjoyed this book as much as we enjoyed creating it.

—Norman, Steve, Jane, Betty, Martyne, Dale, and David